SECOND EDITION

Job Search
Career Planning Guide, Book II

Career Planning Guides by Robert D. Lock

Book I: Taking Charge of Your Career Direction, Second Edition

Book II: Job Search, Second Edition

Book III: Student Activities for Taking Charge of Your Career Direction
(Second Edition) and Job Search (Second Edition)

SECOND EDITION

Job Search
Career Planning Guide, Book II

Robert D. Lock
Jackson Community College

Brooks/Cole Publishing Company
Pacific Grove, California

Brooks/Cole Publishing Company
A Division of Wadsworth, Inc.

© 1992, 1988 by Wadsworth, Inc., Belmont, California 94002.
All rights reserved. No part of this book may be reproduced,
stored in a retrieval system, or transcribed, in any form or
by any means—electronic, mechanical, photocopying, recording,
or otherwise—without the prior written permission of the
publisher, Brooks/Cole Publishing Company, Pacific Grove,
California 93950, a division of Wadsworth, Inc.

Printed in the United States of America

10   9   8   7   6   5   4   3   2

Library of Congress Cataloging in Publication Data

Lock, Robert D., [date]
    Job search / Robert D. Lock. — 2nd ed.
        p.   cm. — (Career planning guide ; bk. 2)
    Includes bibliographical references and index.
    ISBN 0-534-13657-5
    1. Job hunting. I. Title.   II. Series: Lock, Robert D., [date]
Career planning guide ; bk. 2.
    HF5382.7.L63   1991
650.14—dc20   91-17843
                                                          CIP

Sponsoring Editor: *Claire Verduin*
Editorial Associate: *Gay C. Bond*
Production Editor: *Kay Mikel*
Manuscript Editor: *Laurie Vaughn*
Permissions Editor: *Karen Wootten*
Interior and Cover Design: *Sharon L. Kinghan*
Art Coordinator: *Cloyce J. Wall*
Typesetting: *Shepard Poorman Communications Corporation*
Cover Printing: *Lehigh Press Lithographers/Autoscreen*
Printing and Binding: *Arcata Graphics/Fairfield*

To my family, students, and colleagues

Preface

This book, *Job Search,* the second volume of the Career Planning Guide series, makes an assumption about you, the reader. It assumes that you have made at least a tentative career choice and feel relatively comfortable about it. The best job-seekers are those who know exactly what occupation they want to enter. They have already completed a thorough investigation of their own personalities and of the world of work. If these sentences do not describe you, obtain a copy of the first book in this series, called *Taking Charge of Your Career Direction,* and move through it either with the help of a career planning class, instructor, or counselor, or on your own. After you have established a career goal, come back to this book. *Job Search* concerns implementing your career decision. An occupational choice remains only a decision until you actively put it into practice.

Users of the first edition will notice that this edition of *Job Search* contains ten chapters instead of the original seven. The sequence of material has not changed; each of the middle three chapters was divided to shorten those chapters in the second edition.

Many people have contributed to the completion of this book. I would like to acknowledge the understanding and support of my family, the constructive comments of my students, and the productive ideas of my colleagues. I would like to thank Carole France for her word-processing expertise. For their thoughtful reviews of the manuscript I would like to thank Karla Delle Carmichael, Sul Ross State University, Alpine, Texas; Suzanne Connett, California State University—Fullerton, California; George A. Dennis, Lower Columbia College, Longview, Washington; Chris Kroeger, Washington University, St. Louis, Missouri; and Robert McClure, St. Petersburg Junior College—Clearwater, Florida. I would also like to thank Claire Verduin, Gay C. Bond, Karen Wootten, Sharon L. Kinghan, and Kay Mikel at Brooks/Cole and manuscript editor Laurie Vaughn for their warm and professional help.

Robert D. Lock

Contents

CHAPTER 4

Job Application Forms and Other Problems of the Job Search

92

CHAPTER 5

Using Your Research Skills to Get a Job: Geographical Areas

108

CHAPTER 6

Using Your Research Skills to Get a Job: Work Organizations

124

CHAPTER 7

Using Your Speaking Skills to Get a Job: Interviewing for Information   *163*

CHAPTER 8

Using Your Speaking Skills to Get a Job: Interviewing for Jobs   *177*

CHAPTER 9

Into the Working World

CHAPTER 10

The Social and Economic Aspects of Work

1

Overview of the Job Search

Nearly everyone experiences the job search, but many people enter this undertaking with a sense of dread and foreboding. You could be job-hunting at any time in the future; even the best workers, through no fault of their own, can be laid off or forced to resign. The greatest job security is the confidence that you possess the skill and knowledge to conduct a competent job search. However, job-hunting skills are seldom taught, so job-seekers often feel left out, with no one to help them. Most people recognize that they are responsible for their own job search, but they needn't feel isolated. Help is available, and some of it will come through this book.

One basic approach to the job search is the use of all the usual methods, because no single technique is very good. Another approach emphasizes getting through to the hidden job market, where (it is claimed) the great majority of jobs are found. Job search theories have many ideas in common, so you might try a "combination" approach.

A discussion of the "basic truths" of the job search reveals many common elements in the several approaches. A brief survey of theories and basic ideas will start you thinking about the puzzles and problems of job-hunting. Despite differences in method, no one really questions the necessity of the fundamentals: take personal responsibility, learn, start now, seek information, evaluate workplaces, persist, and show enthusiasm, just to name a few. No one argues about the need to be organized, either. An exercise at the end of this chapter will start you toward finding a job efficiently and systematically. Do it right; your job and your work are at the very heart of your life.

The Job Search Mystery

Few subjects are more vital to a person than the job search, but few topics are shrouded with more mystery. Nearly everyone has been frustrated by the job search, but everyone still has plenty of advice to give.

No book or system can offer you a foolproof guarantee of landing a job. One fact can be stated with certainty, however. A job search campaign is hard work: "It's a job to get a job." You will need all your detective skills to win a job in your chosen occupation. As in any process of investigation and discovery, there are times of discouragement and disappointment. Fear and anxiety are part of the picture, too, for a job-seeker feels vulnerable and open to rejection. This book can assist you in acquiring the skills that will enable you to overcome many problems in the job search. A major purpose of the book is to reduce the fears and frustrations of job-hunting and help you face the task of gaining employment in the occupation of your choice with a sense of hope, confidence, inventiveness, and mastery.

The phrase *occupation of your choice* implies that you are relatively certain of your career goal. If this is not so, you are urged to first go through a career decision-making process such as the one described in the first volume of this Career Planning Guide series, then come back to this book. To receive the maximum benefit from this book, you will need to use a definite, or at least a tentative, occupational choice as a target for the job search process this book describes. Your current major occupational choice will be used as an example. (Of course, you have the right to change your career goal. After all, the first book in this series, *Taking Charge of Your Career Direction,* leaves you with a ranked list of occupational alternatives, a set of backup occupations to which you can turn in case your Number One career goal doesn't work out.)

Approaches to the Job Search

Ways of going about finding a job can be broken down into basic, traditional methods; newer, nontraditional methods; or a combination of the two. A *traditional approach* to job-hunting emphasizes using all the methods you have available to communicate with as many employers as you can. For that reason, it is sometimes referred to as the "numbers game." The *nontraditional approach* involves identifying and targeting employers through personal research of the "hidden job market"—employment needs that are not officially advertised through regular communication channels. The two strategies have many features in common, such as self-assessment, researching of work organizations, and adequate preparation for interviews. You may wish to take the common elements, add individual parts of each approach that appeal to you, and devise your own distinctive *combination approach*. All these techniques call for time, effort, planning, and preparation on the part of the job-seeker. Still another way, which is favored by all too many people, could be called a "no-approach approach." Many people would rather conduct a job search with no involvement of time, effort, planning, or preparation. We could call it a *punt approach*, because it's like the situation of a football team that doesn't know whether it wants to run or pass the ball on first down, so it punts.

Traditional Approaches

Traditional methods of job-hunting involve contacting as many employers as possible and hoping that some of them will respond and suggest an interview. Talking with large numbers of employers over the telephone or sending large numbers of résumés in stamped envelopes requires time, expense, verbal skill, and persistence. This is the "numbers game," which its critics believe to be ineffective and unproductive, considering the time spent on it. Traditional approaches also involve getting help from career search professionals in placement offices and employment services, developing personal contacts and informal sources of job leads, and using advertised sources of job openings in newspapers and trade journals.

The reason for this multitude of activities, according to proponents, is that no single method of job-hunting works very well. The Census Bureau, under the direction of the U.S. Department of Labor, conducted a study that revealed that even the best job search method (applying directly to employers) failed to produce results more than half the time. Since no single method is all that effective, logic dictates using as many job search methods and contacting as many employers as possible. For the most part, traditional methods operate by connecting job-seekers with employers in the following ways.

- Using college career counseling and placement office referrals
- Checking public and private employment agency listings of job vacancies
- Answering help-wanted advertisements in newspapers and magazines
- Placing position-wanted advertisements in trade journals
- Sending résumés and application letters in direct-mail campaigns
- Filling out application forms at personnel and employment offices
- Registering with professional and trade association job clearinghouses
- Attending "career days" and "job fairs" sponsored by various organizations
- Dropping in unannounced on people with hiring authority
- Telephoning businesses listed in the Yellow Pages or other directories
- Applying and taking tests for civil service positions in government
- Sending telegrams or mailing special-delivery letters of application
- Printing well-designed brochures outlining your talents and credentials
- Going to places where employers come to meet or hire workers
- Registering at a union hiring hall
- Contacting friends, parents, relatives, acquaintances, neighbors, former employers, teachers, or anyone who may know about job leads

Obviously, using just a few of these job search techniques would entail a lot of hard work. You may agree with the critics of the numbers game and deride this approach as not worth the time, money, and energy spent. However, if some solid job leads develop, you go to two or three interviews, and an attractive job offer results, you may consider this work well worth the effort.

Newer, Nontraditional Approaches: Targeting Employers

The nontraditional approaches aim to make the job-seeker a proactive rather than a reactive agent in the job search. Job-hunters select employer or work-organization targets based on their personal research, penetrate the "hidden job market," and acquire a job through a technique in which they never ask for one.

The job-hunt is basically an information-hunt, says Richard Nelson Bolles, author of *What Color Is Your Parachute?* (1986). He suggests that you read as many pertinent publications as you can get your hands on, such as business directories, company promotional literature, newsletters, trade magazines, government reports, business magazines, annual reports, and business sections of newspapers. When you have exhausted your written resources, you fill in your knowledge gaps by turning to people who know (or can refer you to those who know) what's happening on the inside of companies in which you are interested. You keep acquiring new information and ideas by continuing to go back and forth between publications and people until you are satisfied you have learned everything you possibly can about the organizations and employers that interest you in the area you want to live. The information-gathering process may take weeks or months.

Essential to the job search is an understanding of the "hidden job market." Information about job vacancies is circulated mainly by word of mouth among people who have hiring authority, executives, department heads, friends, acquaintances, and a whole informal network of contacts that a job-hunter should cultivate. Most job openings are never publicized in employment agencies and help-wanted sections of the newspaper, because these openings are often filled first (Jackson & Mayleas, 1981). The idea for a new job opening may develop from the company's plans for expansion into a new product line, a new problem that has emerged, changes in the marketplace, a promotion or retirement that leaves a job temporarily vacant, or a change in management policy. Meanwhile, months can go by before the personnel department publicizes it. This is the time when your personal contacts can help you penetrate the hidden job market by informing you of the job that is unknown to other job-seekers. More discussion of the hidden job market is found in Chapter 6 of Jackson's *Guerrilla Tactics in the New Job Market* (1991).

You collect, read, and digest company and employer information, but you do not make a formal request for a job when you interview people. For this reason, the strategy goes by such names as "nonjob interview survey" (Billingsley, 1978), the "remembering and referral (R & R) interview" (Haldane, Haldane, & Martin, 1976), or "researching your ideal job" (Bolles, 1986). At this point, you are not conducting a job interview. In the research phase of the job search, you interview people only for the purposes of obtaining information and to be remembered so your name can be referred to other people if they have a job to give. You can be remembered by stimulating interest in your proven skills—those abilities you have used to produce achievements. Creating a favorable impression will help people remember you. For example, increasing the volume of business or cutting the costs of producing things or services are achievements any employer will keep in mind. Being remembered is the key to referral; you don't get referred unless you are remembered. Learning what to say in interviews takes time. It is based on information you have acquired about yourself, occupational targets, work organizations that interest you, and the people you want to interview. Asking for a job, if it happens at all, occurs only after you have been told for certain that a job is open or when you have been referred to a person who has a job to offer. More complete examples and descriptions of this strategy can be found in Chapter 4 of *Job Power Now! The Young People's Job Finding Guide* (Haldane, Haldane, & Martin, 1976).

The nonjob survey, R & R, ideal job research, or informational interview technique has advantages. The rejection is taken out of job-hunting when you don't ask for a job. The pressures and tensions of a job interview are reduced or eliminated when a job is not on the line. Employers can be more relaxed, since there is no obligation to make a decision to hire you or turn you down.

The job search consists not only of discovering job vacancies, but also of job creation. Problems that plague an organization can lead to the creation of new job positions for people who possess the skills to help solve those problems. Bolles (1986) suggests what you can achieve through your research.

- Identify work organizations that have goals compatible with yours and that can use your skills and talents.
- Discover the problems they are experiencing (organizations, like people, have problems).
- Accurately determine whether your skills and abilities can help them solve their problems.
- Identify the person or group who has the responsibility to deal with the problem and has the power to hire.
- Arrange a meeting with that person or group to discuss "mutual concerns" (that is, how you would deal with a problem that has been nagging them), giving the person or group an opportunity to hear your proposals or ideas for solving the problem or contributing to its solution.
- Convince the employer, on the strength of your ideas, to create a position that has not existed before.

If a job is created, you may be the sole applicant for the position; your research, your demonstrated mastery of the subject, and your presentation have carried the day. If you are offered a job position, nontraditional proponents counsel you to delay acceptance until you have evaluated your other options. The job-seeker exercises control over the job search process by developing alternative jobs and companies from which to choose. Even when a job offer is not forthcoming, you have gained vital information, created alternative prospects, developed an understanding of the hidden job market, and devised a way for getting a foot through the employment door without getting your toes broken. The last two chapters of Bolles' annual editions of *What Color Is Your Parachute?* explain the nontraditional approach.

A Combination Approach

You can consider both traditional and nontraditional approaches to the job search and combine parts of each into your own unique method. Relying solely on creative nontraditional methods may strike you as impractical or impossible, but you may be able to connect some of those methods to more traditional approaches and develop a job search plan that is more to your liking and within your capabilities.

For those of you who have completed the first book in the Career Planning Guide series, the combination approach could resemble the career decision-making process, with work organizations taking the place of occupational prospects. "Numbers game" techniques could be used to create and expand a list of workplace prospects. Through researching and informational interviewing, you could reduce the number of alternatives as you research your workplace prospects, study your personal characteristics, and eliminate any alternatives that do not come close to your specifications. A final step in the selection process would be to match your personal characteristics (work values and favorite skills) to those work organizations remaining on your list and arrange the organizations in an order of preference. This results in a prioritized list of workplaces, and you can begin active pursuit of the one at the top of your list. Of course, the one factor you cannot completely control is the job offer, which must come from the employer. (This factor is much like the availability of jobs in the occupation of your choice in the career decision-making exercise.) This is why you work with a *list* of alternatives rather than put all your hopes on one workplace (or one occupational prospect).

Honest questions about either approach can arise. Do traditional methods of job-hunting adequately tap the hidden job market, make job-seekers too dependent upon career counselors or employment agencies, or cause job-seekers to be rejected before they have a chance to see anyone with hiring authority? Can all job-seekers select a prospective work organization and research it thoroughly enough to discover its problems, appraise their skills sufficiently to determine whether they have the ability to solve an organization's problems, and convince people who can hire to create a job position? Are nontraditional techniques more appropriate to professional and managerial types and of limited value to people who plan to enter specialized technical work, skilled trades, and semiskilled occupations?

You are urged not to reject any job search method without giving it serious consideration. Some techniques are more complex than others. You may believe that you cannot follow an elaborate plan completely, but perhaps you can use certain parts of it. Questions and thoughts about both traditional and nontraditional approaches can lead to the formation of a combination approach tailored to your personal needs, interests, and abilities.

You should be aware, however, that traditional and nontraditional approaches may have more similarities than differences. For example, all job search approaches emphasize the importance of self-knowledge and occupational exploration. Making career decisions—knowing exactly what it is that you want to do—is an essential beginning to any job-hunting strategy. Another area of agreement between approaches is the importance of obtaining information about companies from personal research. No career counselor would want to see a client go into an employment interview without knowing the kind of product the company makes or the service it performs. If the employer discovers the job-seeker's ignorance, it is probably the "kiss of death" as far as that job is concerned.

Other broad areas of agreement include the following:

- Giving adequate time to the job search
- Developing a personal contact network
- Being honest and straightforward when interviewing employers
- Using the interview as a learning process
- Practicing answering and asking questions before a job interview
- Creating good first impressions on employers
- Writing thank-you letters after any kind of interview
- Showing enthusiasm about the prospect of working in your chosen occupation

These areas, and other ideas that reflect points of agreement among different approaches to the job search, are developed in the next section.

Twenty Thoughts About the Job Search

Learn More

1. *Job-seekers can always learn more about job-hunting.* Most people know very little about how to search for a job. They think all you need to do is send out a few résumés, make some telephone calls, complete application forms, have an interview—and that's it! They are likely to overestimate their knowledge of the subject. Job search strategies are not usually taught in schools and colleges (although this is changing somewhat), so job-seekers often operate by "seat-of-the-pants" knowledge. Landing a job currently averages between eight and twenty-three weeks, depending on the state of the economy (Bolles, 1991)—indicating that there is more to the job search process than many people suspect. How many graduates have you known or heard of who felt panicky or desperate in their job search and settled for something less than they were worth? That unfortunate situation is called *underemployment*. Some underemployment may be structural (caused by the nature of the economy at the time), but some of it could be avoided with better job search information and techniques. Evaluate yourself on your job-hunting knowledge. Can you honestly claim that you know the following:

- Precisely the work you want to do, so that you could accurately describe your job objective to an employer or on a résumé?
- What to include in your résumé and cover letter and how to design these kinds of business communication?
- What most employers and personnel offices ask on their application forms?
- The information you should try to obtain when you first interview employers?
- Twelve to fifteen sources of job leads in your chosen occupation?

- What you should know about a work organization before you join it?
- The economic trends and social forces influencing your chances of getting a job you desire?
- Where you want to work and live and where the jobs in your occupational choice are located?
- Typical problems encountered by people like yourself who work in your chosen occupational field?
- What to do if you are fired or laid off?

If you can answer "yes" to five of these ten questions, you are in better shape than the average job-seeker. But what about the other five questions, plus the many more that could have been asked?

Start Now

2. *The time to start your job search campaign is now.* Job-hunting is hard work and often frustrating. We'd rather procrastinate than face it. For example, college students are often tempted to say that they will start job-hunting after graduation. There are things you can do to shorten the time span between graduation and full-time work. Become knowledgeable about several sources of job leads. Become acquainted with and keep a record of people who could serve as personal contacts (people who know about jobs, employers, and organizations) when you enter the job market. Identify and research companies you believe would be desirable places to work. Develop the right information to include in your résumé and cover letter. Prepare your credentials for the placement office. Learn other job search methods now so you can move into action immediately when the time comes to search actively for a job. Taking the time now to prepare an adequate information base from which to launch your job search campaign could spare you the grim cycle of initial enthusiasm followed by discouragement, desperation, and depression.

Continuity and Repetition

3. *The job search is a continuous activity, and many job-hunting skills can be used much or all of the time.* A job search is not an isolated event; it happens over and over again. It requires persistence and constant effort. The average person currently changes jobs every three or four years. People are not likely to settle into one job for the rest of their lives as they once did. You may be perfectly happy in your present job, but life can be capricious at times. No one ever plans to have an accident, to be laid off, or to become burned out or disillusioned, but these things do happen. The only true job security lies in being ready to search for a new job at any time. You never know when the seemingly solid ground will shift underneath you. You never know when you will need to have your career-planning bag packed and ready to go. Constant readiness is the only realistic principle for the job world of today.

Tell Everyone

4. *Tell everyone you know that you are looking for a job.* The more people who know, the more likely you are to learn about job positions that are or will be vacant. Keep talking to one person after another until you find one who knows of a job vacancy. Don't be content with the discovery of one job; go on to develop more than one possibility. A job lead does not necessarily lead to a job offer. You need a *list* of several jobs from which you can make a *selection* of those you wish to pursue (unless you are desperate from starvation). Interestingly, more job leads are likely to come from acquaintances than from close friends or relatives, an occurrence that researcher Mark Granovetter (1974) calls "the strength of weak ties." Further research has confirmed this finding.

Hidden Jobs

5. *More job openings exist in the "hidden job market" than are visible and advertised to the general public.* Ask people where they would start looking for a job. Most of them would mention the help-wanted ads in the newspaper. Others might mention listings in public and private employment agencies or placement offices, announcements in trade journals, or notices of examinations for civil service jobs posted on bulletin boards in government buildings. Many job-seekers think most job vacancies are advertised to the general public. Actually, only 15–20 percent of all job openings on any given day are published and circulated. Between 80 and 85 percent of all employment comes through the hidden job market (Haldane, Haldane, & Martin, 1976; Jackson, 1991; Lathrop, 1977). Some labor economists consider these estimates too high, but understanding this concept can give you an advantage many others do not possess.

The hidden portion of the job market exists from the time an idea to create a job enters the mind of a person with hiring authority to the time the job is revealed to the public through newspapers, magazines, announcements on bulletin boards, employment agencies, and placement offices. The intervening time gives you the opportunity to penetrate the hidden job market through your own network of personal contacts. Many employers prefer to hire through an inside system of their own personal contacts rather than by any other method, feeling that it doesn't cost them as much and that the information they obtain is more reliable.

The hidden job market may operate more extensively in small businesses than in large companies, which are more likely to have formalized hiring procedures. Many job-seekers believe that big work organizations offer more employment opportunities. Actually, the reverse is true. Employment growth has been the greatest in small companies in recent years. One study revealed that 66 percent of the new jobs made available between 1969 and 1976 were created in establishments of 20 or fewer employees (Birch,

1981). Large companies are no longer the major source of employment opportunities in the United States (Wegmann, Chapman, & Johnson, 1989).

The Bolles job-creation strategy illustrates another aspect of the hidden job market. After the job-seekers have researched workplaces and interviewed people for information, they can demonstrate their job search and problem-solving skills in the hope of stimulating in the employer's mind a job possibility not perceived until now (Bolles, 1986). The employer is motivated to create a job that has been hidden even from himself or herself.

Use Many Methods

6. *Use as many sources of job leads as you can in your job search.* A survey of 10 million job-seekers, conducted by the Census Bureau in 1972, found the most effective job search method, applying directly to employers, succeeded 47.7 percent of the time (see Table 1-1). From the opposite perspective, even this best method failed over half of the time for those using it. Other job search methods were even less productive. Because no single method of job-hunting works very well, it seems wise to use as many job search resources as you can. Table 1-1 illustrates this principle better than any other recent study does. Confining yourself to one or two methods is better than using no method at all, but it limits you too much. Expanding your use of job search techniques improves your chances of finding a job.

Effectiveness Varies

7. *Effective methods of finding jobs appear to vary from one occupational group to another.* While the multiple-method approach to job-hunting is preferable, an even more effective strategy is to concentrate on two or three methods among the many you use, depending upon the occupation you intend to pursue. Table 1-2, from the same governmental study cited above, shows which methods were most effective for the occupational groups studied. Applying directly to employers was at least 25 percent effective for all groups. Beyond this method, managers found newspaper want ads, private employment agencies, and asking friends about jobs to be more productive than other methods. Craft workers had more success checking union hiring halls and asking friends and relatives about jobs where they work (Egan, 1976). Your research on occupations and organizations should include ways in which people were informed about open job positions and how they applied for them.

Job-Seeker Power

8. *The job-seeker has as much power in and control over the search process as the job-giving employer.* Most job-seekers believe they are powerless. Employers can give or withhold something that job-hunters badly want—namely, a job.

TABLE 1-1 Usage and effectiveness of job search methods

Method	Usage[1]	Effectiveness rate[2]
Applied directly to employer.	66.0	47.7
Asked friends:		
About jobs where they work	50.8	22.1
About jobs elsewhere	41.8	11.9
Asked relatives:		
About jobs where they work	28.4	19.3
About jobs elsewhere	27.3	7.4
Answered newspaper ads:		
Local	45.9	23.9
Nonlocal	11.7	10.0
Private employment agency	21.0	24.2
State employment service	33.5	13.7
School placement office	12.5	21.4
Civil service test	15.3	12.5
Asked teacher or professor	10.4	12.1
Went to place where employers come to pick up people	1.4	8.2
Placed newspaper ads:		
Local	1.6	12.9
Nonlocal	.5	*
Answered ads in professional or trade journals	4.9	7.3
Union hiring hall	6.0	22.2
Contacted local organization	5.6	12.7
Placed ads in professional or trade journals	.6	*
Other	11.8	39.7

[1]Percent of total-job seekers using the method (total was 10 million).

[2]A percentage obtained by dividing the number of job-seekers who found work using the method by the total number of job-seekers who used the method, whether successfully or not.

*Base less than 75,000.

SOURCE: From C. Egan, "Job Search: There's a Method in the Madness," Winter 1976, *Occupational Outlook Quarterly, 20,* p. 18.

However, job-seekers have the power to give or withhold something employers badly want—a worker's time and talent. Employers do have the power to hire (and fire), but it is a power they don't usually enjoy using. Hiring (and firing) is often costly, time-consuming, and full of tension and pressure. Employers usually can't wait to give up interviewing job applicants and get back to their work. When their work organizations get big enough, many employers hire specialists to do this personnel work for them because they dislike it so much.

Pressure affects employers as much as (if not more than) job-seekers, for if they do not select good employees, their organization suffers and declines. (As for firing, employers would like to avoid that ordeal as much as anyone else.) Employers and personnel departments work just as hard at finding good people as job-seekers work at finding good jobs. Qualified, conscientious job-hunters have far more power than they realize.

TABLE 1-2 Effective methods of finding a job, by occupation*

Method	Professional and Technical Workers	Managers	Sales Workers	Clerical Workers	Craft Workers	Operatives, Except Transport	Transport Equipment Operatives	Laborers, Except Farm	Service Workers, Except Private Household
Applied directly to employer	XX	XX	XX	XX	XX	XX	XX	XX	XX
Answered local newspaper ads	X	XX	XX	X	X	X	XX		XX
Asked friends about jobs where they work			X	X	XX	X	X	X	XX
Asked relatives about jobs where they work					X	X		X	X
Union hiring hall					XX	X		X	
School placement office	XX			X					X
Private employment agency		XX		XX					
Asked friends about jobs elsewhere		X							
State employment service						X			
Contacted local organization									X

One X indicates that the method was successful for 20–24 percent of the people using it. A double X indicates the method was successful for 25 percent or more.

SOURCE: From C. Egan, "Job Search: There's a Method in the Madness," Winter 1976, *Occupational Outlook Quarterly, 20,* p. 19.

Screen Employers

9. *Job-seekers should screen employers and workplaces as much as companies screen prospective employees.* It is clear that employers and their personnel departments are going to screen applicants *before* they consider hiring them. A formal test, or some kind of informal, subjective test, may be administered. Employers must receive the right set of "vibrations" before they will hire. Job-seekers, on the other hand, are so anxious to pass the employer's screening devices that they forget to think about screening tests of their own until *after* they are hired. If "they" screen you, there is no reason why you can't screen "them."

Your screening, like that of the employer, should be performed before the question of a job comes up. You are not trying to discover if you are good enough for the job—you did that when you selected an occupation. Instead, you are trying to find out whether the employer's work organization is good enough for you. Your attitude should not be one of begging the employer to give you a job. When you first ask an employer for information so that you can evaluate whether the workplace interests you, you avoid approaching the employer as a suppliant on your knees. The employer is evaluating you, too, as a possible job candidate even though you haven't asked for a job. You and the employer are interviewing each other, and that is the way a job search ought to work.

Job Titles Conceal

10. *In the job search, occupational titles often conceal more information than they reveal.* Occupational titles are useful as general indicators of the activities workers perform on the job in that occupation. We use job titles as a kind of verbal shorthand so that we don't have to use lengthy descriptions to explain what we are talking about. Ask people about the work they do, and they respond in the form of a job title: secretary, manager, nurse, auto mechanic, teacher. The title gives you some information and brings to mind some stereotyped images, both accurate and inaccurate, of what a person is like or does on the job. When you researched occupations to make a career decision, you found that the information from a job title was not enough. You had to ask questions and obtain information about the nature of the work, preparation, training, pay, working conditions, location, typical work associates, advancement opportunities, competition, personal satisfaction, problems to solve, and many other data that went well beyond the title of the occupation.

In some situations, you *must* remove an occupational label. If your job ever becomes obsolete or is shipped out of town or overseas where you can't follow it, and you are laid off, you must peel off the old job label and repackage yourself as a constellation of skills to which you can affix a new job title after you are employed (Bolles, 1986). Those skills are then transferred to the new job title.

Know Your Objective

11. *The best job-seekers are those who have their career goals clearly in mind.*
They think not only of a well-defined job objective, but also of a preferred
geographical location and the names of several workplaces. By now you
should have a ranked list of occupational alternatives based on a knowledge
of your important work values and your favorite, documented abilities. If
this is not the case, you have some personal homework to do. Knowing what
you want to do is the biggest hurdle in career planning. Once you have
decided on a career goal, it is easier to take action in the search for a job in
the occupation of your choice.

Desire and Enthusiasm

**12. *Demonstrating your desire for a job and your enthusiasm about the work im-
presses most employers more than anything else.*** Job-seekers typically worry
about how badly they need a job. Instead, they ought to think in terms of
their desire for a job. Nothing captures an employer's imagination more than
the job applicant's communication of enthusiasm about a job. No one has to
say, "I want this job very much." Employers and interviewers can sense it
without being told. Projecting genuine enthusiasm will put you ahead of
many competitors in the job search. A lot of people expect work to be a form
of imprisonment, a monotonous grind, a life of quiet desperation, or an activity they will come to hate. Who could be creative or feel challenged by
work with expectations such as these? Some jobs *are* too small, flat, dull,
energy-draining, or unchallenging for you. Perhaps you can be spared from
wrong jobs by the quality of your career planning. Develop desire and enthusiasm for your work by building reasonable expectations from a process
of setting appropriate career and life goals.

Select Your Workplace

**13. *The selection of a place to work is just as important for job satisfaction as the
choice of an occupation.*** Some people think that once they have chosen an
occupation, they have completed their career planning. Actually, they have
completed only one phase; more decisions remain for the job search. If you
are serious about your future, your exploration of workplaces will involve as
much effort as your research of occupations. Work organizations have their
own distinctive products and services, group cultures, personality characteristics, and ways of employing people. The environmental context or social atmosphere of the place in which you work has as much to do with your
career satisfaction as does the nature of the work in your occupation.

Some workers find themselves in the wrong places of work after having
chosen the right occupation for them. All too often, they think they have
made the wrong occupational choice and never stop to consider that they

could be in the wrong workplace. A change of work location could bring them the job satisfaction they had originally anticipated.

Competent job-seekers research workplaces and organizations *before* they accept a job offer. They may even reject an organization's offer based on the information they have uncovered about it. Richard Irish underscores the importance of selecting a work organization and an employer when he writes: "Hire yourself an employer. You'll be spending as much time with this person as with your wife or husband, and you'll want a good marriage" (Irish, 1978).

Personal Responsibility

14. *The best job-hunters assume personal responsibility for finding a job.* Make up your mind to take responsibility for your job search from the beginning. Professional career counselors, employment-agency personnel, and placement officials can help, but in the final analysis, the job-seeker must put the words in the résumé, complete the application form, do the company research, and face the employer in the interview. If career counselors offer to relieve you of these burdens, flee from them as quickly as possible, for they are either charlatans or misguided. (Before you pay a career counselor to help you, read the appendix on career counseling in *What Color Is Your Parachute?* by Richard Bolles.)

Another facet of career responsibility can arise after you have accepted employment. If the job becomes monotonous, unchallenging, dreary drudgery, don't waste time blaming the system, those in power, the economy, your horoscope, or whatever. You have three options. (1) Do nothing. (2) Improve the quality of your job if possible. (3) Change jobs as soon as you reasonably can. The problem with the first option is that it leads to chronic complaining; the daily gripe session becomes your only job satisfaction. You can try to improve the nature of your work by thinking of ways to make it more challenging and rewarding, clearing your ideas with your supervisors. Changing jobs, of course, requires a new job search, the subject of this book. Try to do it while you have a source of income from your current job. However bad the job may seem to you now, keep in mind that you can always learn something from it that might be useful later. Keep in mind that you are responsible for your job search; no one else will do it as well as you will.

A Concern for Community

15. *Although we must depend upon ourselves in the search for a job, all of us are dependent in some way on others and on the community at large.* The previous section emphasized the virtues of personal responsibility and self-sufficiency. Most people in the United States believe people should have the freedom to "do their own thing" as long as it doesn't hurt anyone. Individualism encompasses many admirable attributes—the values of independence, autonomy, and self-governance, to name a few. Certainly, this Career Planning Guide series is dedicated to helping people "stand on their own two feet." However, we need to maintain an attitude that balances the emphasis on personal responsibility in career decision-making and self-reliance in job searching with an expression of concern for the human community. In present-day America, too many people view their occupational choice, job-hunt, and work as a means to obtain a prosperous *private* lifestyle without much thought of the common good in such areas as justice, health, and knowledge. For example, the community needs lawyers to serve the cause of justice, nurses and doctors to serve the cause of health, and teachers to serve the cause of knowledge and learning (Bellah, Madsen, Sullivan, Swidler, & Tipton, 1988). An exclusive focus on personal advancement leaves people isolated from one another and confused about the requirements of a good society. When you search for a job, you do not do it apart from the community. You will need help from your network of personal contacts and support from your family as much as you will need to accept personal responsibility in your job search. When you are working, you will need customers, suppliers, co-workers, students, patients, clients, and so on—all from the community—and, if you forget those other people, you will soon be out of business. Whether you are self-employed or part of an organization, you are as dependent on other people as you are on your own hard work and motivation to achieve your career goals.

Support and Sharing

16. *Support systems and sharing of resources are useful strategies in the job search.* Some people go it alone in the job search, too proud or afraid to involve anyone else. Most of us, however, need emotional support from others, particularly those who are close to us, when we face a tough situation. Pooling resources with others can be very helpful, especially if you get bogged down. This is particularly important for those who are job-hunting because they have been fired. Some people conceal their unemployment from their families. They carry the entire burden of guilt and embarrassment in their minds: an understandable reaction, but not a helpful or productive one. They simulate their former working days, getting up as usual and pretending to go to work. The truth becomes known sooner or later; therefore, it's better to be straightforward with your family from the start and ask for their support. Whether you are looking for a job for the 1st time or the 20th time, your family can be a source of great strength. Your nuclear family and your extended family can provide you with moral and even financial support and can be a rich source of job leads. But you must let them know what you are doing and how they could help. Work associates, former employers, neighbors, and social acquaintances can recommend you to their contacts or give you referrals from among their contacts in business and social groups. This information network, both inside and outside the family, represents your best opportunity to crack the hidden job market.

Joining a job club or cooperative can be very helpful in finding a job. Job clubs are small groups of job-seekers guided by a counselor. Club members exchange information about job leads, make phone calls, write letters, rehearse interviews, give each other rides, and offer emotional support at a time when it's most needed. When members get jobs, they notify the others, describe how they did it, and turn over their lists of job leads; the process then continues for other job-seekers (Arzin & Besalel, 1982). Check with your local community action agencies to locate job clubs in your area. Job co-ops are sponsored by governmental agencies, women's resource groups, college placement offices, professional associations, churches, and adult education programs. A job co-op can be an excellent way of getting help in the lonely, frustrating business of job-hunting. Support groups provide the encouragement and reinforcement that you might otherwise lack.

Work as Education

17. *Working on the job is an education in itself.*   People often assume that when their formal education in the classroom is completed, they are ready and equipped to do the work in the occupation of their choice. After you have worked on the job awhile, you discover that you have obtained most of your knowledge about the work on the job, not in school. This is not an indictment of the educational system, which has provided "generalist" skills that can be transferred to the job. Generalist skills, such as reading, communicating, researching, and analyzing, are learned in academic courses. These skills may in the future prove to be more adaptable to work than a specialty, which could become outdated because of advances in science and technology. Almost every job is learned through on-the-job training. Skills learned on the job generally fall into the category of "specialist" skills; many companies provide an in-service education program to train workers in their specialties.

The best way to find out what jobs are like while you are in school is to gain work experience from a temporary, part-time, or summer job. If the work can relate to your career objective, so much the better. This is the idea behind cooperative work-study programs and internships. Work experience during school has advantages other than that of earning some spending money. It places you in situations where you can casually interview people for information you may need for your future job search and where you can develop personal contacts. Employers are more impressed with job-seekers who have previous experience of paid work and volunteer work than with job-seekers who have no work experience. Check with your placement office or public employment agency for part-time and temporary work opportunities.

Howard Figler, author of *PATH: A Career Workbook for Liberal Arts Stu-*

dents (1979), suggests an *interim job* approach to career exploration and preparation for the job search. Interim jobs are temporary, part-time, and summer work experiences that meet the following requirements. Little or no qualifications are needed; the job is available; and it places you in contact with many people in different kinds of work situations. These jobs allow you to talk with people about their work, ask them questions to obtain information, and develop contacts that might prove useful in your future job search. Some "interim jobs" suggested by Figler include opinion poll interviewer, news reporter, retail-store clerk, car driver, marketing research interviewer, bartender, museum guard, hospital orderly, security guard, golf caddie, short-order cook, comparison shopper, receptionist, photographer's helper, mail carrier, and temporary office worker.

Persistence Pays Off

18. *Persistence in the job search is the greatest strength of the job-hunter.* Without persistence and effort, no job search system will work very well. The job-seeker's greatest enemy is discouragement; people *do* give up on finding a job and quit altogether. In the government's monthly unemployment figures, there is a special category for "discouraged workers," those who have stopped looking for jobs. Rejection seems built into the job-hunting system. Even though you know it has nothing to do with you personally, your ego gets battered every time you are turned down. Your résumé draws no response, your letters don't get answered, phone calls are not returned, employers are not in, someone else is chosen after the interview. That's the way the typical job search goes. Sooner or later, you are tempted to quit—but then you would certainly find no job.

Jackson (1991) suggests an innovative way of looking at the job search. He describes it as a NO NO NO NO NO NO NO NO NO NO NO NO NO NO NO YES! process. Every NO gets you that much closer to the YES. Be realistic about job-hunting. Few job-seekers connect with a firm job offer after only two or three hours of work. You can't just send out a few résumés and sit back waiting for job offers to materialize. If you take seriously the hard work and persistence needed for job-hunting, you'll be ahead of most job-seekers on that factor alone.

Most job-hunters spend less than five hours a week on their job search. If you make job-hunting a full-time, 35-hour-a-week job, you speed up the job search process by a factor of seven and increase your chances accordingly. That may seem like a lot of time. But if you are not willing to give it your best shot, then others have a right to ask, "How important to you is getting a job, anyway?"

The Universal Hiring Rule

19. *The key to getting hired is convincing an employer that you will bring more value to the company than you will cost it.* Jackson (1991) calls this the *universal* *hiring rule.* Can you show how you could cut the cost of producing something or providing a service? Can you show how you could increase a company's volume of business? The most effective sales technique in a job interview is to quietly and confidently let employers know what you can do for them. This means you must be very knowledgeable about what the organization does for a living—a practical argument for spending time researching the company. A majority of job-seekers define the job search in terms of their own needs: "I need a job." Instead, take the straight and narrow path to your job search goal. Rehearse your answers to the employer's greatest concern and favorite question: "Why should I hire you?" Give the employer the reasons for doing so.

Self-Esteem

20. *Winning a new job is one of the best ways available for developing self-esteem, whether you are seeking a first job or moving to a better one.* The feeling you get when you learn new techniques of job-hunting and build confidence that you can always land a job is one of the most liberating feelings you can experience. You can get help and support and pool your resources with others, of course, but you rely essentially on yourself. Perhaps the greatest feeling you can have about yourself is the inner knowledge that you can get a job, earn your own money, and take care of yourself.

If you currently work at a job you have come to hate, it's time to change jobs. Of course, there will be problems. "It will cost money." "My family won't support me." "It's risky to change." "It's suicide to change jobs in midcareer." It may be more costly, risky, or suicidal to stay put. Yes, you will face new challenges and problems of adjustment, but you will also experience a rebirth of motivation, enthusiasm for life, and a sense of achievement. Today more people than ever opt for a midcareer job change, from the homemaker seeking a new life outside the home to the employee who suddenly needs to escape the comfortable work routine of the past 15 years. A new job can bring a new lease on life. One cautionary note: job-changing is not hopping helter-skelter from one job to another. Job-changing should be a well-planned strategy, not a change for the sake of change.

In addition to the 20 thoughts listed here, many more will be explored in this book, including the following:

- All interviews, informational or for a job, should be followed up with a thank-you letter.
- The job search campaign requires organization in order to be effective (more about this subject in a moment).

For now, 20 thoughts will suffice, and the ones listed in this section meet with widespread agreement. Of course, other thoughts about job-hunting are more controversial:

- *Avoid personnel departments at all costs, because the only authority they have is the power to screen out job applicants, not to hire them— unless the job is in personnel.* This is true enough in a number of cases, but personnel departments are appropriate targets for entry-level positions, and they are still the main gate to jobs for the new college graduate (Shingleton & Bao, 1977).
- *It is easier to get a job if you are working than if you are not working.* This was once true enough, but this idea has eroded because too many worthy people have been unemployed recently; being out of work doesn't carry the stigma it once did.

Getting Organized for the Job Search

Set up a job search office. Choose an area much like a place you would choose to study. It should include a desk or a table where you can keep supplies, notes, incoming mail, stationery, newspapers, books, and files.

Set a time for your job search efforts. Preferably, this should be 8 to 5, for job-hunting is a full-time activity. If you are working or going to school, reserve a couple of hours in the evening for such activities as visiting libraries, reading job search material, and writing or completing letters, résumés, and applications. Use lunch hours, late afternoons, Saturdays, vacation periods, and personal-business days for contacting potential employers, conducting informational interviews, and researching work organizations.

Set aside space in a desk or on a corner of a desk or table for your supplies: paper for notes, stationery, stamps, envelopes, paper clips, stapler, and file folders (if you don't have a file cabinet). You will need access to a typewriter, Sunday editions of newspapers, a photocopier or printing service, a telephone and phone book, and transportation. If you are not home during the day, a telephone answering machine would be helpful.

Keep accurate records. At the end of this chapter and throughout the book, you will find forms on which to keep records. You can photocopy these record forms for your private use if you need more copies of them.

Keep track of your expenses. As of this writing, any expense associated with the job search is deductible on your federal income-tax return. Travel expenses or fees paid to a career counselor or employment agency can be deducted, whether or not you succeed in landing a new job. These expenses must be recorded and verified in case you are audited. Keep receipts to substantiate your transportation, telephone, stationery, lodging, and food costs. Even this book could be deductible. You cannot deduct the costs of education you need to qualify for a new job, nor are expenses deductible if you are job-hunting for the first time or changing occupations. For expenses to be deductible, there must be substantial continuity between a new job and the last job. Technically, you cannot deduct expenses if you are changing from one career field into another.

EXERCISE 1-1   *Getting Started: A Daily Job Search Plan*

Keep a record of your daily job search activities. First, make several photo-copies of the "Daily Job Search Action Plan" form provided in this exercise so as to have copies available as you need them. Next, set your weekly goals, either week-by-week or over an entire month. How many hours do you pro-pose to spend on your job search? How many job leads will be explored, letters and résumés sent, applications completed, areas and organizations researched, informational and job interviews held? Each day you conduct your job search, fill out the Daily Job Search Action Plan. To do this, record the amount of time you spent on the job search that day and tally the number of job leads you explored, the number of letters or résumés you sent to job targets, and so on. Keep a count of employers who contact you. Later chap-ters will supply forms for the names and addresses of contacts, employers, and organizations. A "miscellaneous" category, for a count of job search activities not elsewhere classified, is provided in the record.

   After a one- or four-week period, check to see whether you have accom-plished your goals. Were you too optimistic about how much you would do? Do you need to do more? Should you reset your goals in each category, considering the information you have received from your performance to date? Are your goals achievable, believable, and controllable?

EXERCISE 1-2   *Establishing Clear Career Goals*

This exercise is intended for those who have not completed the career deci-sion-making exercise in the first volume of the Career Planning Guide series. Refer particularly to the lists of possible occupational interests, achieve-ments, abilities (skills and aptitudes), and work values provided in *Taking Charge of Your Career Direction* for help in supplying the information for this exercise. The first step in job-hunting is knowing what you want and what you can do. Fill in the following blanks.

   1. Five achievements I have attained in the past are as follows:

1. _____

2. _____

3. _____

4. _____

5. _____

Title these five achievements and provide details (on a separate sheet of paper) of how you made each one happen. Circle the skills, aptitudes, and abilities you used in producing the achievements.

(continued on page 25)

Daily Job Search Action Plan								
Month: ____ Day/ Date	Time Spent on Job Search	Number of Job Leads Explored	Number of Letters/ Resumes Sent to Job Targets	Number of Job Applica- tions Com- pleted	Pieces of Data Collected on Areas and Companies	Number of Inter- views Held	Number of Employer Contacts to You	Other or Miscel- laneous*
Weekly Goals								
Mon. ___								
Tue. ___								
Wed. ___								
Thurs.___								
Fri. ___								
Sat. ___								
Weekly Total								
Mon. ___								
Tue. ___								
Wed. ___								
Thurs.___								
Fri. ___								
Sat. ___								
Weekly Total								
Mon. ___								
Tue. ___								
Wed. ___								
Thurs.___								
Fri. ___								
Sat. ___								
Weekly Total								
Mon. ___								
Tue. ___								
Wed. ___								
Thurs.___								
Fri. ___								
Sat. ___								
Weekly Total								
Reset Goals?								

* Network contacts, job search training or counseling sessions, and the like.

Daily Job Search Action Plan								
Month: ___ ___ Day/ Date	Time Spent on Job Search	Number of Job Leads Explored	Number of Letters/ Résumés Sent to Job Targets	Number of Job Applica- tions Com- pleted	Pieces of Data Collected on Areas and Companies	Number of Inter- views Held	Number of Employer Contacts to You	Other or Miscel- laneous*
Weekly Goals								
Mon. ___								
Tue. ___								
Wed. ___								
Thurs.___								
Fri. ___								
Sat. ___								
Weekly Total								
Mon. ___								
Tue. ___								
Wed. ___								
Thurs.___								
Fri. ___								
Sat. ___								
Weekly Total								
Mon. ___								
Tue. ___								
Wed. ___								
Thurs.___								
Fri. ___								
Sat. ___								
Weekly Total								
Mon. ___								
Tue. ___								
Wed. ___								
Thurs.___								
Fri. ___								
Sat. ___								
Weekly Total								
Reset Goals?								

* Network contacts, job search training or counseling sessions, and the like.

2. Ten of my strongest and most enjoyable abilities, documented or proven, include the following:

Name of Ability	*Proof or Evidence*
1. _____	_____
2. _____	_____
3. _____	_____
4. _____	_____
5. _____	_____
6. _____	_____
7. _____	_____
8. _____	_____
9. _____	_____
10. _____	_____

3. Ten of my most important work values, defined or explained so that I know each one is distinct from the others, are as follows:

Name of Work Value	*Definition*
1. _____	_____
2. _____	_____
3. _____	_____
4. _____	_____
5. _____	_____
6. _____	_____
7. _____	_____
8. _____	_____
9. _____	_____
10. _____	_____

4. (a) Plan A: My Number One occupational goal is _____

_____ .

(b) Typical jobs in this occupation are _____ ,

_____ , and _____ .

5. (a) Plan B: My Number Two occupational goal is _____

_____ .

(b) Typical jobs in this occupation are _____ ,

_____ , and _____ .

6. (a) Plan C: My Number Three occupational goal is _____

_____ .

(b) Typical jobs in this occupation are _____ ,

_____ , and _____ .

Summary

1. There are three basic approaches to the job search. The traditional approach consists of including as many methods and contacting as many probable sources of job openings as possible. The nontraditional approach focuses on self-selected job targets (often hidden from public view) through research of potential workplaces and employers. A combination of these two sets of procedures can also be applied, using the shared ideas of the other systems of job-hunting.

2. Twenty basic ideas about the job search are common to all approaches. Everyone needs to know more about job-hunting. You should start your job search now, while you are in college or in a secure job position. The job-seeking process is continuous and repetitive. Tell everyone you know that you are looking for a job. The majority of job openings are located in the hidden job market. You should use as many sources of job leads as you can. The effectiveness of particular job-finding methods varies among occupational groups. Job-seekers have as much power in the job-hunt as employers. Job-seekers should screen employers and workplaces. Job titles can conceal as much as they reveal. You need a clear objective in the job search. It is important to show enthusiasm for your intended work. Selecting a work organization is just as important for job satisfaction as is choosing an occupation. You should take personal responsibility in job-hunting. The job-seeker should consider family and community concerns in addition to personal needs. A support system and work experience are essential. Work is an education in itself. Persistence is the most important job search skill. You need to convince the employer that you will bring the company more value than cost. Landing a job greatly enhances self-esteem.

3. Organization and efficiency are the keys to job-seeking. Establishing a job search office, setting aside time and space for gathering information and storing materials, and keeping accurate records will permit you to structure

and analyze your job hunt. As you start your campaign, recording a daily count of job search activities will put into action the principle of being efficient and organized.

References

Arzin, N. H., and Besalel, V. B. (1982). *Finding a job.* Berkeley, CA: Ten Speed Press.

Bellah, R. N., Madsen, R., Sullivan, W. M., Swidler, A., & Tipton, S. M. (1988). *Habits of the heart: Individualism and commitment in American life.* New York: Harper & Row.

Billingsley, E. (1978). *Career planning and job hunting for today's student: The nonjob interview approach.* Santa Monica, CA: Goodyear.

Birch, D. (1981). Who creates jobs? *The Public Interest, 65,* Fall, 3–14.

Bolles, R. N. (1986). *What color is your parachute?* Berkeley, CA: Ten Speed Press.

Bolles, R. N. (1991). *What color is your parachute?* Berkeley, CA: Ten Speed Press.

Egan, C. (1976). Job search: There's a method in the madness. *Occupational Outlook Quarterly, 20,* Winter, 18–19.

Figler, H. E. (1979). *PATH:. A career workbook for liberal arts students* (2nd ed.). Cranston, RI: Carroll Press.

Granovetter, M. S. (1974). *Getting a job: A study of contacts and careers.* Cambridge, MA: Harvard University Press.

Haldane, B., Haldane, J., & Martin, L. (1976). *Job power now! The young people's job finding guide.* Washington, DC: Acropolis Books.

Irish, R. K. (1978). *Go hire yourself an employer.* Garden City, NY: Doubleday/Anchor.

Jackson, T. (1991). *Guerrilla tactics in the new job market* (2nd ed.). New York: Bantam Books.

Jackson, T., & Mayleas, D. (1981). *The hidden job market for the 80s.* New York: Times Books.

Lathrop, R. (1977). *Who's hiring who?* Berkeley, CA: Ten Speed Press.

Shingleton, J. D., & Bao, R. (1977). *College to career: Finding yourself in the job market.* New York: McGraw-Hill.

Wegmann, R., Chapman, R., and Johnson, M. (1989). *Work in the new economy: Careers and job seeking into the 21st century* (rev. ed.). Indianapolis, IN: JIST Works, and Alexandria, VA: American Association for Counseling and Development.

2

Sources of Job Leads

Many people in many places are ready to assist you in your job search. Some are very helpful; some are not so helpful. Some will offer assistance free of charge; others will charge you a fee. You should feel free to obtain help in finding a job, but it is important to remember that you are the only person who can convince an employer to give you a job.

Everyone needs help at some point in the job search, except perhaps people who go into business for themselves. The rest of us are employed by others. This chapter will describe where you can go and what you can do to obtain help in locating job leads. By way of introduction, we'll list some possible job-lead sources.

If you are in college or have attended college, you should contact your school's *career planning and placement office,* which arranges for students and graduates to meet with company recruiters and employers. *State employment agencies* and their local branches offer a free job-finding service. *Private employment agencies* provide job-finding services for a fee, usually paid by the employer, but sometimes by the job-seeker, and sometimes by both. *Temporary help agencies* can provide both a route to a permanent, full-time job position and extra money during one's job search. The *help-wanted ads* in newspapers, journals, and newsletters are often disparaged because of their visibility to everyone, but if employers as well as job-hunters did not find them useful, they would have disappeared long ago. Some people *place ads* for themselves in these publications to indicate their availability. *Other parts of the newspaper* contain articles that can imply a job opening without actually announcing it, such as through articles that report a retirement, a resignation, or the opening of a new business. Some job-seekers organize a *direct-mail campaign* of letters and résumés to hundreds, and even thousands, of work organizations. *Applying directly to personnel and employment offices* is the most extensively used job search method, according to the Census Bureau's study of 10 million workers cited in the previous chapter. Personnel departments represent a good source of job leads, because personnel workers assist managers and executives in filling vacancies.

Many professional and trade associations sponsor *job clearinghouses and registers* to serve as intermediaries between their job-seeking members and employers. A few *executive search firms* help people find jobs, but generally these firms work for employers to recruit for management positions those already employed. A good source of contacts is *career days* or *job fairs* sponsored by schools, chambers of commerce, and the like. *Drop-in visits* or "cold-turkey" calls on heads of businesses or departments are quick and sometimes effective ways of reaching the person with hiring authority, if you are assertive enough. Instead of dropping in unannounced, you can *telephone employers directly* to get in touch with the person who has the power to hire. Job clubs use this approach; the telephone procedure you can use is outlined in this chapter. *Internships and work/study* provide ways of gaining work experience and future employment. *The government,* the largest single employer in the country, should not be overlooked. About one sixth of all people in the American labor force work for federal, state, and local governments. A competitive examination is usually required in the application process for government jobs. *The military* is also a source of employment; it has its own recruiters and training programs. *Publications and directories,* such as the *College Placement Annual,* carry helpful information about companies and corporations. People have attracted employers through all sorts of *unusual methods,* such as long-distance calls, telegrams, and artistically crafted brochures. Some unusual methods are very creative and enterprising; others are just plain kooky.

It may seem strange to you that we haven't yet mentioned the most productive source of job leads. Job search experts tell us that about 80 percent of all employment is gained through the job-seeker's *personal contact network.* A personal contact is someone you know who can give you valuable inside information about potential job openings or refer you to a person who has a job to offer. Personal contacts can be parents, relatives, neighbors, friends, friends of the family, friends of friends, work associates, school alums, present and former employers, teachers, and members of professional associations, service clubs, social groups, labor unions, and religious institutions. Methods of contact are often informal and casual. Make personal contacts, by all means, for they are the major source of job leads, but make them for the motives of friendship and helping others as well as for the purpose of job search. People will want to hear about how you are doing, but if you use them only as sources of job leads, they could come to regard you as self-serving, interested in your own career and nothing else. A personal contact network is like a mutual aid society; you help your contacts and they help you. Your contacts can give you information and advice and can often open doors to the hidden job market. Your initial approach to a potential personal contact is generally the informational interview, which will be discussed briefly in this chapter and more fully in Chapter 7.

Getting Help in the Job Search

Some people are afraid to ask for help. Sometimes, that can be a tragic mistake. A 30-year man wrote the unsigned note to columnist Mike Royko (1982), quoted in part below.

> I had to tell someone before I take my life. I am married with a family of three, religious, and never been in trouble with the law. For the past five months, I have been frantically searching for some kind of employment. I am now at the point of no return. My family and I are about to be evicted because I can't pay the rent. The debts are piling up. I would like to live longer and enjoy my family, but I can't support them. I have tried seeking employment. No matter what it may be, no one has a job opening. I'm not asking for charity or a handout. All I'm asking for is a chance to work and support my family. How do you explain to your children when they say, "Daddy, why can't I have boots for the snow?" When you don't have a job, you have to cut back on everything just to survive. But small children don't understand. I always believed that one

must help himself before he can get help from someone else. I'm desperate, totally desperate. Please tell anyone who has a job that they are the luckiest people in the world, no matter what the pay or conditions. At least they can tell their family when payday comes that they can buy food and clothes and pay the rent.

The columnist responded by acknowledging the man's plight and urging him to hang on. His wife and children would rather have an unemployed living husband and father than the memory of a dead one. He wasn't alone in his unemployed condition; it was nothing to be ashamed of. A lot of jobless people had no control over the trends that cost them their jobs. Our welfare system, although far from perfect, would still provide the bare basics, so the family wasn't going to starve or be out in the freezing cold.

No one should be embarrassed to receive help in the job search; everyone needs it at some point, and plenty of people make their living giving job-finding assistance. You have been introduced to the sources of job leads. The following paragraphs describe each one in more detail.

College Career Planning and Placement Offices

The placement service of a college's career planning office develops contacts with employers, who notify the placement office whenever they have job openings; sets up interviews for students and company recruiters; and offers career planning and job search information and counseling. Students can register with the placement service office when they seek employment. The placement service brings job vacancies to the attention of qualified student registrants. The word *placement* can be misleading in that the placement office does not place people in jobs; it only lets people know where job openings exist. You have to win the job through your own job search skills.

Companies send recruiters to colleges all over the country, mainly for the purpose of interviewing graduating students for potential employment. Up to 2000 recruiters descend upon the campus of a large university in a given year (Shingleton & Bao, 1977). You should use this service while you are in college, for you'll probably never again have the opportunity to interview so many employers from so many different organizations so easily in one place.

You can register for company interviews at your college's career planning and placement office by completing a registration form (for a quick review by employers) or by establishing a *credentials file* that contains your transcript of courses and grades and your letters of recommendation from former teachers, previous employers, and other people who know you well. Students can select the companies and the interviewers with whom they would like to talk. Career counselors in college emphasize that you need to begin using campus interviews about nine months before graduation—in other words, at the start of your last year of full-time study. Before your interview, read all the information you can about the recruiter's organization. Most placement offices have annual reports of and descriptive information about the companies that send recruiters to them. Don't expect the recruiter to offer you a job on the spot, no matter how well the interview goes. If you are invited to visit the company's home office, this indicates a second phase in their employment process; it usually means you have passed some kind of initial screening test in the college career planning and placement office.

State Employment Agencies

Public employment agencies are operated by state governments in major cities and towns. Their services are free to job-seekers, although citizens have paid for them through taxes. Some people focus on the unemployment benefit function, but state employment commissions emphasize that they are first and foremost a job service. Local offices of the state employment service maintain a daily listing of job openings in the local area, the state, and the entire nation through a computerized job bank. Job-hunters complete a registration form and are sent to job interviews with appropriate employers. Some employment services offer training programs in job search skills or refer you to programs conducted by government agencies, unions, or employers.

More people use the public employment service than private agencies, because public employment services charge no fee. Sometimes, you hear the complaint that public employment agency workers are indifferent to the needs of jobseekers; it is said that state employment workers feel less pressure to fill job vacancies because they are paid a salary whether they locate job openings for their clients or not. However, keep in mind that private agencies can be equally bureaucratic and that public employment offices often handle a large volume of business with very little money on which to operate. Despite any negative comments you may encounter, you should not overlook state employment services. Not only do they provide a free job search service, but generally they list more job openings than does any other single source of job leads.

Private Employment Agencies

Some job-seekers use private employment agencies on the assumption that they will work harder at uncovering employment opportunities because their agents work on a commission basis, not for a salary. They must produce results to stay in business. Who pays the costs for the use of private employment agencies? Most of the time, the employer pays. In the minds of agency managers, employers represent repeat business, whereas job-seekers are considered only one-time clients. When the employer pays the fee, the agency advertises its job vacancies as free to job-seekers. In this case, remember that the agency is working for the employer, not for you, the job-seeker. All kinds of payment arrangements exist. Sometimes you and the employer share expenses. If the agency collects a fee from you as a job-seeker, you will be asked to sign a contract that requires you to pay them should they be successful in locating a job that you accept. You could be billed 60 percent of your first month's pay or 5 to 15 percent of your first year's salary. Many companies will reimburse you after you have been with them for a certain period of time. Avoid any contract that demands "exclusive listing" or "exclusive handling"—it keeps you from using other job-finding services, and if you find a job from your own efforts, you could still be bound to pay the agency a fee. Be certain you understand the payment structure and the nature of the services offered before you sign an agreement.

How do you select a private employment agency? You need to do some research to answer this question. You can ask others who have been clients of an agency, but even this will leave you in some uncertainty, because an effective agency for them may not be a good one for you. A local newspaper office could help. Chances are good that private employment agencies in the area have advertised in the paper, and the advertising editor may be able to give you information on the subject. Check whether the agency is listed in the annual membership directory of the National Association of Personnel Consultants (1432 Duke Street, Alexandria, VA 22314), the organization that certifies private employment agencies.

Private employment agencies may concentrate on certain industries in a local area, or they may cover a wide assortment of occupations over a large territory. Reliable agencies can save you hours of time by referring you to only those job vacancies that match your job qualifications. Inexperienced agents can waste a lot of your time by inappropriate referrals. Ask your agent to be selective in suggesting job targets for you. Sending résumés "shotgun style" is something you could do without the added expense of the agency fee. Do not sign with any private agency that wants to sell you lots of extras such as testing, résumé writing workshops, and interviewing practice. Such services are often free or of low cost at a college career planning and placement office. Do not allow yourself to be pressured into applying for a job vacancy in an occupation other than the career objective you have established. Some devious agencies have been known to play the "bait-and-switch" game, luring you with one job prospect but later trying to entice you to apply for an inferior position. Some experts advise college graduates and other first-time job-seekers to use private employment agencies only as a last resort. They believe that such agencies provide a better service for job-changers who have been working for a number of years.

Temporary-Help Agencies

These private business services provide employers with workers for a limited time, as in the case of seasonal work needs or peak production periods. At one time, most temporary help agencies confined themselves to supplying clerical workers, but now they have expanded to include professional employees such as engineers, accountants, systems analysts, programmers, and so on. The number of "contingent," or temporary and part-time, work-ers has increased rapidly, resulting in a growing number of temporary-help agencies. The attractions of temporary and part-time employment are that people can supplement their income, explore a variety of jobs and work-places; try out new work experiences; and possibly, with a demonstration of excellent skills and work habits, interest an employer in offering permanent, full-time work. Employers see temporary help as a way to lower labor costs, screen potential candidates for permanent jobs, and gain flexibility in adjust-ing to changing demands for labor. Disadvantages in temporary and part-time work are lower pay rates, less job security, fewer benefits, and unpre-dictable hours.

Help-Wanted Listings in Newspapers

Many job-hunters start by scanning the help-wanted advertisements in the classified advertising section of the daily newspapers. However, not all job openings are publicized in the local paper. Generally, the higher the salary paid for a job, the less the likelihood it will be advertised in the newspaper. The greatest disadvantage of help-wanted ads is that the publicity of a job opening in the newspaper forces you to compete with many more job appli-cants. Because of the volume of replies an advertisement produces, you must answer many ads in order to bring about any response. Sunday editions of daily newspapers contain the largest number of help-wanted listings. Local newspapers concentrate on local job vacancies. Large city newspapers such as the *New York Times,* the *Chicago Tribune,* the *Los Angeles Times,* and the *Wall Street Journal* carry large sections of help-wanted ads for all re-gions of the country as well as for local job openings.

In general, four types of want ads can be identified: (1) open ads, (2) blind ads, (3) employment agency ads, and (4) catch ads.

Open ads (Figure 2-1) are the best kind from the job-seeker's viewpoint because they give the name of the work organization that offers the job open-ing. These ads often include the company's address and telephone number, the nature of the work, what the organization produces, salary and fringe benefits paid, and the qualifications required of the applicant. One disadvan-tage of open ads is that they attract the largest number of responses, so you are likely to have more competition for the jobs advertised this way.

Blind ads (Figure 2-2) do not reveal the name of the work organization that advertises the job opening. The ad instructs the job applicant to send a letter of inquiry or a résumé to a box number at a postal address. Some information is usually given about the work and the kind of business the employer operates. Employers use blind ads when they don't want to deal with huge numbers of job applicants, some of whom are probably unquali-fied. By using blind ads, the company doesn't have to respond to all appli-cants and won't be bothered by unwanted telephone calls or walk-in applicants. A blind ad also allows a work organization to maintain secrecy

FIGURE 2-1 *An open ad*

> ### BROADCAST JOURNALIST
>
> Professional broadcast journalist for reporter/
> editor/newscaster position at WJOB. Must
> have college degree, 3-5 years' experience in
> broadcast news, and demonstrated capabili-
> ties as a field reporter, writer, and broad-
> caster. Send résumé, letter, writing samples,
> and tape to: O. K. Doke, News Director,
> WJOB, 1000 Anystreet, Anytown, Anystate
> 99999. No telephone calls, please.

with respect to its competitors and its own employees. (Sometimes a person
makes the mistake of responding to a blind ad placed by his or her own
company.) An employer can use blind advertisements to test the job market
for certain positions; the company may have no job opening but wishes to
ascertain the quality and numbers of job-seekers available. Blind ads do have
an advantage, though. Since they cut down on the number of responses,
there is usually less competition for the jobs advertised that way.

Employment agency ads (Figure 2-3) are placed by public or private
employment agencies for their employer clients. These ads function like
blind advertisements because you don't have the name of the employer who
is using the agency. Sometimes an agency will run ads for fictitious job positions in order to attract résumés in an effort to impress potential employer
clients with "evidence" of the large number of hopeful job-seekers on file.

Catch ads (Figure 2-4) should be avoided. They promise big money, easy
working conditions, a need for few or no qualifications, or short work hours

FIGURE 2-2 *A blind ad*

> ### QUALITY CONTROL DIRECTOR
>
> Manufacturing company in southwest part
> of the state is looking for a person with a
> strong quality control background and su-
> pervisory experience. Must meet require-
> ments in all phases of manufacturing, in-
> cluding plastics, die cast, stampings,
> finishings, and assembly operations. Degree
> preferred but not required if otherwise quali-
> fied. Send complete résumé to Box Z-101,
> Times Tribune, Anytown, Anystate 99999.
> All replies held in strict confidence.

FIGURE 2-3 *An employment agency ad*

```
CLERK/TYPIST

Experienced clerk/typist needed with typing
speed of 60 wpm or more. Prefer one- or two-
year community college or business school
grad. Must be familiar with office practices.
Apply at Ace Personnel Agency, 2222
Anystreet, or call 999-0000 for an appointment.
```

with large financial returns. They may use fancy titles such as "executive position" or "public relations manager," which appeal to vanity and status values. A catch ad hides the fact that the job often involves door-to-door selling. This type of ad sounds almost too good to be true, so you are tempted to respond and find out if it really is true. You may be required to buy the product you will sell. Companies using catch ads often make their money by selling products to would-be salespeople, who must in turn sell them to would-be customers. You could end up stuck with a hundred hard-to-sell sets of encyclopedias or whatever. Never sign on with a company that asks you to pay money first in order to get the job.

A study of the use of help-wanted ads, made by Walsh, Johnson, and Sugarman (1975), indicated that a relatively small percentage of the 900 employers surveyed hired workers through help-wanted ads. Of the employers surveyed, 85 percent in San Francisco and 76 percent in Salt Lake City hired no workers through want ads in 1972. Employers who did use want ads hired almost half their workers through them. Large firms were more likely to use want ads, especially in the manufacturing and service industries. Finance, insurance, and real estate companies were among the least likely to use them. Most want ads did not offer the job-seeker adequate information. Over 85 percent failed to provide wage figures, 60 percent did not

FIGURE 2-4 *A "catch" ad*

```
A CAREER IN ADVERTISING AND
PUBLIC RELATIONS

Well-known national company seeking dy-
namic, enterprising people who desire an
opportunity to earn up to $2000 per week
and more with experience. Will train the
right individual. No experience needed. Must
have dependable auto. Call Buffalo Bart at
001-0001.
```

identify the employer, and one third of them did not designate the industry. The authors of the study concluded that employment agency ads were mainly advertising for the agencies themselves. Two thirds of the 846 job-seekers surveyed in San Francisco and Salt Lake City used want ads in their job search. Of these job-seekers, one fourth said they had actually found jobs through them.

Placing Advertisements for Yourself

This job-seeking tactic involves "position-wanted" advertisements in news-papers and trade magazines. Every week or month, thousands of job-seekers place such ads in newspapers and magazines, hoping to attract a few poten-tial employers. Most of the time, however, this strategy doesn't work. There are exceptions, but most people who have tried placing ads for themselves feel they have wasted their money. Those job-seekers who do get responses from position-wanted ads tend to get them from small companies that offer lower salaries or from small employment agencies that want to sell their career planning and job-finding services. If you plan to use this method of locating job leads, the specialized trade publications may provide the best value for your time and money. There are thousands of trade magazines; you can obtain many of their names and addresses from libraries. A typical posi-tion-wanted ad in a newspaper might look like this:

> RECEPTIONIST/CLERK If you would like a friendly, tactful, well-dressed person to receive customers and visitors in your office, call (telephone number) or write (name and address). I have office management skills, can type 65 wpm, am well organized, and enjoy meeting people.

Some local newspapers run free position-wanted ads for young people as a community service at the beginning of summer, usually for about a week. Don't sound desperate for work; emphasize your skills and personal qual-ities.

Other Parts of the Newspaper

In using the newspaper in your search for job leads, read beyond the want ad section. Many excellent job leads never appear in the want ads, but you can still find them in the newspaper. Look for articles on retirements, promo-tions, and resignations. Such announcements may indicate that there is an unfilled position at some level, possibly at an entry level if the "chain reac-tion" caused by a vacancy at a top level goes all the way through the organizational chart. Some people have even studied the obituary columns for notices of deaths of employed people; a new employee may be needed to fill the vacant position. Watch for new businesses that are opening or old businesses that are expanding; they will need employees. New building permits can result in construction jobs. When a lease is signed, this tells you that someone is moving into a new location; chances are they need more space for an expanding business. A new contract for a manufacturer or the development of a new line of products may mean that more people will be hired. Whenever you read about people leaving the community, their jobs may remain unfilled. The business and financial pages of the newspaper contain many such articles. Employers are likely to credit you with creative thinking if you turn information gleaned from the pages of the newspaper into sources of potential job leads.

Direct-Mail Applications to Employers

A direct-mail campaign usually consists of sending large numbers of résumés and cover letters to employers. A *blanket* mailing to companies can be time-consuming and expensive and produce only a low rate of response. It is much like a mass sales drive. What happens to most advertisements you receive in the mail? They go into the wastebasket; you may not even look at some of this mail. What will happen to your résumés and cover letters? The more you personalize your letter and the better you design your résumé, the greater chance you have of their being read and answered. A *selective* direct mailing is based upon your investigation of work organizations and your identification of the ones that impress you most. Choosing your targets carefully may take as much time as mass mailing because of the research involved, but the rate of response should increase.

Whom do you contact in the work organization? For entry-level positions, you would probably write to a personnel manager or a vice president of personnel, unless you have identified a person higher up in the organization who has the authority to hire. In your research of the company, if you discover the name of the vice president or manager in charge of the department in which you would work, you can send your letter to that person. Addresses of companies and names of executives and departmental managers can be found in directories of corporations. For the names of directories, refer to Chapter 6. You can find these directories in most public libraries or college career planning and placement offices. If you know of a person who has been recently promoted in an organization, that person may want to recruit his or her own new team of people from outside the organization. Your source of names here could be from the business pages of newspapers, trade magazines, or college alumni magazines.

One strategy in the direct-mail campaign is to begin with a personal letter and follow it with a résumé and cover letter if your initial letter draws no response. Letters that are personally typed and signed will receive more attention than mass-produced ones (Powell, 1981). What should you include in a personal letter that inquires about employment in an organization or indicates your interest in a company? You should briefly summarize your previous work experience and education, emphasize your past accomplishments, state what you can do for the organization, and express your interest in an interview. Use your personal stationery. If at all possible, send your letter to a person by name rather than by title alone. The personal touch makes a more favorable impression; the employer knows that you took the time and trouble to locate his or her name. Keep sentences and paragraphs short; they are more likely to be read that way. Five or six sentences is enough for a paragraph. Do not start the letter by asking for or "wondering if there is" a job. Write about your achievements in a way that will indicate the benefits you can bring an employer. In your request for an interview, you might say that you have some ideas that may be of interest to the employer and could benefit the work organization.

If you do not hear from the employer in two weeks, consider following up your personal letter with a copy of your résumé and a cover letter. (These communications will be discussed thoroughly in the next chapter.) Don't expect to hear from every employer. The direct-mail campaign offers a quick method for generating interviews, but the rate of response from employers can be discouragingly low. If you receive a 5- to 10-percent return rate, you have been doing something right. Generally, the higher the salary you seek, the lower the response. The low response figures for the direct-mail method are mentioned here because some job-seekers bank on this method—when other sources of job leads should be used as well—and they lose confidence in their ability to find jobs when this technique fails. Well written letters and résumés and contacting the right person in the right work organization can greatly increase the effectiveness of a direct-mail campaign.

Personnel and Employment Offices

Medium-sized and large work organizations have personnel departments or employment offices. Personnel officers help managers and administrators fill job vacancies. They recruit applicants, screen candidates to eliminate the least qualified, and send on the rest to supervisors, managers, and executives who have hiring authority. Personnel officers seldom have the power to hire unless the job-seeker is applying to the personnel department itself. However, personnel recommendations often carry considerable weight, so it is important for job applicants to create good impressions in their contacts with them.

In your job search, you should consult with the company employment officers. You should check whether they hire people with your particular occupational interests and skills and determine if they have job openings in your particular field of preparation. You can ask them for the names of supervisors and administrators who hire people with your qualifications; most personnel officers can give you this information. Later, you can consider contacting these people in a direct-mail campaign or by telephone. The personnel department represents the best single source of information about the company. However, they are not likely to know about all possible job openings in their organization because some hiring authorities in the company may only be thinking about creating a new job position, waiting for the right applicant to come along.

If the personnel officer says flatly there are no job openings for you in the organization, ask him or her to suggest other work organizations, employers, or managers who could possibly be looking for a person with your occupational goals and abilities.

Professional and Trade Associations

Thousands of professional and trade associations act as intermediaries between job-seekers and employers. They provide employment clearinghouses for their members. Your library may have directories that list the names and addresses of such associations. You send an association a membership fee that makes you eligible for placement help and notices of vacancies in their trade journals. These associations hold local or regional meetings and annual conventions that offer opportunities for job-seekers to form relationships with people established in their field of work. Associations also print material that can help you discover job information available only through hidden job market sources and networking.

Executive Search Firms

People working for executive search firms are often called *headhunters*. They work for employers, not for job-seekers. They concentrate their activities on people who already have jobs. When an employer hires an executive search firm to recruit applicants for them, the search firm's assignment is to find qualified candidates for a specific position that the employer has available. This job search method has limited value to job-seekers. A direct application to an executive search firm will not usually receive much attention unless you know of an executive recruiter who gives time to job-seekers.

Career Days or Job Fairs

You can make several contacts in a couple of hours at a Career Day or a Job Fair sponsored by a college placement service, chamber of commerce, or professional association. Many small companies send representatives to career days because they are less expensive than recruiting trips. You can talk with employers about your qualifications and ways you might fit into their work organizations. Dress as you would for a job interview. Bring extra copies of your résumé. Ask probing questions to find out what you want to know from employers, such as names of people to contact for a job in the organization, availability of on-the-job training and internships, and academic credentials the company would like to see in its job applicants. As in the case of placement office interviews, don't expect employers to make firm job offers at a career fair. The most you could realistically expect is to be invited to the company's home office for further interviews.

Drop-In Visits to Heads of Companies

This technique is recommended only for the most assertive job-seeker. Some experts extol the virtues of the "cold-turkey" call, in which you walk directly into the office of the chief executive officer and talk about a job. It takes brashness and enormous self-confidence to pull this off. You must know exactly what you are doing, and this method can easily backfire. The cold-turkey approach is sometimes effective, because some executives like an aggressive style. A few people get their jobs this way; most do not. You run the risk of being booted out. Pushing your way past secretaries and receptionists is a very big gamble for beginning job-seekers. It is not suggested for those seeking entry-level positions.

Telephoning Employers

The telephone call is a fast and direct way to find out if the employer will set up an interview with you. The "job club" approach uses the Yellow Pages section of the telephone directory as the single greatest source of job leads. Job club members rehearse what they are going to say on the phone and then make as many as 100 calls per day. The routine for requesting an interview over the telephone is as follows. (1) Give your name; (2) ask for the name of the department head; (3) address the department head by name and introduce yourself; (4) describe your qualifications; (5) ask for an interview; (6) if the person says no, ask for an interview just in case an opening occurs later; (7) if the person still says no, ask for other job leads; (8) ask for permission to use the person's name for leads; (9) ask for a good time to call back in case a job opens up later on (Arzin & Besalel, 1982). You can list each step on a piece of paper before phoning and check steps off as you proceed with the call.

Be prepared to deal with secretaries or receptionists who protect the boss from "unnecessary" calls. You may call at the wrong time; if so, ask the secretary to suggest a good time for you to call back. The best time to reach employers may be just after 5:00 P.M., the usual quitting time. The telephone switchboard is usually still open, the boss often stays late, and the secretary may have left for the day, so the person you most want to speak with just might answer the phone. Other good times to call might be just before the normal lunch hour or just before the workday begins, at 8:00 or 9:00 A.M.

Internships and Cooperative Work/Study Programs

Internships and cooperative work/study programs are agreements between schools and employers to provide students with supervised work experiences while they pursue an education. The arrangement is something like an apprenticeship, where a person agrees to work for a journeyman or master craftsman for a specified amount of time in order to learn a trade. The difference is that apprentices are paid a percentage of the skilled worker's wage, and interns usually are not. Employers like internships because they are getting unpaid help, which can free up their experienced workers to perform more complex tasks. Work/study programs usually operate in one of two ways. Either you split the school day between classes and work, or you alternate between a semester devoted entirely to school classes and a semester of full-time work experience. Some work/study programs operate like apprenticeships in that you are paid for your work.

Students like internships and cooperative work/study programs because they give students the oppportunity for an on-the-job tryout of a prospective occupation. These programs can benefit you in several other ways. You don't have to commit yourself in this situation, for it is considered a learning experience. You can develop contacts to help you in your job search. Your performance could lead to a job with the company that sponsors the internship or work/study program. Your school will award you credit for the experience. The experience looks good on your credentials or résumé. Possible disadvantages are that the length of your education could be increased if the internship credits are less than those of a normal course load, and your program might include only lower-level skills rather than the cross section of experiences you need to prepare you adequately for the practical requirements of an occupation. For more details, consult you counseling office or academic advisor. Over 1000 colleges, universities, and community colleges offer the plan.

Government and Civil Service

The U.S. government is the nation's largest single employer. It employs about 20 percent of all government workers. The largest growth in government employment in recent years, however, has been on the state and local levels. Each state government is the largest single employer in its particular state, employing about 25 percent of the governmental work force. Local governments hire over half of all government employees in the United States. Together, all levels of government in the United States employ about 15 percent of the nation's labor force. Because of the publicity about government job openings, there is usually much competition for such jobs, but great opportunity also exists. For example, the turnover in federal positions produces nearly half a million annual job openings, even though total federal government employment has not expanded lately. Government hires people in almost every occupational group found in private employment. Approximately 150,000 engineers and architects, 120,000 accountants and budget analysts, 120,000 doctors and health specialists, 87,000 scientists, and 45,000 social scientists work for the federal government. Nearly a million people work for the Department of Defense, and another two thirds of a million are in the postal service (Krannich, 1983). There is greater job security for many government positions than for their counterparts in the private sector. You can research departmental budgets on any level in government. (This could be the subject for a term paper in a college political science class.) Increases or reductions in a budget affect the number of job openings in a department, agency, or bureau.

Most applicants for federal positions are hired under the General Schedule (GS) classification. There are currently 18 grade levels. Lower-level entry jobs are numbered GS-1 through GS-5. Higher-level administrative and professional positions are at the GS-13 through GS-18 levels. Entry into federal employment occurs basically through two standardized procedures: individual position announcements and the Professional and Administrative Career Examination (PACE), which is given several times a year. The top three persons qualifying through PACE and other written or multiple-choice tests, and through evaluations of education and experience, are referred to the employing agency. The Office of Personnel Management (formerly the Civil Service Commission) has a central office in Washington, DC, 10 regional offices, and 72 subregional centers scattered throughout the United States. Upon request, it will send you information about career opportunities inside the federal government and about the formal procedures to follow in applying for a federal job. Supplement this information with your own personal research, just as you would investigate companies in the private sector. (Researching work organizations will be covered in more detail in Chapter 6.) Contact agency personnel offices for their job vacancy listings. The *Federal Career Opportunities Report* is published every two weeks by the Federal Research Service, Inc. (P.O. Box 1059, Vienna, VA 22180). *How To Get a Federal Job* by David E. Waelde (Washington, DC: FEDHELP Publications, 1989) and *Information U.S.A.* by Matthew Lesko (New York: Penguin) are two other good sources of federal job information.

Despite standardization, hiring patterns vary in government agencies just as much as they do in private companies. The aforementioned information about federal hiring practices applies for the most part to the state and local levels as well. Each level and unit of government has its own formal employment rules and its own informal recruiting customs. You should research state and local government agencies the same way you would federal departments and bureaus. Use the informational interviewing procedures outlined in Chapter 7. Consult every bit of published material you can find on the agency, and identify the person with hiring authority in each unit. More political patronage probably exists in state and local governments, but efforts to use connections, influence, and pressure could backfire in some places.

The Military

The armed forces currently have nearly 3 million jobs in the United States. If your occupational goal reflects any type of military work, you might consider enlistment in the Army, Navy, Air Force, Marines, or Coast Guard after completing school. The Reserve Officers' Training Corps (ROTC) can help with expenses while you are in college; you can write for information from a college that offers ROTC programs. College catalogs and directories also provide ROTC information. The armed forces will assess your skills and interests to determine the kind of training program most appropriate for you. A number of military occupations are transferable to the civilian labor force. Almost every military assignment teaches some kind of skill that can be useful to civilian employers, including leadership, responsibility, technical know-how, management, experience overseas, loyalty, and discipline— skills that would be attractive to any employer.

Periodicals and Publications

Business magazines such as *Forbes, Fortune,* and *Business Week* are excellent sources of industry information; their "positions open" sections are usually located near the last page of each issue. The *College Placement Annual,* published each year by the College Placement Council, lists hundreds of companies by name and indicates the types of college majors they are looking for. Industrial directories, published in each state, list the names and addresses of companies located in each city. Higher education positions are advertised in the weekly *Chronicle of Higher Education.* You can find directories in the reference section of the library. The amount of material published each year on job openings in work organizations is truly staggering. The information is there; you have to dig it out.

Unusual Methods

Creative job-seekers continue to devise new ways of finding sources of job openings. For example, one young man put his résumé on a *billboard* and received two job offers by the end of the second day. Some job-seekers send employers *telegrams* asking for an interview because they know that a telegram will be read. This is an expensive method of uncovering job leads, as is the use of *special delivery* or *registered mail.* If these methods work, however, they're worth every penny. *Long-distance calls* have also been tried. Job-hunters have prepared *brochures* to advertise their talents. Another source you might consider is editors or publishers of newsletters; they sometimes act as intermediaries between job-seekers and employers, since many newsletters are read by employers at all levels. One student got a job by picketing the company he wanted to work for (not recommended, however). "Open Letters to All Area Employers" have been posted on hundreds of bulletin boards. One college student began her open letter to all area business offices by introducing herself by name and stating, "I am skilled as a legal secretary and would like to do overflow typing work for your firm. Call me if your secretary is swamped or if your typing needs do not require a full- or even part-time secretary. My work is very neat. I can take dictation over the telephone and draft letters." She went on to describe her typewriter and dictaphone, which had a microcassette adapter for transcribing tapes. The message was typed as a business letter, thus serving to demonstrate her skills to any employer who happened to see it posted on the bulletin boards.

Perhaps showing persistence and constant dedication to getting a job qualifies as an unusual method of job-seeking. One personnel director tells a story about an unemployed man, down on his luck, living in a community shelter during the winter. He walked three miles daily for two and a half months, appearing at 8:00 A.M. in the employment office of a local company to apply for a position as building custodian. Each day he was told there was no opening. Most job-seekers would be discouraged to hear this message once or twice, let alone day after day for two and a half months. The employer was sufficiently impressed to create a job for the man. He had demonstrated his persistence and punctuality, which were important qualities to the job-giver. The man had said, in effect, "If I can show up for work on time each day even when there is no job, think of what I will do for you when there is work for me to do and I am being paid for it."

Personal Contacts

You have read about various sources of help in locating job leads, but none are as productive as your personal contacts: people who are knowledgeable about occupations and jobs that interest you, people who know others that are also knowledgeable, people with connections to other people who can hire you, and people with the power to hire. They can operate as a third party to bring the job-seeker and job-provider together. Personal contacts may be your friends and their friends, your parents and relatives and their friends, past and present neighbors, current and former classmates, teachers, counselors, administrators, youth club leaders, co-workers, employers, supervisors, club and association members, and so on. In fact, any person you know could potentially be a part of your personal contact network.

More jobs are obtained through a network of personal contacts than through all other sources of job leads combined (Granovetter, 1974). The term *personal contact network* means a structure of interlocking connections among people you know who could help you in your job search (see Figure 2-5). Work organizations also use their network of contacts to find people to fill their vacant positions. *Networking* is a word used to describe the activity of developing relationships with and cultivating people who could give job-finding assistance. "Cultivating people," in its best sense, means meeting people for the sake of getting to know them and possibly

FIGURE 2-5 *Personal contact network*

(Blank lines are provided for you to insert the names of people as you think of them)

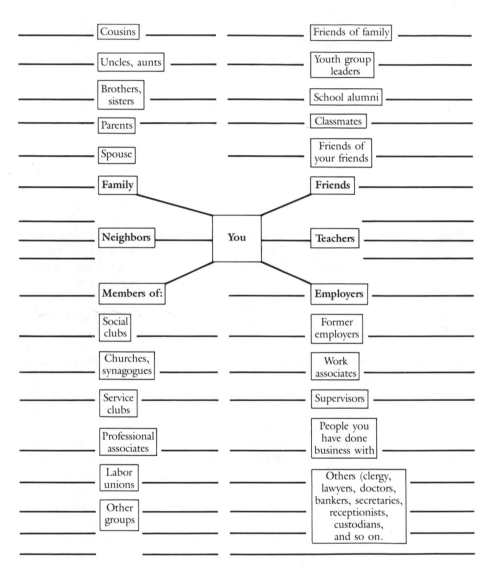

Remember: All these people have personal contact networks of their own. Some may not realize this, so you can share the idea of networking with them.

establishing a friendship. In its worst sense, it means a one-sided manipulation of others in order to get something from them (in this case, a job or a lead on a job), without ever doing anything for them in return. Of course, some people regard the whole contact business as degrading and vow "not to use other people." This attitude can be just as unrealistic as the opposite, selfish one. People like to do favors for others. Helping people is a worthy motive many admire and include in their own behavior. By going it alone in the job search, you could deprive some people of satisfying their need to assist others. You could also lose a tactical advantage in your job-hunting. The job search world floats on a sea of contacts; "who you know" does help get you through the job interviewer's door. ("What you know" helps to convince an employer to offer you a job as well as helping you to keep the job later on.) Research on job-hunting has shown that people find more highly paid and prestigious jobs through personal contacts than through any other method. People who find jobs through personal contacts also report greater satisfaction in their work (Granovetter, 1974). The more you enlist people into your job search network, the better your success is likely to be (Bolles, 1986).

You can start right away to build a network of personal contacts by doing Exercise 2-2, "Record of Personal Contacts," at the end of this chapter. You simply list the names, job titles, addresses, and telephone numbers of people who could be called your personal contacts, indicate your relationship with each one (friend, relative, neighbor), record the dates you have talked with each, note the subjects discussed, and list the names of those who suggested each personal contact and to whom they referred you. You start by brainstorming a list of potential contacts by yourself and then ask other people to suggest possible names for you. Of course, these other people could be contacts, too.

All it takes is one name to start developing a list of personal contacts. A natural way to begin a conversation with people is to ask them about their work. If it is work in which you are interested, so much the better. People love to talk shop. Asking them for details of their jobs is a time-honored way for you to obtain information. Keep in mind that the most important question you can ask concerning your personal contact network is the referral question. "Can you give me the names of any other people who do the kind of work you do? How might I contact them? May I say that you suggested I get in touch with them?" Some people might even write a letter of introduction for you. The referral question is the key to expanding the number of names in your personal contact network. In theory, expansion of contacts is exponential. Take the example of two people multiplied to the "fourth power." You talk with one person, who talks to another about your job search ($1 \times 2 = 2$). Those two each connect with two more people ($1 \times 2 \times 2 = 4$). And then ($1 \times 2 \times 2 \times 4 = 16$). Carry the networking principle one step further, and you arrive at 256 people. Each link between two people creates an exponential expansion (Powell, 1981).

Courtesy is an essential factor in developing a list of personal contacts. You are asking contacts for occupational information, job leads, and referrals to other people for the expansion of your network, so normal courtesy and appreciation of their efforts are appropriate. Always ask for permission to use your contact's name if he or she tells you about a job opening or suggests names of other people to contact. Ask also whether your contact would recommend using his or her name—it is possible that this person is not on good terms with the potential new contact. Express your thanks when you leave, and follow up with a thank-you letter. This is not only a mark of courtesy; it is also practical. You never know when you will want to ask a favor of your personal contact again.

When you approach a personal contact to obtain information about jobs and job openings, the rule is that you *never ask for a job*. Few of your contacts are likely to have hiring authority, much less an unfilled job just waiting for you. Asking for a job will put your personal contact on the spot, make him or her uncomfortable, and possibly create negative feelings toward you. This is an *information-seeking* exercise, not a job interview. What could you ask a personal contact in an informational interview or a casual conversation about work? Here are some suggestions.

- What attracted you to your occupation in the first place? What are the personal rewards of the work for you now? What do you enjoy about your job?
- How long have you worked in your job? How long have you been with your present employer?
- What are your major responsibilities? How are you evaulated by your supervisor?
- What qualifications would you look for in a new employee?
- What are the major frustrations and the most frequently recurring problems in your job?
- What advice would you give to a person coming into a job like yours?
- *Who else could I talk with* about your field of work? How can I get in touch with them? May I give them your name and say you suggested I talk with them?

The referral question is always your last question in an interview for information. A major purpose in talking with people is to generate more personal contacts and keep expanding your network.

EXERCISE 2-1   *Record of Job Leads*

Where have you found job vacancies in the occupation of your choice? Fill in the following information on the blank "Record of Job Leads" form that accompanies this exercise. (1) Write the *name of the company or organization*. Indicate the *source* of the job lead. (2) *Who* is your contact person in the organization? Include *address* and *telephone number*. (3) Keep a record of the actions you took concerning the job opening. Write the *date* you made each contact with an organization and make a note about *what happened*. Photocopy the job leads form if you need more copies. Another option is to record your job lead information on 3 × 5 or 4 × 6 cards.

EXERCISE 2-1 Record of Job Leads

Name of Work Organization (Source of Job Lead)	Person's Name	Address/Telephone	First Contact		Second Contact		Third Contact	
			Date	Result	Date	Result	Date	Result

EXERCISE 2-2   *Record of Personal Contacts*

First, refer to Figure 2-5, where you are encouraged to list the names of contacts as you think of them. Then, on the blank form, "Record of Personal Contacts," that accompanies this exercise, fill in the following information. (1) Write down the *name* of the person, *address,* and *telephone number.* (2) What is this contact's *job title?* (3) What is this person's *relationship* to you? (4) Record the *date* you talked with this person. (5) What *subjects* did you talk about? (6) *Who* suggested or referred you to this person? (7) *To whom* did this personal contact refer you? Photocopy the personal contacts form if you need more copies. Another option is to keep a record of your personal contacts on 3 × 5 or 4 × 6 cards.

Summary

1. Traditional sources of job leads are college career planning and placement offices, public and private employment agencies, newspaper and magazine help-wanted advertisements, direct-mail applications to employers, direct application to personnel and employment offices, telephone calls to employers, career days or job fairs, and government civil service announcements. These methods are criticized by some career counselors because job vacancies from traditional sources are usually advertised and made visible to the public, which places the job-seeker in competition with large numbers of applicants. Most of these sources are free or inexpensive (with the exception of some private employment agencies), so most counselors suggest using various sources in a multiple approach to finding job openings.

2. Some sources of job leads are more selective, in the sense that they are not as well known or used as much by the general public. Examples are drop-in visits, internships, work/study programs, telegrams, or a special brochure targeted to a number of employers. You can make some traditional sources of job leads more selective by researching organizations, eliminating those that do not interest you, and communicating only with those on which you wish to focus your job search.

3. More people discover job openings from their personal contacts than from all other sources combined. Anyone you know can be a personal contact. You should always try to expand your contact network by asking for referrals from your current contacts. Many questions about work are appropriate, but one question you never ask a personal contact is, "Do you have a job for me?" Your purpose is solely to obtain information. If an idea for a job develops, it comes from your contacts, not you. You can tell personal contacts, however, that if they encounter a job opening in your occupational field, you would appreciate hearing about it.

4. Keep a file of your job leads and names of your personal contacts on the forms provided in this chapter or on 3 × 5 or 4 × 6 cards. Your job

EXERCISE 2-2 Record of Personal Contacts

Name of Personal Contact Address—Telephone Number	Job Title	Relationship	Date of Interview	Subjects Discussed	Suggested by Whom?	Referred to Whom?

search will be more organized and effective if you maintain written records of your progress.

References

Arzin, N. H., & BESALEL, V. B. (1982). *Finding a job*. Berkeley, CA: Ten Speed Press.

Bolles, R. N. (1986). *What color is your parachute?* Berkeley, CA: Ten Speed Press.

Granovetter, M. S. (1974). *Getting a job: A study of contacts and careers.* Cambridge, MA: Harvard University Press.

Krannich, R. L. (1983). *Re-careering in turbulent times: Skills and strategies for success in today's job market*. Manassas, VA: Impact Publications.

Powell, C. R. (1981). *Career planning today*. Dubuque, IA: Kendall/Hunt.

Royko, M. (1982, January 21). This is not time to give up on life. *Jackson Citizen Patriot*.

Shingleton, J. D., & BAO, R. (1977). *College to career: Finding yourself in the job market*. New York: McGraw-Hill.

Walsh, J., JOHNSON, M., & SUGARMAN, M. (1975). *Help wanted: Case studies of classified ads*. Salt Lake City, UT: Olympus.

3

Using Your Writing Skills to Get a Job: Résumés and Cover Letters

Your writing skills will be useful in getting a job. A standard feature of most job search campaigns is writing a résumé and cover letter. A *résumé* is a summary of your personal, educational, and employment experiences and qualifications. Résumé preparation may seem a rather prosaic subject, but it is controversial. Some authorities state that résumés are more likely to get in the way of your job search than to help it; certainly, a poorly written résumé will work against you, and a well-designed résumé by itself will not get you a job. Its intent is to obtain a job interview; if you can get an interview without a résumé, more power to you. However, many employers will not see you without a résumé. What then? Unless you intend to practice a little deception with these employers, you'll need to write a résumé. Some career counselors will tell you that résumés are the royal road to job interviews.

No less controversial is the question of what should be included or emphasized in the résumé. Some people advocate omitting the job objective section on the theory that it limits the use of your résumé; others state that it must be included because it indicates to employers that you know what you want. Opinions differ over the preferred type of résumé—chronological or functional? The chronological résumé arranges the schools you attended and your job positions in reverse time order, starting with and emphasizing your most recent experience. This chronological approach appears to be the easiest to follow and may be more appropriate for job-seekers with limited experience (Nutter, 1978). The functional résumé accentuates the functions of job positions you have held, displaying the skills you have used and the qualifications you possess. Quite a few writers discourage use of the chronological format and encourage something close to a functional style, calling it a "qualification brief" (Lathrop, 1977) or a "job power report" (Haldane, Haldane, & Martin, 1976).

A *cover letter* accompanies the résumé. It introduces you to the employer and clearly states your application for a specific job, particularly if your job objective has been expressed in broad, general terms in your résumé. Other functions of the cover letter include presenting particular achievements and personal skills and requesting an interview with the employer. Some job-seekers omit the personalized cover letter when they mail hundreds of résumés in a direct-mail campaign. Research indicates, however, that presenting a résumé together with a cover letter is more effective than presenting a résumé alone.

The skills discussed in this chapter and the next one are part of your general communication abilities. Words are used in special ways to get ideas across to other people, something you have spent a great deal of time on in school. Not only will you relate to other people through résumés and cover letters; you will also relate to others when you write a letter of inquiry, a thank-you letter, or a letter accepting or declining a job offer. Of course, writing is not the only way you communicate in your job search. You use your reading skills when you look for job leads and research organizations, and you use your speaking skills when you interview for information and for a job.

The Résumé

A résumé is a self-designed information sheet written about yourself, a brief account of your qualifications for a job. The words *personal data sheet* or *curriculum vitae* can be used in place of *résumé*. The word *résumé* has an accent mark over each *e,* but standard usage allows you to spell the word without the accent marks. *Résumé* is derived from a French word meaning "summary." A résumé generally summarizes your job objective, education, work experience, personal data, names of references, and any other pertinent information you want to emphasize to employers and personnel officers. The résumé should answer at least two questions for the employer: "What can you do for me?" (explained in the job objective), and "Why should you be considered for this job?" (answered in the sections on education and work experience). In order to complete a résumé, job-seekers need to answer three questions about themselves: Who am I? What do I do well? What do I want? (Irish, 1978).

The great advantage in writing a résumé is that it allows you to present yourself in your own way. Employers' application forms require you to disclose yourself in their terms, but a résumé can emphasize your strong points while minimizing limitations. An employer will be impressed if you have prepared a résumé, particularly if the employer has not asked for one. It shows that you are well prepared and serious about applying for a job. If an employer asks you to complete an application form before an interview, the résumé will help you supply accurate information you might overlook or remember incorrectly. The résumé can be thought of as a verbal picture of yourself that stays with the employer after you leave the interview.

The basic purpose of the résumé is to introduce yourself and secure an interview. It will not get you a job by itself; few employers are going to hire an applicant on the basis of a résumé alone. Résumés and cover letters are meant to get you through the employer's door.

A good résumé is written only by the individual who is searching for a job. Do not rely on an outside résumé preparation service; experienced personnel workers can easily recognize this sort of résumé because it follows a formula, lacks spontaneity, and often presents a misleading picture of the job-seeker. You can do a better job of writing the résumé yourself. It takes time; the résumé is part of your campaign to persuade an employer to hire you, and you must spend several hours working on it.

Neatness and correct spelling are essential. Neatness projects your qualifications on paper, but a messy résumé indicates a careless worker in the minds of many employers. Mistakes in spelling, punctuation, and grammar reflect on your competence and can cost you a job opportunity. Study after study shows that employers strongly prefer résumés that are neat, grammatically correct, and free of spelling errors (Meyers, 1984). If you are unsure about the spelling of a word, use a dictionary. Avoid abbreviations. Have someone proofread your résumé before you send it to employers. When you refer to activities in which you are currently engaged, use the present tense. Use the past tense when you mention anything previous to your current activities.

The writing style should be factual and concise. Avoid the use of the personal pronoun *I*. The reader of your résumé already knows you are the subject of each sentence or phrase. Start each sentence with an action verb. (Table 3-1 has a list of 200 action words to consult when you are writing your résumé.) Then complete the sentence by using a word or a phrase as an object to complement the action verb, and add an adjective or adverb to describe your action. (Table 3-2 offers a list of self-descriptive words.) Readers who have completed Exercises 6-1 through 6-4 in Chapter 6 of *Taking Charge of Your Career Direction* will recognize the functional, content, and adaptive skills that form the structure of résumé writing.

Reasons for Writing a Résumé

There are many good reasons for preparing a résumé. Ten are listed below.

1. A résumé is often a requirement for a personal interview. Some employers and interviewers will not talk to job applicants without first looking at their résumé.

2. A résumé lets you tell your story in your own way. You can be assured that your most attractive features will be presented to the employer. An employer's application form makes you tell your story in a way that might not allow you to present yourself as you would like.

3. The preparation of a résumé reminds you of things about yourself that you should remember as you search for a job. The process of constructing a résumé encourages you to make an inventory of your experiences and abilities. Job-hunters learn a lot about themselves as they prepare their résumés.

4. A résumé represents you when you are not on hand to speak in your own behalf. An attractive, well-written résumé can help you survive an employer's screening of candidates, especially when the competition is relatively equal in other respects. The résumé can help you be remembered after the interview has taken place. Richard Bolles, author of the best-selling *What Color Is Your Parachute?*, makes the point that résumés may serve the very useful function of jogging the employer's memory. Bolles advises not taking a résumé to the interview. If the interviewer requests one, say you'll mail it. Then tailor your résumé to the skills needed in the job and send it with a thank-you note attached to a cover letter (Bolles, 1986).

5. If you apply for a job through the mail, the employer generally expects a résumé whether it was specifically asked for or not. Advertising an attractive job will probably draw many responses from job-seekers. Employers and personnel workers do not have the time or patience to plough through stacks of letters crammed with inappropriate material. A well-designed résumé that is concise, to the point, and presented in sequential order will serve you well in this situation (Biegeleisen, 1982).

TABLE 3-1   Action verbs for résumé writing

Achieved	Determined	Interviewed	Recommended
Acted	Developed	Invented	Reconciled
Adapted	Devised	Investigated	Recorded
Administered	Diagnosed	Judged	Recruited
Advanced	Directed	Launched	Reduced
Advised	Discovered	Led	Rehabilitated
Analyzed	Displayed	Lifted	Reinforced
Anticipated	Distributed	Listened	Remodeled
Appraised	Drafted	Located	Reorganized
Approved	Drew	Maintained	Repaired
Arranged	Drove	Managed	Reported
Assembled	Edited	Measured	Represented
Asserted	Educated	Mediated	Researched
Assessed	Enabled	Memorized	Resolved
Assisted	Encouraged	Moderated	Restored
Attended	Entertained	Monitored	Retrieved
Audited	Established	Motivated	Reviewed
Authored	Estimated	Moved	Revised
Balanced	Evaluated	Navigated	Revitalized
Budgeted	Expedited	Negotiated	Saved
Built	Explained	Nurtured	Scheduled
Calculated	Fabricated	Observed	Shaped
Checked	Facilitated	Operated	Simplified
Classified	Followed	Organized	Sketched
Cleaned	Forecast	Originated	Sold
Coached	Forged	Painted	Solved
Collected	Formulated	Participated	Spoke
Colored	Founded	Perceived	Started
Communicated	Gathered	Performed	Steered
Compared	Generated	Persisted	Streamlined
Compiled	Graduated	Persuaded	Strengthened
Completed	Guided	Planned	Studied
Composed	Handled	Prepared	Summarized
Comprehended	Harvested	Presented	Supervised
Computed	Helped	Printed	Supported
Conceived	Identified	Processed	Surveyed
Conceptualized	Illustrated	Produced	Systematized
Conducted	Imagined	Programmed	Taught
Confronted	Implemented	Promoted	Tended
Consolidated	Improved	Proposed	Trained
Constructed	Improvised	Protected	Translated
Controlled	Increased	Proved	Traveled
Coordinated	Influenced	Provided	Treated
Corresponded	Informed	Publicized	Understood
Counseled	Initiated	Published	Updated
Created	Inspected	Purchased	Upgraded
Decided	Inspired	Questioned	Visualized
Defined	Installed	Raised	Volunteered
Demonstrated	Instructed	Read	Worked
Designed	Interpreted	Reasoned	Wrote

Of course, you can consult a thesaurus to find replacements for these words.

TABLE 3-2   Self-descriptive words for résumé writing

accurately	dependably	industriously	radiantly
actively	determined	intelligently	rationally
adeptly	dexterously	judiciously	realistically
aggressively	diplomatically	kindly	reasonably
alertly	disciplined	logically	reflectively
ambitiously	discreetly	loyally	reliably
analytically	distinctively	maturely	resourcefully
articulately	effectively	methodically	responsibly
artistically	efficiently	meticulously	responsively
attentively	eloquently	modestly	self-reliant
attractively	empathically	objectively	sensitively
businesslike	energetically	observantly	seriously
calmly	enterprising	optimistically	sincerely
candidly	enthusiastically	orderly	sociably
capably	ethically	patiently	spontaneously
carefully	expressively	peacefully	stalwartly
cheerfully	fairly	perceptively	steadily
clearly	firmly	persistently	sturdily
competently	flexibly	persuasively	supportively
confidently	forcefully	pleasantly	systematically
conscientiously	formally	politely	tactfully
considerately	generously	positively	verbally
consistently	genially	practically	vigorously
constructively	gently	precisely	virtuously
cooperatively	gregariously	productively	vivaciously
courageously	helpfully	prudently	voluntarily
courteously	honestly	punctually	warmly
creatively	hopefully	purposefully	watchfully
decisively	humorously	quickly	wisely
deliberately	imaginatively	quietly	zealously
delicately	independently		

Again, you can consult a thesaurus to find replacements for these words. Most of these words are stated as adverbs. For the most part, they can be changed to adjectives by dropping the suffix *-ly*.

6. A good résumé serves as the most effective piece in a direct-mail campaign. Your appeal may include a personalized letter, a favorable clipping about yourself from a newspaper or trade publication, or a reproduced sample of your work. It's the résumé, however, that often gets the most serious attention from prospective employers (Biegeleisen, 1982).

7. A résumé can function as a calling card as you research work organizations. Just as salespeople leave their cards, so can job-seekers leave their résumés in order to be remembered. Give a few copies of your résumé to your personal contacts. They can distribute it to their contacts and thus widen the scope of your job search. A résumé makes it easier for those who know you to recommend you to potential employers.

8. You can transfer information from your résumé to an employer's application form and know that it is accurate because you have spent time making sure the material in your résumé is correct. If you arrive for an interview and

are asked to complete an application form on the spot, you are already under pressure; it's helpful to have a source of reliable information.

9. A résumé helps ease the transition of introducing yourself and getting acquainted with the employer or interviewer. It can provide an outline for discussion during an interview.

10. Even if you are not looking for a job, you should prepare a résumé. The majority of desirable job positions are offered to people who are satisfied in their work and are not seeking a new job (Hizer & Rosenberg, 1985). The job opportunity of a lifetime might suddenly appear—or you could lose a job in an economic downturn. Either way, it is advantageous to have an updated résumé to use in an unexpected situation.

Physical Appearance of the Résumé

The résumé must be typed. Advice from employers and job search writers is unanimous that job applicants should limit their résumés to one page, adding a second page only if necessary (Meyers, 1984). Résumés of two pages may be appropriate for people with several years of work experience and many achievements and responsibilities to cover. Most employers will not take the time to read a long résumé. Use 8½-by-11-inch, high-quality paper. Larger sizes are difficult to handle; smaller sizes could get lost in the shuffle. The traditional plain white bond or an off-white textured bond is usually recommended. Balance the material on the page so that the total effect is attractive and pleasing to the eye. Leave adequate margin space so the page will not appear crowded; margins should be at least one inch on all sides. Avoid careless erasures.

Extra copies of your résumé can be reproduced through high-quality printing and photocopying processes. Investing in good paper, typesetting, and an excellent printing job is well worth the cost. The mechanics of a résumé must be perfect, and the material must be 100-percent accurate. Any mistake could be duplicated 200 or 2000 times. Mimeographed copies of your résumé are not advised, and you should never submit a carbon copy of a résumé.

Should you enclose a photograph of yourself? There are positive and negative answers to this question. If you include a photo, it is easier for an employer to remember you after the interview, especially if the interviewer has talked with ten other people that day. On the other hand, there is the problem of job discrimination. Most states make it illegal for an employer to request photographs from job applicants. A photograph identifies sex, age, and race, although this information can be discerned from other parts of the résumé or through an interview.

Information Sections Within the Résumé

There is no single way to write a résumé—you must create one that is right for you. Some people advocate a chronological résumé; others believe a functional résumé is better. Some say a job objective must appear in the résumé; others prefer to leave it out. If you find out from your personal contacts that an employer in a target company prefers to see certain material included in or left out of a résumé, follow that format, regardless of what you read in this or any other book. Because most people begin with a chronological résumé, that format will be described in this section. Then, in the next section, several salient points about functional résumés will be covered. Figure 3-1 presents the structural outline of a chronological résumé.

The Heading

The heading includes your name, address, and telephone number. It is usually placed at the top center of the page. If you set the heading at the top left side, add some personal data, such as social security number and birth date, on the top right side for the sake of balance. Some people type RÉSUMÉ in capital letters above the name, but this title is not necessary. Give your full name, spelling out your first name and surname. Type your name in capital letters if you want to make it more noticeable. Place your home address just below your name. City, state, and zip code appear together on a separate line. The telephone number of your home address goes on the last line of the heading. Include the area code. If you are currently working, do not list your work number unless you have your employer's permission to do so. Most people prefer to be contacted at home. Use your cover letter to suggest when and how this can be done.

The Job Objective or Career Goal

A difference of opinion exists as to whether a specific job objective or career goal should be a part of the résumé. Most people favor it, because you can communicate your goal clearly, employers are more impressed with those who know exactly what they want, and you can give copies of the résumé to personal contacts without constructing a cover letter to introduce yourself and explain the job position you are trying to obtain.

Some people, however, prefer to omit the job objective, believing that it restricts the scope of their employment possibilities. You can be considered for similar positions to the one you had in mind if you don't limit yourself to a specific job objective. The problem with this approach is that employers are left to guess what you really want. You can prepare a separate résumé for each job position sought, or the job objective statement can be expressed in more general terms so as to include an entire occupational field.

The job objective is the hardest part of the résumé to write if you have not defined your career goals and abilities. Never write "anything available" for a job objective; employers will not take the time to speculate about the meaning of those words. Practice writing your career goal in brief, understandable language before typing it on your résumé. State the job position

FIGURE 3-1   *Structural outline of a chronological résumé*

1. *Heading.* Name, street address, city, state, zip code, and telephone number (with area code) are included here. Place in upper center of the sheet of paper. (Place in upper left-hand corner if you bring personal data into right-hand corner.) Optional: Type RÉSUMÉ in capital letters at the top of the center of the page.

2. *Job Objective.* State clearly and concisely what type of position or occupational goal you are seeking and what type of future you anticipate. Some résumé writers leave out this section, thinking it limits their prospects for a job or has been discussed in the cover letter. We include a career goal statement because then the employer is not left guessing about what you want, and there may be occasions when you use the résumé without a cover letter (for example, when you give copies to your personal contacts).

3. *Education.* Place names of schools in *reverse* chronological order (present or most recent first, then next most recent, and so on). Include dates of attendance, school names, addresses, cities and states, diplomas and degrees earned, specific courses if related to job sought, high grades earned or a good grade point average, and extracurricular activities (especially those that show special skills and leadership qualities). Also mention scholastic honors, scholarships, seminars, workshops, internships, correspondence courses, military training, and the like.

4. *Work Experience.* Again, put these experiences in *reverse* chronological order. Include dates of employment, names of organizations, addresses, cities and states, and job titles. Other information given could be descriptions of duties and responsibilities, names and addresses of supervisors, and work skills used or acquired. List part-time, summer, and volunteer jobs as well as full-time work. Military information (if you have the experience) may be placed here or in a separate section with data on branch of service, dates, rank, Military Occupational Specialty (MOS), duties, and honors or awards. (The work experience section may appear before the education section if you wish to emphasize it.)

5. *Personal Data*—optional. (Insert here if not placed in upper right-hand corner of page.) Include date and place of birth and social security number. Use the following information only if it will strengthen your case: marital status, height, weight, draft status, health information, willingness to relocate, sex, race, and religious preference. Mention hobbies, special skills, and interests, particularly if they relate to your job objective.

6. *References.* Give names and addresses of persons who will testify to your good character. Giving their titles and phone numbers is optional. Always request references' permission to use their names ahead of time. Possible references are neighbors, teachers, clergy, former employers or supervisors (if not mentioned in the work experience section). Do not list relatives. Three references are usually sufficient. An alternative method is to write, ''References available'' or ''References furnished upon request.''

7. *Other, optional items.* Use is dictated by circumstances. These items include salary range, membership in professional and service organizations, offices held in clubs, travel experiences, recreational activities, willingness to travel, availability (when you could report for work), and so on.

you are seeking and combine it with your hopes for the future. Avoid vague job titles such as "business management" or "administrative assistant." Indicate the kind of business, or combine the job title with a particular type of occupation. Keep this section short. A well-constructed phrase or a sentence or two is sufficient. Despite its brevity, the job objective statement is important. Your entire résumé revolves around it (Weinstein, 1982).

The following are some career objective statements:

- A beginning job in _____ , leading to a position in _____ .

- Wish to begin a career as a _____ in the _____ _____ industry. Future goal is a move to _____ _____ , where I can be involved in _____ .
- Interested in joining the _____ staff of a company (or firm, business, agency). Long-term ambition is to _____ .
- _____ position in _____ involving _____ _____ responsibilities.
- Interested in becoming a _____ , with advancement to _____ .

- Desire a _____ position that uses my experience (or education) in _____ and offers an eventual move up to _____ .

- Seeking a _____ position in a (an) _____ _____ organization, with hopes of advancement to _____ .

- Major interest is in _____ , with advancement opportunity to specialize in _____ in the future.

You can express your job objective statement in more general terms. Several goals could be mentioned in the same statement. That's the nice thing about a résumé; you are in charge of the design.

Education

Start with your current or most recent schoolwork and go back in time. If you have college, technical, or business school experience, it is not necessary to go further back than high school. Military training, special seminars or workshops, correspondence courses, in-service industry training, or on-the-job training can be a part of your educational record.

Items that can be covered in the education section include dates of attendance, names of schools and their addresses (with city, state, and zip code), degrees and diplomas earned, educational majors, and specific subjects if relevant to the position sought. If you are short on work experience, emphasize your education. Achievements in school should be mentioned. Some people add a section titled, "Significant Accomplishments in College (or High School)" or "Extracurricular Activities."

If you graduated in the upper third, quarter, or tenth of your class, say so. Include a high grade point average (GPA). If it's not high, leave it out. The GPA can be computed in many different ways to show you in your best light. You may have changed your career and educational direction and established a better record in your last one or two years of college. You could figure your GPA only from the courses you took in your educational major. Notice how the same data can be presented in significantly different ways.

GPA—*four-year senior college:*
Overall (all four years)—2.63
Upper-division (last two years)—3.01
Upper-division courses in major—3.31
Senior-level courses in major—3.40

GPA—*two-year college:*
Overall (both years)—2.88
Last year of school—3.12
Courses in major—3.48

Give the figure that shows you to your best advantage (Figgins, 1976).

Did you work your way through school? Highlight that fact if you did. A perfect or near-perfect attendance record will have a favorable effect on any employer. List any scholastic honors received, scholarships won, or special recognition earned. Definitely include your extracurricular activities, particularly those in which you excelled. Did you hold any class or club office, work as a library aide, or help publish the school paper or yearbook? Were you on an athletic team or in a school play? Anything that will indicate leadership, teamwork, artistic talent, physical dexterity, or creative ability will strengthen your case. The great characteristic of a résumé is that it allows you to present your strengths and abilities without saying a word about any weaknesses or limitations.

The following are some sample statements of educational achievement:

- Graduated in highest _____ of my class.
- Earned special recognition as _____ .
- _____ teams of which I was a member won _____ .
- Financed _____ percent of my educational (or college) expenses.
- Won a _____ scholarship, which partially covered school expenses.

Work Experience

If your employment history is your strongest appeal to an employer, place it ahead of your education section. Again, use reverse chronological order.

Your most recent job is usually given the most space, because it probably represents your highest level of achievement and has the greatest interest to the prospective employer. Provide the following information: dates of employment, name and location of each work organization, your job title, achievements on the job, duties and responsibilities, skills used, and special abilities developed. Be consistent; give the same information for all your places of employment. Give the names of supervisors if you know that they will give you a good recommendation and that they still work for the company. This need not be done for job positions held long ago unless you have a special reason for doing so. Present evidence for jobs well done or responsibilities carried out, especially if you helped your organization achieve its goals.

If your employment record is long, you might consider subtitling a section "Representative Job Positions" after describing your last three or four places of employment. Definitely indicate that your work experience section has been shortened for the sake of convenience (Figgins, 1976). A recent college or high school graduate, on the other hand, is more likely to have the opposite problem and must describe each job position more thoroughly. A waiter or waitress, for example, might say: "Had face-to-face contact with people, suggested food items that would appeal, took orders and remembered them correctly, served people what they ordered, made sure customers had a pleasant time, totaled the check or bill without making errors, brought the correct change to customers and thanked them for coming, cleaned the table and neatly set it for the next patron, and dressed attractively to make a good appearance."

List your part-time, summer, and volunteer work, particularly if you have little full-time work experience. Homemakers, for example, might think they haven't had much work experience until they start to remember all the volunteer jobs they have held. Treat the volunteer effort like any other job— think of the skills you used to complete the volunteer work. Try to show how your previous work experiences can be applied to your present job objective and your future occupational goals.

You can include military information in the work experience section, or you might want to construct a separate section for this. Be certain to mention military experience, because some private employers and many civil-service positions give a preferred status to former military personnel when hiring. List your branch of service, dates of entry and discharge, your rank, your Military Occupational Specialty (MOS), your duties, and other items such as promotions, honors, awards, proficiency ratings, and how your military skills could be converted to civilian jobs.

Whenever possible, show evidence or proof that others can depend on you to carry out your duties and responsibilities. Claiming that you were successful at your last job is only a generality. Supporting that statement with figures, such as a percentage increase of the volume of business or the organization's profits, will be more impressive. A representative sample of activities that brought about the results stated will make your claims more convincing to the employer.

Some writers advise that you list your work experience *functionally* rather than chronologically. A functional résumé features responsibilities, achievements, abilities, and experiences classified by category instead of by time sequence. Reviewing personal achievements and job successes to discover the skills that made them happen prepares you to write a functional résumé.

There is some debate about whether or not to give your reasons for leaving jobs. It is not necessary to state this information in your résumé, but it is worthwhile to write your reasons on a separate piece of paper as preparation for a job interview or for filling out an employer's application form. If you left a job with a previous employer on good terms, here are some sample phrases or sentences you could use:

- Accepted higher position offering greater opportunity for advancement.
- Accepted a more challenging position.
- Left to (complete college education) (expand experience beyond the scope of that job position) (fulfill military obligation).
- Left because new position (offered greater opportunities for use of my skills) (was closer to my occupational goal) (offered promise of more secure employment).
- Work was seasonal and I desired more steady employment.

If your reason for leaving was that you were not on good terms with the previous employer, it is probably best to say: "Am willing to discuss at interview." You can then prepare a response that will explain the circumstances from your viewpoint.

Refer to the list of action verbs in Table 3-1 for help in starting sentences that describe your previous job positions. Use the action verb (or functional skill) first. Next, list the object that completes the action; these are specific-content skills or special knowledges. Finally, add a self-descriptive adverb or adjective if you can; see Table 3-2 for a list. Other sample sentences or phrases that could go into the work experience block are the following:

- Started as _____ , promoted to a position of _____ within _____ years.
- Developed a working knowledge of operation and maintenance of the following equipment: _____ .
- Directed _____ employees in supervisory capacity as _____ .
- Responsibilities as _____ included _____ _____ .
- Have the following clerical skills: Can type _____ words

per minute; can take and transcribe dictation; can operate the following office machines: _____ , _____ , _____ .

- Organized and developed a new class in _____ , which enrolled _____ students.

Personal Data

The personal data section is placed between the work experience or educational section (whichever appears last) and the references section, unless you have placed it in the upper right corner opposite the heading. Personal data can include your social security number, birth date, height, weight, marital status, health condition, draft status, number of dependents, sex, race, religious preference, citizenship, hobbies, special skills, interests, and willingness to relocate. All this information is optional; mention only what relates to your employment history.

Information concerning your availability for work can be included in the personal data section. If you are currently unemployed or can start one or two weeks after you accept a job offer, you can indicate that you are "immediately available." If you are employed, state the amount of time you need to notify your employer and close out your affairs. You can write "Availability: _____ days' notification required," or indicate the date you would be available.

The personal data section has been deemphasized recently, perhaps as a result of antidiscrimination laws and right-to-privacy legislation. How much of this information you want to put into your résumé is a subjective decision for you to make.

If you decide to include personal data in your résumé, keep in mind the following points. State your date of birth rather than your age; that way, you won't need to write a new résumé after your next birthday. Health condition should be listed as "good" or "excellent," never "perfect." If you have a medical problem or physical disability, you may direct the reader to "see attachment." The situation can then be explained in greater detail on a separate sheet of paper attached to your résumé, with doctor's statements if necessary. You can use the same technique to deal with other sensitive material, such as a criminal record. If you are divorced or separated, you are, for all practical purposes, single. The single person may have some advantages if a job involves travel. You may wish to state that you own a car if an employer expresses concern about how you are going to get to work.

References

You should be able to list the names of at least three people who will attest to your good character, professional competence, or potential in your chosen occupation. However, it is not required that you include this information in your résumé. You may simply state, "References available upon request," or omit this section completely. Always secure the permission of your references to use their names *before* you list them.

Whom can you ask? References can be neighbors, former teachers, clergy, previous employers or supervisors if not already listed in the work experience section, or almost anyone who knows you well or remembers you and will give a good recommendation. Do not use relatives as references. If you have recently changed your surname or reverted to a maiden name, you will need to inform prospective employers that your references will remember you by a different last name.

Other Information

Most résumés contain information sections for the job objective, education, work experience, personal data, and references, but this is not a rigid format. You can list other items in the résumé under a heading such as "Related Skills and Activities" or "Miscellaneous Data" and place it just below the education and work experience sections.

All this information is optional, so select only those items that you believe will strengthen your résumé. You can show your involvement in professional functions, civic projects, volunteer work, memberships and offices held in clubs or organizations, travel experiences, and recreational activities. You can also emphasize special skills: proficiency in a foreign language, ability to operate specialized equipment, typing or shorthand speed, knowledge of computer languages, skills in first aid or lifesaving, or possession of special certificates and licenses. The subject of pay is best left for the interview.

Avoid filling a résumé with nonessential or irrelevant information. If you have any doubt about the relevance of an item, leave it out. Long lists of factual data are boring to read and detract from the important things you want to say.

What Is Most Important About a Résumé to Employers?

A survey of employers in large American corporations, appearing in the *Journal of College Placement* (Rogers, 1979), reported employers' views concerning what items should or should not be included in résumés. In terms of correctness of content, poor grammar was ranked as the greatest deficit. Spelling errors ran a close second, followed by poor organization of the résumé itself. The survey findings are presented in Table 3-3.

Of these employers, 66 percent felt that a one-page résumé was usually sufficient, and 83 percent thought the résumé should never exceed two pages. Beyond the initial contact with the employer, résumés were seen as having two important functions. One function is to serve as an outline around which the interview can be structured. The other function is to be a

TABLE 3-3 *Inclusions preferred in résumés*

Section or Topic	Should Appear	Neutral	No Need to Appear
Job objective	87%	8%	5%
Extracurricular activities	86%	13%	1%
All colleges attended	86%	13%	1%
College grades	72%	18%	10%
Interests and hobbies	57%	37%	6%
Education prior to college	34%	41%	25%
Statements about personality, background	31%	42%	27%
Personal data (age, sex, etc.)	26%	46%	28%
The statement: "References furnished upon request"	17%	52%	31%
List of references	8%	47%	45%

SOURCE: From "Elements of Efficient Job Hunting" by E. Rogers. Fall, 1979, *Journal of College Placement.* Reprinted with the permission of the College Placement Center, Inc., copyright holder.

concrete reminder to the employer of the job applicant after the interview is over (Rogers, 1979).

Figures 3-2 and 3-3 are sample chronological résumés that can serve as models. Do not repeat them verbatim; use your own imagination to create your own résumé. Exercise 3-1 provides a worksheet for the preparation of a chronological résumé. Exercise 3-2 (later in this chapter) concerns preparation of a functional résumé. You may wish to work on Exercise 3-2 first in order to make a better presentation of your previous (or current) job functions, achievements, and skills. Always prepare a rough draft of your résumé before you type your final copy. Your résumé must be perfect before you send it to an employer.

EXERCISE 3-1   *Draft Your Own Résumé*

Before you begin, make several copies of the blank worksheets on pages 71 and 72 so you will have extras when you need them. Fill in the information where indicated on the worksheets. You will then use this information to develop a final copy of a résumé that you can send or give to potential employers.

FIGURE 3-2   *An example of a chronological résumé for an experienced worker*

WILLIAM D. MASTERS
937 N. West Avenue
Riverside, California 92514
(555) 762-4567

JOB OBJECTIVE

Teaching political science and history, with opportunities for career and academic counseling on the community college level.

WORK EXPERIENCE

July 19__ to present, Riverside Community College, Riverside, California 92506. Experience includes teaching political science, western civilization, and psychology courses, and counseling students in student services office.

September 19__ to June 19__ , Modesto High School, 4000 Seventh Ave., Modesto, California 95350. Head counselor; organized a complete guidance program; administered schoolwide testing program; taught career guidance courses; coached basketball and track.

September 19__ to June 19__ , Northern High School, 2489 Foothill Drive, Santa Barbara, California 93109. Taught American government, U.S. and world history, and psychology. Coached varsity basketball, track, and cross-country. Served as faculty advisor to National Honor Society chapter.

March 19__ to February 19__ , U.S. Army. Basic training, infantry and artillery; counterintelligence training.

Other part-time and summer work experience: <u>Recreation director,</u> Central Methodist Church, 1145 N. Pacific Ave., San Jose, California. <u>Playground supervisor</u> in San Jose summer recreation program. Mowed lawns, painted houses, delivered newspapers, and cleaned rooms to pay for college expenses.

EDUCATION

September 19__ to March 19__ , Michigan State University; East Lansing, Michigan 48825. Educational specialist degree in counseling and educational psychology. Participated in counseling and guidance institutes at University of Maryland and San Francisco State College.

April 19__ to June 19__ , California State University at Fullerton, Fullerton, California 92634. Master's degree in counseling and guidance, with minor in psychology. Assisted in group and individual therapy sessions at Community Counseling Center. 3.7 GPA (4.0 = A) .

September 19__ to December 19__ , San Jose State University, San Jose, California 95192. Bachelor's degree in political science, with minors in history and physical education. 3.4 GPA (4.0 = A). Member of Spartan YMCA.

PERSONAL DATA

Born September 30, 19__ , in Davis California; good health; married, three children; enjoy athletics, reading, travel, music, ceramics; active member of St. Paul's Episcopal Church, lay reader, church school teacher, member of Vestry.

REFERENCES

Dr. John H. MacPherson	Robert C. London	Dr. Wilma R. Curry
Professor	Principal	Associate Professor
Political Science Dept.	Modesto High School	Department of Counseling
San Jose State University	4000 Seventh Ave.	and Educational Psychology
San Jose, CA 95192	Modesto, CA 95350	Michigan State University
		East Lansing, MI 48825

FIGURE 3-3   *An example of a chronological résumé for a student graduating from college*

TERESA M. MORGAN

Campus Address   Permanent Address
1252 River St., Apt 808   1111 W. Franklin
East Lansing, MI 48823   Jackson, MI, 49203
(555) 332-6086   (555) 782-0819

OBJECTIVE   To pursue a career in interior design or a related field, in which I can
                       use my design training. Willing to relocate after June 19__ .

EDUCATION   **Michigan State University**, East Lansing, MI 48825. Bachelor of
Sept. 19__   Arts in interior design, with emphasis in design communication
June 19__   and human shelter. Courses include lighting, introduction to
                       computers, public relations, and history of art. (F.I.D.E.R. accredited)
                       3.0 GPA (4.0 = A).

July 19__   **Michigan State University overseas study**, England and France,
Aug. 19__   decorative arts and architecture. 4.0 GPA (4.0 = A).

Sept. 19__   **Jackson Community College**, Jackson, MI 49201.
June 19__   Associate in Arts. 3.5 GPA (4.0 = A).

EMPLOYMENT   **Food Service and Maintenance**, Owen Graduate Center,
Sept. 19__   Michigan State University.
Present   • Prepared and served food.
                       • Managed upkeep of adjacent Van Hoosen Residence Hall.

Dec. 19__   **Food Service and Maintenance**, McDonel Residence Hall.
June 19__   • Served food and cleaned facility.
                       • General building maintenance.

June 19__   **Interior Decorator**, H. R. Smith Decorators, 201 S. Brown
                       Jackson, MI. 49203
Dec 19__   • Contacted clients to determine decorating preferences for offices
                          and homes.
                       • Ordered fabrics and materials.
                       • Supervised installation of design.

HONORS   • Community College Transfer scholarship from MSU.
AND   • American Society of Interior Design Publicity Chairman;
ACTIVITIES   Executive board, MSU Chapter.
                       • Wharton Center of the Performing Arts (MSU), usher.
                       • MSU Student Foundation member.
                       • Sigma Chi Little Sisters.
                       • Independent European travel, summer 19__ .
                       • Stage manager and performer in plays and musicals.
                       • Jackson High School Senior Class Treasurer.
                       • Jackson High School Yearbook Assistant Editor.

REFERENCES and PORTFOLIO available upon request.

A Worksheet for Developing a Chronological Résumé

Name _____

Street Address _____

City, State, Zip Code _____

Telephone (_____) _____

JOB OBJECTIVE

_____

_____

_____

EDUCATION (List in <u>reverse</u> chronological order.)

Dates: _____ to _____ School Name _____

City / State _____

Degree / Courses _____

Activities _____

_____

Dates: _____ to _____ School Name _____

City / State _____

Degree / Courses _____

Activities _____

_____

Dates: _____ to _____ School Name _____

City / State _____

Degree / Courses _____

Activities _____

_____

WORK EXPERIENCE (List in <u>reverse</u> chronological order.)

Dates: _____ to _____ Company Name _____

    Address _____

    Title / Duties _____

_____

    Accomplishments / Skills Used _____

_____ Supervisor* _____

Dates: _____ to _____ Company Name _____

    Address _____

    Title / Duties _____

_____

    Accomplishments / Skills Used _____

_____ Supervisor* _____

Dates: _____ to _____ Company Name _____

    Address _____

    Title / Duties _____

_____

    Accomplishments / Skills Used _____

_____ Supervisor* _____

Dates: _____ to _____ Company Name _____

    Address _____

    Title / Duties _____

_____

    Accomplishments / Skills Used _____

_____ Supervisor* _____

*Optional

PERSONAL DATA (optional) - Health, special skills, interests, etc.

_____

_____

MILITARY INFORMATION

    Dates: _____ to _____ Branch of Service _____

    Rank (when separated) _____ MOS / Duties _____

_____

REFERENCES

Name _____	Name _____	Name _____
Address _____	Address _____	Address _____
_____	_____	_____
Telephone _____	Telephone _____	Telephone _____

The Functional Résumé

The functional résumé highlights work functions rather than summarizing education and work experiences chronologically. It provides a way of displaying your abilities and relating your strengths to the job you are seeking. The reader concentrates on your achievements. Some résumé writers prefer the functional style, claiming it is more interesting to read and is more likely to attract attention. They feel that the chronological or "historical" résumé tends to obscure a person's accomplishments and skills with too many names, dates, addresses, and positions held.

The functional résumé emphasizes different abilities, depending upon the qualifications required by the job goal. Those who have had years of work experience often favor the functional résumé because they have accumulated many skills from work they have done. College graduates can emphasize the skills they developed in school, on part-time and summer jobs, and from life experiences. Functional résumés are also favored by people who have changed jobs frequently. A chronological résumé would reveal many job changes; not listing jobs in order can disguise the frequency of changing from one job to another. If your career direction has changed several times or you have several gaps in your employment record, a chronological résumé could portray you as unstable or unreliable in the minds of some employers. A functional résumé, on the other hand, could make your job changes appear more logical and sensible. You should not mislead your reader, however, for personnel workers are aware of the ability of the functional résumé to withhold information about your work history. If your employment background does not have frequent interruptions, you are probably better off using a chronological résumé.

Title each part of the work experience section with the name of a work function, and underline or capitalize it to make it more prominent. For example, you could write:

Advertising Experience   Public Relations Skills
Hospital Nursing   Research Functions
Merchandising Management   Technical Accomplishments

If you have had just one kind of work experience, you could divide it into several titles. For example:

Administrative and Management Skills   Accounting Experience
 • District Sales Manager   • Develop Annual Budget
 • Purchasing Director   • Cost Accounting
 • Retail Store Manager   • Billing and Collection

Then you describe your achievements, responsibilities, and skills under each title. Exercise 3-2 organizes your work experience into a presentation of important qualifications of your job objective.

Figure 3-4 provides an example of a functional résumé. Notice that the

FIGURE 3-4   *Example of a functional résumé*

JAMES K. JEFFERSON
1077 Second Avenue
Miami, FL 33161
(305) 592-8170

CAREER OBJECTIVE

Sales management position that uses my experience in motivating people and creating effective programs contributing to increased sales and greater profits for the organization.

EXPERIENCE

Management	Directed and coached twenty representatives in sales and customer service, improved staff morale and reduced turnover rates, administered quality control program, implemented two-year plan to upgrade operation efficiency of a production unit, identified errors made by employees before they became a liability to the company.
Sales Representative	Sold advertising and promotional campaign services in a territory covering Central and Southern Florida, increased sales volume over 50 percent in a two-year period, trained and motivated a sales force of twelve people, successfully introduced new product lines.
Public Relations	Designed advertising artistically for a major retail company, developed media and promotional materials, established contacts with editors and producers, wrote press releases and program scripts imaginatively.
Training	Supervised training procedures for office personnel, prepared training manual, produced 30-hour training programs for field representatives, taught sales and retailing class at a local community college.
Sales Clerk	Assisted customers with orders and purchases of appliances and furnishings for their homes, placed orders on worldwide network, cleaned and displayed merchandise creatively, won salesman of the year and month awards.
Financial	Tallied daily sales receipts accurately, deposited monies carefully, prepared monthly and quarterly financial reports for management, assisted in budget preparation.
Cooperative Relationships	Negotiated settlements for customer complaints courteously, organized non-profit child care center for employees, served as consultant for small minority-owned businesses, counseled employees supportively.

EMPLOYMENT

19__ to present	Johnson Advertising Services, Inc., 1221 N. Adams, Miami, FL 33167. Sales manager.
19__ to 19__	Emory Home Furnishings Company, 508 Beaufort Avenue, Atlanta, GA 30314. Personnel and public relations director.
19__ to 19__	J.C. Hill and Company, 163 Fourth Street, Tampa, FL 33606. Sales clerk.

EDUCATION

19__ to 19__	University of Florida, Gainesville, FL 32611. Master of Business Administration degree.
19__ to 19__	University of South Florida, Tampa, FL 33620. Bachelor of Arts degree. Majored in Business Administration.
19__ to 19__	Seminole Community College, Sanford, FL 32773. Associate degree in Arts and Science.

REFERENCES   Available upon request.

FIGURE 3-5   *Example of a combination functional and chronological résumé*

JASON R. SMITH
4121 Howard Road
Carlson, Michigan 49210
(517) 787-0899

EMPLOYMENT OBJECTIVE

Major interest is in Office Management with an opportunity for advancement to a Manager of a Sales, Purchasing, or Payroll Department.

BUSINESS EXPERIENCE

May 19___ to present.   XYZ Corporation, 126 W. Storybook Lane, Carlson, Michigan 49212. Supplier of machine parts to Ford Motor Co. James Littlefield, manager.

Bookkeeping — Simple accounting, posting accounts, statements, payroll tax reports (state and federal), weekly payroll, invoicing, accounts payable, accounts receivable.
Purchasing — Purchased office machines and supplies for a 25-person office, purchased stamping machines and drill presses for manufacturing division.
Sales — Established sales organization of independent dealers in Michigan, Ohio, and Indiana; set sales policies and dealer discount schedules.
Collections — Set credit limits to dealers, terms of payment, collection procedures on late accounts.
Inventory — Instituted card system on 150 to 200 items for fast cost analysis and control.
Pricing — Determined list and net prices on manufactured goods such as machines, accessories and replacement parts; prepared price lists for end users, stocking and non-stocking dealers.
Advertising — Layout and design of product literature, with photographs, descriptions, and specifications of product; direct mail advertising to dealer and end user; coordination of publicity campaign with an advertising agency.

June 19___ to May 19___.   ABC Corporation, 3480 Donneybrook Road, Turkeyville, Michigan 49998. Manufacturer of farm equipment. Alan Praeger, supervisor.

Bookkeeping — Simple accounting, posting accounts, payroll, book closing (monthly and annually), control of cash receipts and disbursements.
Financial Statements — Depreciation schedules, tax returns, annual partnership returns.
Invoicing — Product sales and miscellaneous labor sales.
Purchasing — Machinery, tools, and operating supplies.

EDUCATION

September 19___ to June 19___.   Carlson Community College, 1112 Emmons Road, Carlson, Michigan 49201. Associate in Applied Arts and Science degree with a major in Business Management. Grade point average: 3.25 (4.0=A). Distributive Education club member; Track and Field athlete; received scholarship from Business Department.

September 19___ to June 19___.   Carlson High School, 445 Wildwood, Carlson, Michigan 49210. National Honor Society Vice-President; Track and Field team captain; Cross Country athlete; Junior class Treasurer; Junior Achievement member.

REFERENCES

Furnished upon request.

focus of this type of résumé is on the work experience section. Each sentence begins with an action verb (the functional skill), which is followed by the object (a specific-content skill or special knowledge) and, often or occasionally, a self-descriptive adverb (an adaptive skill). Figure 3-5 is an example of a résumé that includes both functional and chronological features. The business experience section is in the functional style for each place of employment; everything else is arranged chronologically.

EXERCISE 3-2   *Functional Résumé Worksheets I and II*

There are two worksheets for this exercise. On the first worksheet, you will find four columns. In Column 1, title your job objective and identify its major functions. The *Dictionary of Occupational Titles* (DOT) can help you specify the functions performed in the job you are seeking. (The DOT is published by the U.S. Department of Labor and can be found in most libraries and career resource centers.) Another idea is to obtain an organization's description of a position that interests you. In Column 2, record your work experiences by job title and name of organization. Include any volunteer work. (Homemakers can consider their home responsibilities as work experience.) Describe your work experiences in Column 3 by listing the functions you performed in them. Functions are the same as responsibilities, duties, and achievements in the work you have done. Where any function listed under your job objective in the first column is the same as or similar to any function already performed in the third column, record it in Column 4. Refer to Figure 3-6 for an example of this first worksheet.

On the second worksheet, transfer the job objective and the functions from Column 1 of Worksheet I to Column 1 of Worksheet II. The functions can be expressed in a shorter form on Worksheet II. Next, find the functions in Column 4 of Worksheet I that match the functions in Column 1 of Worksheet II and write them in greater detail in Column 2 of Worksheet II. See Figure 3-7 for an example.

When you have completed the second worksheet, you have the basis for the work experience section of either a functional or chronological résumé. Work experience should be 80–90 percent of the functional résumé. The job objective functions in Column 1 become your work experience titles on the résumé. The list of responsibilities, duties, and achievements in Column 2 can be fleshed out in greater detail under these functional titles. An employer knows from a glance at your titles and descriptions for each job function that you understand to a great extent what the job involves. As you complete these worksheets, you will begin to realize that you have already performed many functions of your future job in various ways during your previous work experiences (Angel, 1980).

FIGURE 3-6 Example of the first worksheet for the functional résumé

Column 1	Column 2	Column 3	Column 4
Title and Functions of Your Job Objective	*Record of Work Experiences (Job Title, Workplace)*	*Description of Each Work Experience (List Functions Performed)*	*Same or Similar Work Experience Function to Job Objective Function*
Title: Social Services Aide *Functions:* Assisting caseworkers cooperatively. Counseling individuals and families supportively and empathically. Gathering information about personal and family problems. Compiling records about clients' past histories and experiences. Developing programs for small groups of clients on topics such as substance abuse, employment and family problems, interpersonal relationships, etc. Organizing, coordinating, and leading small groups. Referring clients to other agencies. Providing other services to caseworkers as needed, such as caring for children of clients while they are talking with the caseworker.	1. Volunteer at Emergency Counseling Center. 2. Teacher aide at Western Elementary School. 3. Church school teacher at United Community Church. 4. Housewife (or househusband) at 1033 Adams Street, Homeville, Texas.	1. Counseled, interviewed, listened to, and referred people; collected information on clients. 2. Assisted regular teacher, instructed small groups of students, helped individual students with learning problems, developed programs for students with special needs, maintained records for student evaluation. 3. Taught units on religious subjects and supervised care for babies and small children in nursery school. 4. Gathered and prepared food for the family, mended and cleaned clothing, maintained a home, budgeted money, supervised and participated in various family activities, counseled and advised members of family.	Counseling, interviewing, and listening to individuals. Referring people to other agencies. Compiling and maintaining records on clients accurately. Assisting supervisors (teachers and caseworkers) cooperatively. Organizing and leading small groups in programs that meet their needs and interests. Creating and developing programs of instruction that deal with personal and family problems. Instructing students competently. Caring for small children responsibly. Teaching clients about buying and preparing food, mending and cleaning clothes, maintaining a home, handling money, supervising and participating in family activities, counseling family members empathically and supportively.

FIGURE 3-7 *Example of the second worksheet for the functional résumé*

Column 1	Column 2
Title and Functions of Your Job Objective	*List the same or similar functions in the form of responsibilities, skills, and achievements from previous work experiences. (Use past tense unless currently using the function.)*
Title: Social Services Aide *Functions*:	
1. Assisting Caseworkers.	1. Assisted and followed directions of supervising caseworkers and teachers competently and cooperatively. (Specific responsibilities can be listed here.)
2. Counseling Individuals and Families.	2. Counseled, interviewed, and listened to people in an emergency counseling center and in my family. (More specific counseling skills could be indicated such as reflecting feelings, paraphrasing or summarizing statements, asking appropriate questions, giving advice or feedback, etc.)
3. Gathering Information.	3. Collected information about clients in performing responsibilities at an emergency counseling center. Assembled data about students in an elementary school for grading and evaluation purposes.
4. Compiling Records.	4. Maintained precise records about clients' and students' past family, school, work, and learning experiences.
5. Developing Programs.	5. Created (or planned, designed, outlined, devised, conceived) programs for student, church, and family members on personal, religious, and special needs topics.
6. Organizing Groups.	6. Coordinated small group activities in programs designed to meet the needs and interests of group members. (The names of specific groups and subjects of programs should be cited here.)
7. Referring Clients.	7. Learned the functions of 20 other social agencies in order to accurately refer clients from an emergency counseling center to them.
8. Providing Other Services.	8. Experienced in (and could teach about) buying and preparing food for a family, mending and cleaning clothes economically, maintaining a home efficiently, caring for small children, handling money carefully, coordinating small group and family activities, and counseling family members supportively. (With these "other" or "catch-all" functions, only the limits of the imagination restrains one here!)

Functional Résumé Worksheet I

Step 1. Complete columns 1, 2, and 3. If any column does not give you enough space, use separate sheets of paper.

Step 2. In Column 4, write the name of any job objective function from Column 1 beside any same or similar function (or responsibility) you have performed in a previous experience listed in Column 3.

Column 1	Column 2	Column 3	Column 4
Title of your job objective: _____	Record of work experiences (job title, workplace):	Description of each work experience. List the functions you performed:	Same as or similar to a job objective function:
Functions of your job objective:	1. _____	1. _____	_____
_____		_____	_____
_____		_____	_____
_____	2. _____	2. _____	_____
_____		_____	_____
_____	3. _____	3. _____	_____
_____		_____	_____
_____	4. _____	4. _____	_____
_____		_____	_____
_____	5. _____	5. _____	_____
_____		_____	_____
_____	6. _____	6. _____	_____
_____		_____	_____
_____	7. _____	7. _____	_____
_____		_____	_____

Functional Résumé Worksheet II

Step 1. Complete Column 1. This column is the same as Column 1 on the first worksheet. You may shorten the descriptions of your job objective functions by using only the action verb and its object.

Step 2. In Column 2, list and briefly describe all the functions in Column 1 of this worksheet that are the same or similar to each job objective function. (Column 2 of this worksheet expands on and reorganizes the information in Column 4 on Worksheet I.)

Step 3. Transfer this information to the work experience section of your résumé. Titles of functions will come from Column 1, and descriptions of those functions already performed in work experiences will come from Column 2.

Column 1	**Column 2**
Title of your job objective:	List the same or similar functions in the form of responsibilities, duties, skills, and achievements of your previous work experiences. (Use the past tense unless you are currently performing the function.)
_____	
Functions (titles):	

1. _____   1. _____

2. _____   2. _____

3. _____   3. _____

4. _____   4. _____

5. _____   5. _____

6. _____   6. _____

7. _____   7. _____

8. _____   8. _____

9. _____   9. _____

The Cover Letter

The purposes of a cover letter (also called a letter of application) are to introduce yourself to a prospective employer, to bring attention to your enclosed résumé, and to create a desire in the employer to send you an application form and have an interview with you. The cover letter is the first thing employers notice when they open your envelope. Most organizations receive letters from many more job-seekers than they could ever interview. Many employers or personnel officers will immediately start looking for reasons to reject your application and not grant you an interview. Therefore, only correct, concise, and carefully composed cover letters stand a chance of getting through the screening maze.

Cover letters are usually sent to discover job openings, initiate contacts, respond to an advertisement, or follow up a referral by a personal contact or an employment agency. In some cases, you must make a judgment call on whether to send your cover letter without a résumé. Some job-seekers prefer to use the cover letter as a letter of application and present the résumé only after an interview has been held. Cover letters are not necessary for on-campus interviews in a college placement office or when arrangements for an interview have already been made.

Addressing a cover letter to a specific person by name is far more effective than using "Dear Madam," "Dear Sir," or an official title. If you do not know a specific name, telephone the organization and request the name and title of the appropriate person to receive your letter. Explain the reason for your call; a secretary or receptionist will give you this information. You can also find names in business and industrial directories from libraries. Not addressing a specific person by name makes your letter impersonal; some employers say they would rather have the wrong name on the address than a "Dear Madam or Sir." It makes a better impression when the job-seeker has at least gone to the time and trouble of learning the name of a person in the organization.

The cover letter should not exceed one page; three or four paragraphs are all that is needed. Almost all personnel managers in one survey agreed that one page is sufficient (Meyers, 1984). In your own style, you can say: "I am interested in your organization; let me give you some reasons why you should be interested in me; I would like to have an interview with you." Always type your cover letter. If you can't type or don't have a typewriter, find someone who can do the job correctly for you, and pay them if necessary. Résumés can be mass-produced by a print shop; cover letters are more personal.

Heading, Inside Address, and Salutation

In the upper right corner, about 10 or 12 spaces from the top of the page, depending upon the length of your letter, type your return address and the date. If you prefer the block-style letter, it is equally correct to type the return address and date even with the left margin. See Figures 3-8 and 3-9 for examples of both styles. The block style aligns everything in the letter at the left margin.

The inside address is the same information you place on the outside of an envelope. It includes the name of the person you are writing; his or her title, if available; the name of the organization and its address; and the city, state, and zip code.

The salutation should read: "Dear Mrs. Smith:" or "Dear Mr. Doe:." Use "Dear Madam or Sir:" if you do not know the name of a person, as in the case of a blind ad. The colon (:) is correct after the salutation. Use a comma when you personally know the individual to whom you are writing. Some people

FIGURE 3-8   *Example of a cover letter (regular style)*

```
                                        4811 N. Pacific Avenue
                                        Anyville, California 94201
                                        Telephone (555) 011-0011

                                        September 15, 19__

Ms. Jane Thompson
Personnel Director
Crown and Smith Publishing Company
1001 Woodland Avenue
Anytown, California 94910

Dear Ms. Thompson:

I am seeking a junior management position with a progressive company
in the publishing business. My education and experience in writing and
publishing could be valuable to your organization. I have earned a
college degree, majoring in journalism at the University of Califor-
nia, Berkeley. Practical, on-the-job experience includes working as an
assistant editor with a university press and as a teaching assistant
in a college English department. I am capable of learning quickly and
can grow with an organization such as yours.

As a trainee for a management position, I could contribute much while
learning how a private publishing company operates. I have prepared
several authors' manuscripts for publication by the university press.
My experience includes delegating work assignments and arranging
schedules of employees. I have taught four courses for the Communica-
tions Department at Oregon State University.

I am articulate, a good correspondent, and able to motivate people. I
am eager to put my ideas and experience to work for you. I am willing
to relocate and travel as required.

The enclosed resume summarizes my education and work experience.
Please contact me by phone or mail; I would be pleased to meet with
you at your convenience.

                                        Sincerely,

                                        Daryl K. Jones

                                        Daryl K. Jones
```

FIGURE 3-9   *Example of a cover letter (block style)*

4312 Carlton Blvd.
Atlanta, Georgia 30341
Telephone (404) 933-5980
April 18, 19__

Mr. William A. Harrison
General Manager
Machinery Installation Systems
P.O. Box 560
Atlanta, Georgia 30342

Dear Mr. Harrison:

I am a resourceful, diligent, achievement-oriented person looking for
a challenge. I can bring experience of a varied and thorough business
background to your growing company. Please consider this letter and
the attached resume as my application for a management position within
your organization.

While researching potential employers relevant to my aspirations and
career goals, I was intrigued by the presentation of your unique
product offerings and varied engineering services in the latest issue
of the Journal of the Fabricator. My innovative and creative skills,
talents, and interests, as well as my experience and education, would
fit well at your company and operate to our mutual advantage.

It would be a pleasure to meet with you at your convenience to discuss
your firm's employment opportunities, particularly coordination and/or
supervision of your clerical, accounting, and financial processes. I
can be reached at the above telephone number after 5:00 p.m. and on
weekends or at my present office number (404) 934-8060 between 8:00
a.m. and 5:00 p.m. Monday through Friday.

I shall look forward to hearing from you. Thank you for your attention
and consideration.

Sincerely,

Ruth A. Davisson

Ruth A. Davisson

Enclosure (Résumé)

have difficulty framing a salutation. A few years ago, newspaper columnist
Ann Landers received suggestions from her readers for substitutions for the
traditional approach. One was "Ladies and Gentlemen," but it sounded too
much like the opening of a speech. "Good morning" is a homey touch,
according to another suggestion. One reader wanted to replace the salutation with the company's name: "Dear Sears," or "Dear General Motors." The
prize went to "Yoo-hoo. Yes, I'm talking to you." Save yourself the trouble;
obtain the person's name.

First paragraph.   *State why you are writing and why you want to work in
that job position and for that particular organization; attract attention
and create the desire to read further.*

The first two or three sentences of the cover letter are very important. They must attract attention and motivate the reader to continue reading. The first paragraph is the hardest part of the cover letter to write. You must use words and phrases that will capture the imagination of the employer or personnel manager. Some writers estimate that you have an average opportunity of about ten seconds with the reader. Within that time span, the reader will decide whether to continue reading or to go on to something else. You must develop language to make the employer read further, to identify the purpose of your message, and to express what motivated you to write. However, you should do this in a way that is not so flamboyant it brands you as a show-off.

Here are some suggested openings:

- My education and experience in the field of _____ could be valuable to your company (or organization).
- With _____ years experience in the _____ field, I believe I am suitably qualified to apply for . . .
- I am an energetic, hard working college graduate interested in a _____ _____ position.
- I know the _____ business! For the past _____ years, I have been working in the _____ _____ industry. I began as a . . .
- _____ , a former supervisor of your organization, suggested that I contact you for . . .
- My _____ skills and _____ abilities in the field of _____ may be of great interest to you.
- A recent advertisement of your company in the ____(name of publication)____ indicated your desire to hire a _____ for _____ _____ .

Whatever the opening, it needs to generate enough interest to cause the employer to continue reading. Some writers prefer a very simple, straightforward approach. Some readers do, too! For example:

- Please accept my application for . . .
- I am qualified to be considered for . . .
- My background and experience prepare me for . . .
- I am applying for. . . .

Second paragraph.   *State your qualifications for the job opening; mention an achievement (or two), particularly if it is relevant to the job being sought.*

The second paragraph gives the employer reasons why he or she should hire you. Some writers might want to use two paragraphs for this. You should briefly summarize your qualifications, your skills and abilities, and mention one or two achievements, especially if they are appropriate to the job position you seek. Review significant aspects of your education or previous work experience. Some writers like to identify their strongest abilities or reinforce a strength that is mentioned but not highlighted in the résumé. Consult any achievement experiences you have written, and use a couple of key sentences in this part of your cover letter. Exercise 3-2 contains worksheets for the functional résumé that could give you some help stating your qualifications.

The following are examples of sentences you could use in this paragraph:

- At ____(name of company or school)____ , I was responsible for _____ _____ , using my _____ skills.
- I handled the following details for ____(name of organization or employer)____ : _____ .
- Sales increased by _____ percent when I _____ _____ for ____(name of organization)____ .
- I was able to produce _____ more efficiently, saving (name of employer or organization)____ time and money.
- My skills in _____ were demonstrated at ____(name of school or workplace)____ when I _____ .

Third paragraph.   *Urge the reader to continue the correspondence; bring attention to the enclosed résumé; request an interview; and state how the employer can contact you (or how you will contact the employer).*

The last paragraph summarizes the purpose of your cover letter. You want the employer to contact you, send a letter expressing interest in you or call on the telephone, send an application form, read your résumé, and grant you an interview. A more assertive style is to inform employers that you will contact them for an interview; a less assertive style leaves the interview to the employer's discretion. The following are examples of statements that you could adapt:

- I hope to hear from you as soon as possible.
- Please send me information regarding employment with your organization.
- The attached résumé should prove to be of interest to you.
- Enclosed is a copy of my résumé, which summarizes my qualifications, education, and work experience.
- I am willing to discuss my qualifications with you in person at your earliest convenience.
- If you are interested in my qualifications (or application) for this position, I will be available _____ to meet with you in person.
- I will make an appointment for a personal interview with you next _____ .
- I will telephone your office next _____ in the hope of setting up an appointment with you.

- I can be contacted at the above address or by telephone _____(days)_____ after _____(time)_____ or on weekends. My telephone number is _____ _____ .

There is no one right way to write a cover letter. Some people write four or five paragraphs; others are content with two.

Complimentary Close and Signature

This is a brief, simple courtesy. Merely say: "Yours truly," "Sincerely," or "Respectfully." Follow the close with a comma. Then sign the letter in ink (preferably blue or black), and type your name about four spaces below the complimentary close, to avoid any misreading of your handwriting. Remember to sign your name. An optional item is to type the word "Enclosure" in the lower left corner of the cover letter. This refers to the résumé, alerting the reader to the fact that more is included in the envelope. "Enclosure: (résumé)" is also correct.

Physical Appearance of the Letter

A cover letter is placed on top of a résumé and is received before a job interview occurs, so it conveys a first impression to the employer. The impression you want to create is that you are a competent person with a lot to offer. The way to do this is to send a clean, neat, and technically perfect cover letter. Spelling mistakes, awkward sentence structure, grammatical errors, and typographical oversights detract from the quality of your letter; not paying attention to these details will cause your cover letter to work against you rather than for you.

Always use a current dictionary to check the spelling and definition of every word you are not sure of. Misspelled and mistyped words may be regarded as evidence of the job applicant's carelessness and inattention to detail, even though the applicant is normally intelligent and proficient.

Proofread your cover letter and résumé very carefully, word for word. A typographical error is as bad to the reader as a misspelled word. Ask a friend, spouse, or parent to proofread your work critically and catch all errors while there is still time to correct them. Never mail your letters and résumés without proofreading them.

Always type your cover letter using high-quality white paper. The size of the paper should be 8½ by 11 inches. The importance of neatness cannot be overemphasized. When employers or personnel directors begin to look through cover letters and résumés, they often begin by eliminating those that look messy or contain misspelled words and errors in grammar.

EXERCISE 3-3 *Draft Your Own Cover Letter*

Your address _____

City, state, zip code _____

Date _____

_____ Employer's name

_____ Name of organization

_____ Address

_____ City, state, zip code

Dear _____ :
(name)

First paragraph (Attract attention and create the desire to read further; state why you are writing and want to work in that job and for that organization.)

_____

_____

_____

Second paragraph (State your qualifications for the job; mention an achievement or two, particularly if they are relevant to the job being sought.)

_____

_____

_____

Third paragraph (Urge the reader to respond; bring attention to the enclosed résumé; request an interview; state how you can be contacted.)

_____

_____

_____

Sincerely yours,

_____
(Your signature)

Enclosure (résumé)

(Type your name below your signature)

Other Types of Written Communication

Résumés and cover letters are not the only communications you will write when you seek a job. Thank-you letters, follow-up letters, an acceptance letter, and letters declining offers are also a part of the job search. Ideas for and models of these letters are presented in this section. After reading this section, you should have a general idea of how to write these letters, but do not copy them word for word.

Thank-You Letters

Within three days after each interview, you should write a brief note to the person with whom you talked, expressing your thanks for the time he or she spent with you. You never lose when you say, "Thank you." You can mention something specific from the interview to indicate that your letter is personally written to the reader, not just a form letter. Two or three short paragraphs are usually enough. (See Figure 3-10.)

Writing a thank-you note takes only five or ten minutes, yet it is one of the most important things you can do in your entire job search. The employer notices that you are a person with courtesy. You are probably the only one of a hundred job-seekers who writes this kind of a letter. All career counselors advise it, and almost all job-seekers forget it. Some people have obtained jobs on the strength of their thank-you letters. That's not why you write, but it does happen. The thank-you letter was the one thing that set them apart from the other job candidates; it made the essential difference. Also, keep secretaries or receptionists in mind. Get their names and send them thank-you letters. After all, you probably had to go through a secretary to see the employer. The secretary will appreciate your simple courtesy and remember you for it.

Follow-Up Letters

You write a follow-up letter when you do not receive any response from an employer after sending an application or résumé and cover letter. The pur-

FIGURE 3-10 *Example of the body of a thank-you letter*

I am grateful for the opportunity to meet with you last _____(day)_____ . I value the information you gave me concerning _____ .

Should any opening occur in a job position for which you believe I would be qualified, I would greatly appreciate being informed about it. Let me know if I can provide you with any additional facts about my career goals and qualifications.

Thank you once more for the interview. I hope we can meet again soon.

FIGURE 3-11 Example of the body of a follow-up letter

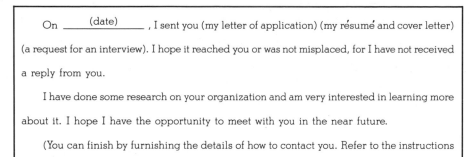

On _____(date)_____ , I sent you (my letter of application) (my résumé and cover letter) (a request for an interview). I hope it reached you or was not misplaced, for I have not received a reply from you.

    I have done some research on your organization and am very interested in learning more about it. I hope I have the opportunity to meet with you in the near future.

    (You can finish by furnishing the details of how to contact you. Refer to the instructions for the third paragraph of the cover letter.)

pose of the follow-up letter is to remind employers of your contact with them, show interest in their organization, and give additional information that could strengthen a previous impression. (See Figure 3-11.) There is no standard amount of time to wait before writing a follow-up letter. Some career counselors advise giving the employer two to three weeks' time to reply to your original letter. You can also write a follow-up letter when you receive no response after an interview. One job-seeker got a job after writing three follow-up letters; the employer was impressed by the job-seeker's persistence and obvious interest in the company.

Accepting or Declining a Job Offer

Accepting an offer.   Start with a statement accepting the job offer and follow with any necessary details, such as additional papers needed and when you can report. End with a sense of optimism toward the time you will be working for the employer. See Figure 3-12 for an example.

Declining an offer.   Decline the offer and express your appreciation for the organization's interest in you and the time they have given you. Leave an opening for future opportunities with the company. (See Figure 3-13.)

Summary

    1. The résumé is a self-designed personal data sheet that contains information about your job objective, education, and work experience. The two major styles of résumés are *chronological* and *functional*. Chronological résumés present your education and work experience in a time sequence, whereas functional résumés highlight work functions you performed on previous jobs.

    2. A cover letter can accompany the résumé when you communicate with employers. The cover letter introduces you to the employer, explains

FIGURE 3-12 *Example of the body of an acceptance letter*

I am truly pleased to accept your company's offer of a position as a (an) _____

_____ at a salary of $ _____ per year. I look forward to facing the

challenges the company provides and will give every effort to fulfill your expectations. It

will be a pleasure to work with _____ and share your interests in

_____ .

Enclosed are the completed information forms you requested contingent upon my

acceptance. I will be most grateful for any assistance the company can give me in arranging

for an apartment or house. I will be ready to report for work on _____

when I conclude my responsibilities at _____ .

Please inform me of any other details you believe I should know. I am eagerly anticipating

my new assignment and wish to thank you for placing your confidence in me.

FIGURE 3-13 *Example of the body of a letter declining an offer*

After considerable thought and deliberation, I have decided not to accept your offer of

a position with _____ . This decision was a very difficult

one to make.

I am very impressed with your organization and hope the door will be open for future

opportunities. I sincerely appreciate the time and consideration you have given me.

why you are writing, states your qualifications for the job objective, and asks
for an interview.

3. Other forms of communication with employers are thank-you notes
after interviews, follow-up letters when you have received no response to
your letter or résumé, and letters accepting or declining job offers.

References

Angel, J. A. (1980). *The complete résumé book and job-getter's guide*.
New York: Pocket Books.
Biegeleisen, J. I. (1982). *Job résumés: How to write them, how to present
them, preparing for interviews*. New York: Putnam.

Bolles, R. N. (1986). *What color is your parachute? A practical manual for job-hunters and career changers.* Berkeley, CA: Ten Speed Press.

Figgins, R. (1976). *Techniques of job search.* San Francisco: Canfield Press.

Haldane, B., Haldane, J., & Martin, L. (1976). *Job power now! The young people's job-finding guide.* Washington, DC: Acropolis Books.

Hizer, D. A., & Rosenberg, A. D. (1985). *The résumé handbook: How to write outstanding résumés and cover letters for every situation.* Boston: Bob Adams.

Irish, R. K. (1978). *Go hire yourself an employer* (rev. ed.). Garden City, NY: Doubleday/Anchor.

Lathrop, R. (1977). *Who's hiring who?* Berkeley, CA: Ten Speed Press.

Meyers, H. H. (1984). Writing résumés right. *Journal of College Placement, 44*(2), 19–21.

Nutter, C. F. (1978). *The résumé workbook: A personal career file for job applications.* Cranston, RI: Carroll Press.

Rogers, E. J. (1979). Elements of effective job-hunting. *Journal of College Placement 40*(1), 55–58.

Weinstein, B. (1982). *Résumés for hard times.* New York: Fireside/Simon & Schuster.

4

Job Application Forms and Other Problems of the Job Search

Giving information about yourself on an employer's application form is the most common element of the job search. Because the application form is so much a part of the usual routine, the importance of this document can be easily overlooked. The words you write on the form are permanent. They can be verified or refuted, and they will be used as part of your evaluation. The application form becomes a paper with legal standing if you are hired. After you have filled out the tenth application form in, say, three days, there is an understandable tendency to give it short shrift and become careless and sloppy about it. You must resist that temptation. Approach the employer's application form as if it were a test—which it actually is. It is a test of your written expression, accuracy, honesty, neatness, spelling, ability to follow directions, and a test of how well you represent yourself. Like the résumé, the application form by itself will not be enough to get you the job, but you must master it well enough to stay in the running.

After discussion and exercises pertaining to job application forms, the rest of this chapter considers several special problems that can emerge from a job search. Illegal questions on application forms (and in job interviews as well) present a dilemma. Opinions differ about how best to handle them. One idea is to ignore them if they do not personally bother you. Another strategy is to suggest politely that the inquiry is not relevant to the job position being sought, thus protecting not only yourself but also those whom the law is trying to protect.

Concluding this chapter are two exercises on strengths and problems of the job search. Some job-seekers have the problem of concentrating only on their weaknesses and ignoring their strengths. Exercise 4-3 may help you gain a better perspective on the strong points you already possess. Exercise 4-4 may help you to cope with certain special problems that could arise on a job application form or during a job interview. Recognizing possible difficulties in advance allows you time to develop responses that could reduce or eliminate the negative impact of an unprepared answer.

Completing an Employer's Application Form

The application form is an innocuous-looking piece of paper, but it can be loaded with danger. There is a temptation to become careless when completing an employer's application form. There are so many of them to fill out that you can become punchy after a while. If you find yourself answering "Dad" for father's name or "womb" for place of birth, you have symptoms of the "application blahs." Study the application form carefully. The employer may discover far more than you could ever imagine from this simple piece of paper. If you make mistakes on the application blank, ask for another one. It is better to take time on it than to leave a poor impression of yourself. Give the application form the same consideration you give any other part of your job search—that is, consider it very important. The application could become the most important link between you and the employer.

Here are some helpful aids in filling out employer's applications.

1. Read the entire application form carefully before you attempt to give information on any items or answer any questions.
2. Use your résumé as a source of dates and other information.
3. Fill out the form in *ink,* and *print* responses unless otherwise directed. *Write* your signature.
4. Answer all questions, even if you must print "not applicable" or "none" as a response. Unanswered items become conspicuous to some employers.
5. Follow directions carefully. This sounds trite, but not following directions trips up more people than you can imagine. Read each item *before* you respond to it.
6. Compose your answers on a blank or scrap sheet of paper first if you are not sure how to reply.
7. Answer all questions honestly. If you are hired, your application form becomes a part of your permanent record.
8. Keep the application form clean and neat. You are giving a written impression of yourself to a prospective employer. Complete a second application form if the first one is sloppy.
9. Check the accuracy of your spelling.
10. Obtain the permission of your references *before* you use their names.
11. Base requested salary figures on your research of the organization. Write "open to negotiation" if you are not sure of an appropriate amount.
12. Don't forget to sign your name!

EXERCISE 4-1   *Application for Employment*

The application form in Exercise 4-1 is a composite of many employers' applications used in the past; use it for learning or teaching purposes only, because it contains several items that are now illegal to ask an applicant before he or she is hired. Fill out the sample Application for Employment, and circle the items you think are illegal. After the exercise, check your knowledge of legal and illegal questions asked before hiring takes place by consulting the Pre-Employment Inquiry Guide.

Legal and Illegal Questions

The application form in Exercise 4-1 is more complex than the ones you will usually encounter. Actually, it is a composite drawn from several actual forms used in the recent past, and it contains a number of areas of inquiry that are now illegal. Most of them appear in the "personal information"

APPLICATION FOR EMPLOYMENT (To be completed in applicant's own handwriting in ink)	Not an actual application. To be used for teaching purposes only.

PERSONAL INFORMATION

Date _____ Social Security number _____

Name _____ Age _____ Sex _____
    Last   First   Middle (maiden name)

Present address _____
    Number and street   City   State   Zip   Phone

Permanent address _____
    Number and street   City   State   Zip   Phone

Birth _____ U.S. Citizen? _____ Height _____ Weight _____
    Date   Place

Married   Single   Widowed   Divorced   Separated _____

Number of children _____ Dependents (other than spouse and children) _____

Have you ever been convicted of a crime? _____ If yes, explain. _____

Do you own a car? _____ If yes, give details: Make _____ Year _____ License number _____

Do you have a driver's license? _____ License number _____ What state? _____ Date license expires _____

Driver's license ever suspended or revoked? _____ If yes, when and why? _____

Do you have any personal responsibilities or problems that might prevent you from coming to work at times? _____ If yes, explain. _____

EMPLOYMENT DESIRED

Position _____ Date you can start: _____ Salary expected: _____

Other job interests _____

Are you willing to relocate? _____ In what city or area would you prefer work? _____

If related to anyone in our organization, state name and department. _____

State reasons for preference of work desired. _____

EDUCATION

	Name and location of school	Years attended	Graduation date and degree	Name of major or program
College				
High school				
Other				

Do you plan to further your education? Explain. _____

Membership in professional, technical, honorary associations _____

List any special skills you have developed. _____

List hobbies, special interests, and things you like to do. _____

MILITARY _____	Branch of service	Date of entrance	Date of discharge
Rank when discharged	Military Occupational Specialty		Type of discharge
Received disability payments?	Nature of disability		

EMPLOYMENT RECORD   (Start with your present or latest employer)

Date (month/year)	Name and address of employer (Include name of your supervisor)	Title or position	Highest salary	Reason for leaving
From _____				
To				
From _____				
To				
From _____				
To				
From _____				
To				
From _____				
To				

Explain any periods of unemployment
or part-time work not listed.

Attendance record: Average number
of days absent per month in last job.

PHYSICAL RECORD: General health   Excellent ___   Good ___   Fair ___   Poor ___

Serious illness in the past five years?	If yes, state the nature of your illness.	
Any physical handicaps or limitations?	If yes, explain.	
Have you ever had a work injury for which you have received disability benefits?	If yes, when and for what reason?	

Indicate whether you have had any of the following: Diabetes___   Heart condition___
High blood pressure___   Defective sight___   Mental problems___   Epilepsy___
Back ailments___   Hernia___   Defective hearing___   Frequent or serious headaches___
Other _____

Has any insurance company rejected your application for life insurance?	If yes, explain.

FINANCIAL

Have you ever been sued or had wages garnisheed or assigned?	If yes, explain.

List two businesses where   1.
you have established credit
(Name, address, telephone). 2.

REFERENCES Give names of three persons. (Do not list relatives or former employers.)

Name	Address	Telephone	Business or Occupation

I authorize investigation of all statements in this application. I understand that misrepresentation or omission of facts called for is cause for dismissal. All information I have given in this application for employment is true to the best of my knowledge.

DATE _____   SIGNATURE _____

section. All the items on this application form have appeared at some time on real applications.

What should you do if you encounter an illegal item on an application form? There is no simple answer to this question. Basically, you have three options.

1. You could write "not relevant for the qualifications required by the job" or "not an appropriate question before hiring" or (more directly) "this question is an illegal inquiry and I am not required to answer it." These responses are somewhat risky because you may feel that they make you appear uncooperative to the employer. You have the law on your side, but it may not help much. It takes time to prosecute repeated discrimination. Also, the employer may not realize that a particular question is illegal. Some employers know very little about the legalities of hiring employees and thus may be unaware that the question is illegal.

2. You can answer the question and ignore its illegality. Many job-seekers answer questions they know to be illegal because they are desperate for a job or because the subject is of no great concern to them. Some people feel differently. They argue that job-seekers should not aid and abet a clearly illegal procedure.

3. Tell the employer you will inform the nearest office of the Civil Rights Commission or the Equal Employment Opportunity Commission (EEOC). Before doing this, try the first option above and give the employer a chance to comply with the law. Otherwise, kiss the job good-bye. Successful prosecution of employers who illegally discriminate in their hiring practices is difficult. You must be able to show a repeated pattern of illegal job discrimination by the employer. Your best chance of winning your case is to get in touch with an advocacy group that has competent legal resources.

To become knowledgeable about the legality or illegality of items on employment application forms (and also in job interviewing situations), refer to the Pre-Employment Inquiry Guide on pages 98–101.

Employers may apply for an exemption on the basis that religion, national origin, age, height, weight, or sex is a bona fide occupational qualification essential to the normal operation of the business or enterprise. Upon sufficient showing by the employer, an exemption may be granted.

The information given in the Pre-Employment Inquiry Guide is drawn mostly from the Michigan Department of Civil Rights. Relevant legislation includes the Equal Employment Opportunity Act (Title VII), the Higher Education Act (Title IX), and the Age Discrimination Act on the national level and Public Acts 220 and 453 of 1976 for Michigan.

If you are job-hunting and do not have a résumé prepared, complete the worksheet in Exercise 4-2 and take it with you when you apply for a job position in person. It will help you remember accurate information about yourself. Another variation of this exercise is to write needed information on 3 × 5 or 4 × 6 cards, which may be easier to handle than a larger sheet of paper. Exercise 4-2 appears on pages 102–103.

Pre-employment inquiry guide

Subject	Lawful Pre-Employment Inquiries	Unlawful Pre-Employment Inquiries
1. Name	a) Applicant's full name. b) Have you ever worked for this company under a different name? c) Is any additional information relative to a different name necessary to check work record? If yes, explain.	a) Original name of an applicant whose name has been changed by court order or otherwise. b) Applicant's maiden name. c) To ask if a woman is a Miss, Mrs., or Ms.
2. Address or Duration of Residence/Housing	a) How long a resident of this state or city? b) Place and length of current and previous address? c) To ask for applicant's phone number or how he or she can be reached if a number is not available.	a) To ask applicant if he or she owns a home or rents or lives in an apartment or house.
3. Age	a) Require proof of age by birth certificate *after hiring*. b) Are you 18 years old or older? (This question may be asked for the purpose of determining whether applicants are of legal age for employment.)	a) How old are you? b) What is your birth date?
4. Birthplace		a) Birthplace of applicant, parents, spouse, or other close relatives. b) To ask that applicant submit birth certificate or naturalization or baptismal record.
5. Religion or Creed		a) Inquiry into an applicant's religious denomination. b) To request recommendations from church officials.

6. Race or Color	a) To ask about race, for affirmative action plan statistics, *after hiring*.	a) Any inquiry that would indicate race or color.
7. Photograph	a) May be required *after hiring* for identification purposes.	a) Requirement that an applicant attach a photograph to an employment form. b) Request that an applicant, at his or her option, submit a photograph. c) Require a photograph after an interview but before hiring.
8. Height		a) Inquiry regarding applicant's height.
9. Weight		a) Inquiry regarding applicant's weight.
10. Marital/Parental Status	a) Status (only married or single) *after hiring*, for insurance purposes. b) Number and ages of dependents and/or spouse *after hiring*, for insurance purposes.	a) Requirement that an applicant provide any information regarding marital status or children. b) Are you single or married? c) Do you have any children? d) Is your spouse employed? e) What is your spouse's name?
11. Sex		a) Any inquiry that indicates sex, unless job-related, such as locker-room or restroom attendant.
12. Health	a) Do you have any impairments, physical, mental, or medical, *which would interfere with your ability to do the job for which you have applied?* b) Inquiry into contagious or communicable diseases that may endanger others. If there are any positions for which you should not be considered or job duties you can't perform because of physical or mental handicap, please explain.	a) Do you have a disability or handicap? b) Have you ever been treated for the following diseases? c) Do you use any adaptive device or aid? d) Requirement that women be given pelvic examinations.

(continued)

Pre-employment inquiry guide (continued)

Subject	Lawful Pre-Employment Inquiries	Unlawful Pre-Employment Inquiries
13. Citizenship	a) Are you a citizen of the United States? b) If not a citizen of the United States, does applicant intend to become a citizen of the United States? c) If you are not a United States citizen, have you the legal right to remain permanently in the United States? d) Do you intend to remain in the United States permanently?	a) Of what country are you a citizen? b) Whether an applicant is naturalized or a native-born citizen. c) Requirement that an applicant produce naturalization papers or first papers. d) Whether applicant's parents or spouse are naturalized or native-born citizens of the United States; the date when such parents or spouse acquired citizenship.
14. National Origin	a) Inquiry into languages applicant speaks and writes fluently.	a) Inquiry into applicant's lineage, ancestry, national origin, descent, parentage, and nationality. b) Nationality of applicant's parents or spouse.
15. Education	a) Inquiry into the academic, vocational, or professional education of an applicant and the public and private schools he or she attended.	
16. Experience	a) Inquiry into work experience. b) Inquiry into countries applicant has visited.	
17. Criminal Record	a) Have you ever been convicted of a crime? If so, when, where, and nature of offense? b) Are there any felony charges pending against you?	a) Inquiry regarding arrests.
18. Relatives	a) Names of applicant's relatives, other than a spouse, already employed by this company. b) Name, address, and relationship of person to be notified in case of emergency, only after hiring.	a) Address of any relative of applicant, other than address (within the United States) of applicant's father and mother, husband or wife and minor dependent children. b) Name and address of nearest relative to be notified in case of accident or emergency.

Subject	Lawful	Unlawful
19. Military Experience	a) Inquiry into an applicant's military experience in the Armed Forces of the United States or in a state militia. b) Inquiry into applicant's service in a particular branch of the U.S. Army, Navy, or the like	a) Inquiry into an applicant's general military experience.
20. Organizations	a) Inquiry into the organizations of which an applicant is a member, excluding organizations the name or character of which indicates the race, color, religion, national origin, or ancestry of its members.	a) List all clubs, societies, and lodges to which you belong.
21. References	a) Who suggested that you apply for a position here?	
22. Work Schedule	a) To ask about willingness to work required work schedule. b) To ask if applicant has military reservist obligations.	a) To ask about willingness to work any particular religious holiday.
23. Physical Data	a) To require applicant to prove ability to do manual labor, lifting, and other physical requirements of the job, if any. b) Require a physical examination.	a) To ask height and weight, impairment or other non-job-related physical data.
24. Handicap	a) To inquire about handicap for the purpose of determining applicant's capability to perform the job. (Burden of proof for nondiscrimination lies with the employer.)	a) To exclude handicapped applicants as a class on the basis of their type of handicap. (By law, each case must be determined on an individual basis.)
25. Other Qualifications	a) To inquire about any area that has a direct reflection on the job applied for.	a) Any non-job-related inquiry that may present information permitting unlawful discrimination.

EXERCISE 4-2   *Worksheet for Completing Job Application Forms*

Name _____

Present address _____

Permanent address _____

Telephone _____ Business telephone _____ Social Security number _____

Person to contact in an emergency _____ Phone _____

OPTIONAL INFORMATION

Date of birth _____ Height _____ Weight _____

Marital status _____ Maiden name _____ Number of children _____ Their ages _____

Child-care arrangements _____

Driver's license no. _____ Make of car _____ Year _____ License no. (car) _____

Job objective _____ Date you can start _____ Desired salary _____

Other job interests _____

Willing to relocate? _____ Area preferences _____

Education	Name and location of school	Years attended	Degree	Program: major/minor
College				
High school				
Other (including conferences workshops, seminars)				
Honors, achievements extracurricular activities, hobbies, interests				

Employment Record (in reverse chronological order)

Dates of employment	Name and address of organization	Title or position	Duties and responsibilities	Name of supervisor	Reason for leaving

Professional, union, social memberships _____

Military Service Branch of service _____ Date of entrance _____ Date of discharge _____ Rank _____

Military assignments/ occupational specialty _____

Explain any special circumstances: personal responsibilities or health problems that might prevent you from coming to work; defects in hearing, vision, or speech. _____

References	Name	Address	Telephone number	Received permission?	Business/ occupation

Take this completed worksheet with you when you are applying for job positions. Use this worksheet if you have not developed a résumé.

Job Search Strengths and Problems

Job search difficulties must be studied if you find yourself in situations that produce these problems, but it is your job search strengths and assets that get you hired. Many people do a poor job of studying their strengths. If you get the most mileage possible from your strengths, you will obtain a higher-level job with higher pay and more personal satisfaction than if you give little attention to these critical factors.

EXERCISE 4-3   *Job Search Strengths*

Check any of the following statements if you think they describe your situation.

_____ I can list a job objective that I am capable of doing well.

_____ I can list at least seven skills that I perform competently on the job.

_____ I can list at least seven values that lead to personal satisfaction expressed in the jobs I can do.

_____ I have completed my high school education or its equivalent (GED) and have received a diploma.

_____ I have pursued additional education in college (beyond my high school studies).

_____ I have taken a trade school course, completed vocational technical training, studied one or more correspondence courses, participated in a continuing educational program, or participated in some kind of special educational program.

_____ I have been given on-the-job training by a former employer for a specific task.

_____ I have been trained to operate some kind of special equipment.

_____ I plan to continue my education or training.

_____ I am a member of a technical or professional organization, association, or club.

_____ I have a technical or professional certificate or license.

_____ I have worked several years in one previous job.

_____ I have a good work record, and a former employer will recommend me as an excellent worker.

_____ My attendance record at school or in previous jobs is excellent.

_____ My hobbies, interests, and things I like to do are related to the job I want to get.

_____ I have special military training and work experience that relates to the civilian job I would like to have.

_____ I have several excellent character references who know my work habits and who will give me a good recommendation for work attitude and competence.

EXERCISE 4-4 *Major Job Search Problems*

Check any of the following statements if you think they describe your situation.

_____ It is difficult for me to name a job objective that I want to do and feel capable of doing.

_____ One of my major problems in obtaining a job is that I am young and have little work experience.

_____ One of my major problems in obtaining a job is that I am considered too old by employers, so no one will hire me.

_____ I am a member of a minority group, and this is one reason I believe I will have trouble finding employment.

_____ Getting a job is difficult for me because I am not a U.S. citizen.

_____ My recent separation or divorce seems to cause me difficulties when I apply for a job.

_____ A major problem in my getting a job is that I have a criminal record. I think employers will not hire me if they know I have an arrest record.

_____ My lack of transportation prevents me from finding or keeping a job.

_____ I don't have a driver's license, and this prevents me from getting a job.

_____ I don't have a high school diploma, and this makes it difficult to find a job.

_____ My attendance record at school or on previous jobs is poor.

_____ The reasons I left my previous job(s) are a big problem for me when I apply for a new job.

_____ One reason employers will not hire me is that I have poor health.

_____ I can't get a job because employers will see my physical handicap and will not hire me because of it.

_____ Employers will not hire me because of my past workers' compensation claims.

_____ Employers do not hire me because I have one of the following medical problems: diabetes, heart condition, high blood pressure, defective sight, mental or emotional problems, epilepsy, hernia, back ailments, defective hearing, frequent or serious headaches.

_____ My dishonorable discharge from the armed forces gives me problems when I look for a job.

_____ My past financial problems are a source of trouble when employers interview me for a job.

If you checked any of these statements, try to formulate the best response you could make if the subject arises. Possible answers are suggested in the following pages.

How can you handle any of these or other job search problems should they require a response on a job application form or in an interview? The best thing to do is to be open and honest with the interviewer and with yourself. This isn't easy; you may be turned down sometimes—but the alternative is to lie or misrepresent yourself. Employers and interviewers have an uncanny ability to sense when something is wrong. They will check your background very thoroughly, especially if they are both interested in you and suspicious of you.

Emphasize the positive aspects of your previous experiences and play down the negatives. *If you have to mention something negative, indicate your desire to change and to be given the chance to prove yourself.* For example:

Too young? Mention that you are looking for a job you can keep for some time. (Employers worry that young people are unsettled or have poor work habits.) Stress your skills, particularly if you think the employer regards you as inexperienced.

Too old? You will want to emphasize your experience and the abilities you have acquired over a long period of time. Your wisdom and experience may be well worth the higher benefit rates your employer may have to pay for you.

Divorced or separated? Indicate your ability to get along or cooperate with other people, particularly co-workers and supervisors. Some employers have negative feelings toward divorced people because they feel that home problems will become work problems.

Criminal record? The most important message you can give an employer is that you have changed. You realize you made a mistake and did a foolish thing, and now you desire to work and go straight. Provide evidence of improved behavior since imprisonment or during probation. Get recommendations from probation or parole officers, a rehabilitation counselor, a chaplain, a caseworker, or some other person. If you were released early for good behavior, mention this. Don't make excuses for the behavior that got you into trouble; show that you take responsibility for your actions. You have to overcome the employer's natural fear that one misdeed will lead to another or that he or she will be "ripped off." On the application form, answer this question with the statement that you are willing to discuss it during the interview.

Lack transportation? Possible solutions include riding with a person who works at the organization (offer to pay if necessary), asking a relative or friend for help, public transportation, or walking. Employers want to be reassured that your attendance record will be good.

Alcoholic? This problem must be under control, or else you will get no job. Offer to sign a statement that says you will keep your job only by staying away from alcoholic beverages. This would probably be a condition of employment, anyway.

Fired, quit, laid off last job? If you were laid off, obtain a good recommendation from your former employer and include it with an explanation that the layoff was due to lack of seniority, a plant or office closure, or downsizing of the company, and had nothing to do with your work performance. If you quit, was it to get a better job? If you were fired, don't make excuses, and state that you have changed whatever it was that caused you to be fired. Employers are afraid of hiring unmotivated employees, drifters, or people with poor work attitudes.

Poor health? Indicate that you are taking steps to correct this. Employers think that bad health will cause absences and constant complaining on the job. Seek help from a doctor, and tell the employer you are doing so.

Physically handicapped? Tell the interviewer or employer how the handicap will not interfere in the performance of your work duties. Be sure, however, that you can do the job. Your doctor's report and an assessment of your job abilities and goals from your rehabilitation counselor are valuable documents as you try to gain employment.

Medical problems? Mental problems, heart condition, epilepsy, and back ailments are probably the greatest obstacles to getting a job. Other medical problems include diabetes, bad eyesight, poor hearing, hernia, and serious or frequent headaches. If the problem is under control through medication or medical restoration, indicate this and state on the application form that you are willing to discuss it during the interview. Medical reports, doctor's recommendations, and rehabilitation counselor's reports can help you with these problems.

Financial problems? (Bankruptcy, wages garnisheed, poor credit rating.) These problems indicate poor planning and irresponsibility to the employer. Try to clear up any debts before you apply for a job. Paying your creditors may be the way to turn this liability into an asset; you can tell the employer that you have fulfilled your obligations.

These are but a few quick answers to complex problems, but they indicate what the nature of your response could be.

Summary

1. Completing employers' application forms is often an exercise in persistence, patience, and paying close attention to detail. Application forms are usually straightforward, but employers and personnel workers can glean a great deal of information from them. It is illegal for employers to ask applicants certain questions.

2. Inventory your job search strengths, for they will be your key to finding a job. Be knowledgeable about your problems, for that is the only way you can deal with them adequately. Preparing answers ahead of time for application forms and interviews will help you to handle difficult questions that develop in the job search.

5

Using Your Research Skills to Get a Job: Geographical Areas

Research is something you have become accustomed to doing in school and college. You have developed skills in gathering information, reading it, examining it critically, and compiling all your newly discovered knowledge into a term paper, complete with footnotes and references. This chapter invites you to use those same investigative skills on your own behalf to obtain information about geographical areas in which you could live and work. Many people allow their work to determine where they will live. Others, however, would rather determine for themselves where they want to live and then find their preferred work environments within those geographical areas.

Researching Geographical Areas of Interest to You

Where you live may have even more impact on your lifestyle than your choice of occupation or workplace. Some people work in a less desired occupation because it allows them to make a living in the geographical area they prefer. The assumption that your job determines where you spend your life does not apply to as many people as it once did. The conflict between job availability and choice of a place to live may not occur in occupations that are spread throughout all parts of the country, unless local employment trends provide a higher supply than demand of workers in a certain occupation. Secretaries, mail carriers, nurses, and teachers, for example, find employment in all parts of the country. People in advertising, on the other hand, are concentrated mainly in big cities and are thinly scattered elsewhere. Television actors and actresses are centered mostly in New York City and Los Angeles. Oceanographers must live near the ocean. Personal and family living preferences will also need to be considered, along with employment trends and the location of jobs in the occupation of your choice.

Whether you stay where you are or relocate to another community, weighing the costs and benefits calls for research. You might decide to stay put because you are emotionally attached to your community and its familiar network of relatives, friends, schools, churches, neighborhoods, activities, and places of work. Even if you would be willing to move, your spouse may be happily employed; you don't want to make him or her give up a good job. Whatever the reason, staying where you are is your choice for now. Even so, you still need to research your home base, particularly the work organizations that employ people in your occupational preferences within reasonable commuting distance.

It is surprising how many people decide to relocate without first conducting any research on the place to which they will move. If you anticipate leaving your present job and moving to another community, start your investigation immediately. Lack of information about an area can be costly, both financially and emotionally. If a company is asking you to relocate, your research may turn up some compelling reason not to move. If you are offered choices, you have all the more reason to compare them through your own investigation. If unemployment is forcing you to look elsewhere, you should research target areas before you commit to another location. Recently, massive unemployment hit the author's home state; people pulled up stakes and took the family where the jobs were supposed to be. Many came back bitterly disappointed, having encountered hostility (due to the competition they represented) and much lower pay rates for any jobs they were offered. The biggest problem for these people was their lack of adequate preparation. They did not assess their own skills or identify qualifications they could offer; they had neither developed contacts and referrals nor enlisted the help of job search resources; they never researched companies and employers in the area, nor did they check out living conditions and housing in the "promised land." They just threw themselves, unprepared and unorganized, into their search, and most of them returned sadder but wiser for the experience.

Sources of Area Information

Whether you are investigating a distant place or your hometown, most of the research principles are the same. How do you start? Where do you find information about a particular geographical location? Here are a few ideas.

1. *Local chambers of commerce* publish lists of businesses and manufacturers in the area they serve. These directories contain addresses, telephone numbers, names of officers, products made or services rendered, and the number of employees working for each company. The information you can obtain from them is worth the nominal fee you may pay for the service. The local chamber usually publishes a free booklet describing the educational, cultural, religious, recreational, governmental, and economic life of the community. Their job is to attract new people to the area, so ask them for all the information they can send. Write to the Chamber of Commerce of the United States, 1615 H Street N.W., Washington, DC 20062, for the address of the local chamber in your target city.

2. *Local newspapers.* Subscribe to the local newspaper of your target area for several weeks or months if it isn't sold on your hometown newsstands. The newspaper office in your home city should have the name of the newspaper in your target area; its circulation department will mail copies to you. Sunday editions carry the most data about the market for advertised jobs. Other important information a newspaper might tell you about the community concerns culture, lifestyle, housing, recreation, climate, politics, and education.

3. *City, township, and county government offices.* The office of the city manager or county executive; a city, township, or county clerk's office; or a regional planning office can send you information about an area you are investigating. Local governments may also have an economic agency that is

trying to lure new business into the area. Ask for the same information they would send a prospective business. In addition, many areas have a consumer affairs department or a better business bureau that can furnish information about the background of local businesses.

4. *The Yellow Pages of the local telephone book.* Most people look in the Yellow Pages to locate a product or service, so businesses make sure they are listed and advertise there. Headings and cross-references are listed alphabetically, from "Abattoirs—see Slaughter Houses" to "Zippers—Repairing." Your nearest telephone exchange should have the telephone book for your target area.

5. *The city directory.* City directories are large volumes divided into several major indexes that contain alphabetical lists of names of businesses, manufacturers, institutions, and residents and their occupations. Business firms purchase advertisements to publicize their products or services in greater detail. A buyer's guide serves as an intermediary between buyers and sellers in the community. A classified business directory arranges every business by type in alphabetical order, whether the business pays for it or not. A street directory of householders and businesses lists names, addresses, and telephone numbers. This information is collected by door-to-door canvassing. A numerical telephone directory is often provided, as well as a statistical and historical record of the city. Write to the local chamber of commerce, city government, or public library and ask how you can purchase a copy.

6. *The library in your target city.* This is usually the public library, but it could also be a college or hospital library. Determine the information you need to know about the area you are researching, then politely ask the reference librarian in your hometown library to locate and obtain the material you need from the library in the community under consideration. This will involve mailing requests, interlibrary loans, and time. Offer to pay the expense for photocopying and mailing this material.

7. *Business and industrial directories.* Commercial publishers print such directories on a statewide basis. State governments publish directories of public agencies. (National directories, covered in the next chapter, are not usually indexed by geographical area.) Your hometown library may either have state directories in the reference section or borrow them for you through an interlibrary loan. You can photocopy the geographical section that covers your target area. Usually, areas or cities are listed alphabetically. Each listing contains names of businesses and manufacturing industries, names of company officers, products made or services provided, addresses, and telephone numbers.

8. *Local companies and corporations.* As a public service, organizations in the community often publish promotional material about the area in which they do business or have a home office.

The sources of geographical area information described so far provide published material, but you can also develop personal contacts from written sources. Talking with an expanding number of personal contacts can be an important source of information.

9. *Personal contacts.* When your target area is the community in which you currently reside, communicating with personal contacts is relatively easy. Researching a geographical area at a distance, however, requires more effort: making long distance telephone calls or, better yet, a visit to the target area. Some people may balk at the idea of visiting a potential place to live before making a commitment to that area, but consider the comparable situation of buying property or a home sight unseen in a faraway place. Some people who have done this, for example, in Florida and Arizona, have invested their life savings in a section of swamp or desert. The costs of being uninformed can be great.

So do your homework on the target area. Before you visit the area, line up several informational interviews, starting with anyone you know. If you do not know anyone there, you may have a personal contact in your hometown who does. Ask for a referral. Have the person write a letter of introduction for you, or write one yourself if he or she is not willing. Your college or high school alumni organization keeps track of your classmates; one of them may now be living in your target area. Your religious denomination may have a church or synagogue in the area. The clergy are interested in helping people and enlarging their congregations. A group or association to which you belong may have a branch in the community; this is a good place to develop additional personal contacts. The variety of groups is almost endless; there are service clubs, labor unions, professional associations, political parties, veterans' organizations, ethnic groups, and special interest groups. Don't forget family groups; you may have relatives living in the target area who would be pleased to meet you.

As soon as you have several contacts lined up, set the dates for your visit and let people know you are coming. When you get there, use the techniques of informational interviewing outlined in Chapter 7. Always ask your initial contacts to suggest more people for you to interview for information. The referral is the key to expanding your personal contacts. Remember to write thank-you letters to those who help you in your investigation.

In addition to the names of more personal contacts, what are you trying to learn about a geographical area as you talk with people and read material?

- population figures
- civic groups and service clubs
- housing
- police and fire protection
- schools and colleges
- banks and financial institutions
- climate and weather
- type of local government
- churches and synagogues

- cultural activities
- utility services and costs
- recreational facilities
- library facilities
- tax rates
- transportation
- human resources
- health care

The preceding list provides plenty of topics for any informational interview. Notice that specific jobs, types of industries, employers, and work organizations haven't even been mentioned yet.

Use Exercise 5-1, the Quality of Life Inventory, to review or identify elements of geographical areas that are important to you.

EXERCISE 5-1   *Quality of Life Inventory*

Interesting work, earnings, and work environment are important considerations to people making decisions about occupations and workplaces. Another factor is location, the geographical area where a person lives and works. This inventory can help you determine what is important to you about a geographical area. Use the following key to rate each item in the inventory:

3 means the item is *very important* to you.
2 means the item is *of average importance* to you.
1 means the item is *of little importance* to you.
0 means the item is *of no importance;* it does not affect you.

1. *Costs of living.* I want to live in an area where:

____ state and local income and sales taxes are low (or nonexistent).
____ property taxes are reasonable.
____ the cost of a house is low.
____ food costs are low or below average.
____ housing repairs, furniture, and appliances are low-priced.
____ people can afford single-family homes.
____ utilities (gas, oil, electricity, water) are inexpensive.
____ mortgages and rents are reasonable.
____ college expenses are low or moderate.
____ health care costs are low or below average.

2. *Jobs.* I want to live in an area where:

____ the population is growing rapidly or above the national average.
____ the employment rate is high (or the unemployment rate is low).
____ employment growth is forecast to be high or above average.
____ the business climate is good (lower taxes, welfare costs, and so on).
____ the economic climate and job outlook for an entire region of the country are good.
____ the income growth rate is expected to be high or above average.
____ unemployment benefits are adequate or above average.
____ there are "recession-resistant" industries; job security is good.
____ salaries are higher than the national average.
____ employers emphasize the quality of work and life.

3. *Crime rate.* I want to live in an area where:

___ the population is not crowded together; the area is not densely populated.

___ there are fewer males aged 14 to 25 in relation to the rest of the population than in most areas.

___ more middle-class and well-to-do people than poor or poverty-stricken people live.

___ there are strong ethnic neighborhoods.

___ there is a stable population whose characteristics stay basically the same.

___ the rates of arson, alcoholism, drug abuse, divorce, and suicide are low.

___ the weather is cold or mild, but rarely hot and humid.

___ the police force is considered strong and effective.

___ community attitudes favor tougher laws and stiffer sentences for criminals.

___ citizens and neighbors keep an eye out for each others' safety and property and offer information, identification, and testimony to help stop crime.

4. *Health care and environment.* I want to live in an area where:

___ there is an adequate supply of doctors in relation to the population.

___ there are sufficient hospital beds in relation to the local population.

___ there are medical schools or teaching hospitals.

___ medical costs are reasonable or low.

___ there are cardiac rehabilitation centers or acute stroke centers.

___ there are comprehensive cancer treatment centers.

___ drinking water is clean, free of chemical and organic pollutants.

___ fluoride is in the drinking water.

___ there is clean air to breathe, a low degree of air pollution and smog.

___ there is little or no ragweed pollen (or other allergens) in the air.

5. *Transportation.* I want to live in an area where:

___ there are airports and regular airline service.

___ there is passenger rail service.

___ there are interstate highways.

___ there are uncongested roads, streets, and freeways.

___ there is a good public transportation system.

___ there is a good road system, well planned and well maintained.

___ trucks and rail lines are routed away from heavily traveled car routes.

___ traffic laws are strongly enforced against drunk and reckless drivers.

___ the costs of owning and driving a car (insurance rates, taxes) are low.

___ the life of a car is longer than average.

6. *Education.* I want to live in an area where:

_____ the student-teacher ratio in schools is low; class sizes are small.

_____ more than an average amount of money is spent per student in schools.

_____ teachers are paid an above-average salary, even if it means higher taxes.

_____ many options for training and education are available in local colleges.

_____ teachers are held accountable through good supervision and competency testing.

_____ there is a selection of private schools.

_____ student absentee rates are low.

_____ there are many adult, continuing, or lifelong learning education programs.

_____ tuition rates are low or reasonable in local colleges or private schools.

_____ the quality of education is considered to be excellent or above average.

7. *The arts.* I want to live in an area where:

_____ colleges and universities make cultural contributions.

_____ there are symphony orchestras.

_____ there are opera companies or dance companies.

_____ there are theaters or acting companies.

_____ there are public television stations.

_____ fine arts radio stations offer classical music.

_____ art and natural-history museums are available.

_____ there are public libraries with a wide selection of books and services.

_____ many artists, actors, authors, dancers, and musicians live.

_____ quality newspapers are available.

8. *Recreation.* I want to live in an area where:

_____ there are many public or private golf courses.

_____ there are many bowling alleys.

_____ above-average amounts of money are spent on public parks and recreational facilities.

_____ there are movie theaters, television stations, and dramatic performances.

_____ there are neighborhood bars, pool halls, nightclubs, or social gatherings.

_____ there is a zoo or an aquarium.

_____ there is an amusement park or a family theme park.

_____ there are many sports events to attend.

_____ there are horse or dog racetracks or automobile racetracks.

_____ there are skiing facilities, hiking trails, beaches, or sailing opportunities.

9. *Climate (and terrain).* I want to live in an area where:

_____ I can establish my own kind of recreation and leisure-time activities.

_____ I can keep heating and/or cooling costs down.

_____ the temperatures are mild, not too hot or too cold.

_____ the humidity does not get too high and uncomfortable.

_____ there is a lot of sunshine (or there is a lot of snow).

_____ the weather is the same year-round (or the weather is changeable and varied).

_____ there is little risk of severe thunderstorms, hail, tornadoes, or hurricanes.

_____ there is little risk of earthquakes or floods.

_____ there are mountains and hills (or the terrain is mostly flat).

_____ there is a lot of vegetation, forest growth, and adequate rainfall.

10. *Miscellaneous.* I want to live in an area where:

_____ there are churches or synagogues of my religious affiliation.

_____ there is good fire protection and quick response to fire alarms.

_____ there is a chapter of my professional association or labor union.

_____ there is a branch of my service club, lodge, or social group.

_____ government is effective, offers good service, and operates efficiently.

_____ people are civic-minded and take pride in their community.

_____ there are fine restaurants.

_____ there are resources to help people find employment.

_____ there are many trees and shady places.

_____ (add one item important to you but not on this list) _____

Scoring the Quality of Life Inventory.   Go back through the inventory and check or circle at least ten items you consider most important. Save these for future use and thought. This exercise should help you determine which factors to research as you investigate an area. If you want to discover which category is most important to you, add the points you gave the ten items in each category and record the totals below. Totals in each category can range from 0 to 30.

Category	Points	Rank
1. Costs of living	_____	_____
2. Jobs	_____	_____
3. Crime rate	_____	_____
4. Health care and environment	_____	_____
5. Transportation	_____	_____
6. Education	_____	_____
7. The arts	_____	_____
8. Recreation	_____	_____
9. Climate	_____	_____
10. Miscellaneous	_____	_____

After you score the inventory, refer to the *Places Rated Almanac* (Boyer & Savageau, 1989), which rates 333 metropolitan areas. An area qualifies as a metropolitan area if it has a central city of at least 50,000 people or it has an urbanized area of one or more towns of at least 50,000 located in one or more counties with at least 100,000 people (75,000 in New England). Metropolitan areas are usually found within single states, but 35 of them cross state boundaries. Metropolitan Cincinnati, for example, includes three counties in Ohio, three in Kentucky, and one in Indiana (*1990 Statistical Abstract of the U.S.*).

Places Rated Almanac provides detailed information and rankings of each of the 333 metropolitan areas for the first nine categories of the *Quality of Life Inventory*. There is also a cumulative score and an overall ranking for each area at the end of the book. Approximately 75 percent of the U.S. population lives in these 333 areas. As you might imagine, ratings such as these stir up quite a bit of controversy. Areas ranked near the top are pleased; those near the bottom think they have been handled unfairly and challenge the conclusions. Be cautious in using the information this almanac provides. The publisher warns that the book "is published for general reference and not as a substitute for independent verification by users when circumstances warrant." In other words, the book contains a lot of good information, but you must confirm it through your own personal research. Table 5-1 lists the 333 metropolitan areas alphabetically.

TABLE 5-1   *333 Metropolitan areas in the United States*

Metropolitan Statistical Area	1988 Population (1,000)	Percentage Change 1980–88	Metropolitan Statistical Area	1988 Population (1,000)	Percentage Change 1980–88
Abilene, TX	122	+9.9	Augusta, GA-SC	396	+14.5
Akron, OH	653	−1.1	Aurora-Elgin, IL	355	+12.7
Albany, GA	116	+3.6	Austin, TX	748	+39.3
Albany-Schenectady-			Bakersfield, CA	520	+29.0
Troy, NY	851	+1.8	Baltimore, MD	2,342	+6.5
Albuquerque, NM	493	+17.4	Bangor, ME	85	+1.2
Alexandria, LA	138	+2.2	Baton Rouge, LA	537	+8.7
Allentown-			Battle Creek, MI	139	−2.1
Bethlehem, PA	677	+6.6	Beaumont-Port		
Altoona, PA	133	−2.9	Arthur, TX	364	−2.9
Amarillo, TX	196	+12.6	Beaver County, PA	190	−6.9
Anaheim-Santa Ana,			Bellingham, WA	119	+11.2
CA	2,257	+16.8	Benton Harbor, MI	167	−2.3
Anchorage, AK	219	+25.9	Bergen-Passaic, NJ	1,292	−0.1
Anderson, IN	132	−5.0	Billings, MT	116	+7.4
Anderson, SC	143	+7.5	Biloxi-Gulfport, MS	205	+12.6
Ann Arbor, MI	268	+1.1	Binghamton, NY	260	−1.1
Anniston, AL	123	+2.5	Birmingham, AL	923	+4.4
Appleton-Oshkosh-			Bismark, ND	86	+7.5
Neenah, WI	313	+7.6	Bloomington, IN	103	+4.0
Asheville, NC	173	+7.5	Bloomington-Normal,		
Athens, GA	145	+11.6	IL	125	+5.0
Atlanta, GA	2,737	+28.0	Boise City, ID	201	+16.2
Atlantic City, NJ	309	+12.0	Boston, MA	2,845	+1.4

(continued)

TABLE 5-1 (continued)

Metropolitan Statistical Area	1988 Population (1,000)	Percentage Change 1980–88	Metropolitan Statistical Area	1988 Population (1,000)	Percentage Change 1980–88
Boulder-Longmont, CO	218	+14.7	Dayton-Springfield, OH	948	−0.6
Bradenton, FL	187	+26.4	Daytona Beach, FL	348	+34.4
Brazoria, TX	185	+8.8	Decatur, AL	133	+10.8
Bremerton, WA	181	+23.1	Decatur, IL	124	−5.3
Bridgeport-Milford, CT	444	+1.1	Denver, CO	1,640	+14.8
Bristol, CT	79	+6.8	Des Moines, IA	392	+6.5
Brockton, MA	187	+2.1	Detroit, MI	4,352	−3.0
Brownsville-Harlingen, TX	264	+25.7	Dothan, AL	131	+7.4
			Dubuque, IA	91	−3.2
Bryan-College Station, TX	117	+24.7	Duluth, MN-WI	241	−9.7
			Eau Claire, WI	138	+5.3
Buffalo, NY	959	−5.5	El Paso, TX	586	+22.1
Burlington, NC	106	+7.1	Elkhart-Goshen, IN	151	+10.2
Burlington, VT	129	+12.2	Elmira, NY	92	−6.1
Canton, OH	401	−0.7	Enid, OK	58	−7.9
Casper, WY	65	−9.7	Erie, PA	277	−1.1
Cedar Rapids, IA	172	+1.2	Eugene-Springfield, OR	270	−1.8
Champaign-Urbana-Rantoul, IL	172	+2.4	Evansville, IN-KY	281	+1.8
			Fall River, MA-RI	154	−1.9
Charleston, SC	511	+18.8	Fargo-Morehead, ND-MN	148	+7.2
Charleston, WV	261	−3.3	Fayetteville, NC	256	+3.6
Charlotte-Gastonia-Rock Hill, NC-SC	1,112	+14.5	Fayetteville-Springdale, AR	111	+11.0
Charlottesville, VA	124	+8.8	Fitchburg-Leominster, MA	98	+4.3
Chattanooga, TN-GA	438	+2.6			
Cheyenne, WY	75	+8.7	Flint, MI	431	−4.2
Chicago, IL	6,216	+2.6	Florence, AL	136	+0.7
Chico, CA	174	+20.8	Florence, SC	118	+7.3
Cincinnati, OH-KY-IN	1,449	+3.4	Fort Collins-Loveland, CO	182	+22.1
Clarksville-Hopkinsville, TN-KY	159	+6.0	Fort Lauderdale-Hollywood-Pompano Beach, FL	1,187	+16.6
Cleveland, OH	1,845	−2.8	Fort Myers-Cape Coral, FL	309	+50.7
Colorado Springs, CO	394	+26.9	Fort Pierce, FL	232	+52.6
Columbia, MO	106	+6.0	Fort Smith, AR-OK	181	+11.0
Columbia, SC	456	+11.2	Fort Walton Beach, FL	151	+37.3
Columbus, GA-AL	247	+3.3	Fort Wayne, IN	367	+3.7
Columbus, OH	1,344	+8.0	Fort Worth-Arlington, TX	1,291	+32.7
Corpus Christi, TX	358	+9.8			
Cumberland, MD-WV	102	−5.6	Fresno, CA	615	+19.4
Dallas, TX	2,475	+26.5	Gadsden, AL	103	0
Danbury, CT	191	+12.4			
Danville, VA	108	−3.6			
Davenport-Rock Island-Moline, IA-IL	364	−5.2			

TABLE 5-1   (continued)

Metropolitan Statistical Area	1988 Population (1,000)	Percentage Change 1980–88	Metropolitan Statistical Area	1988 Population (1,000)	Percentage Change 1980–88
Gainesville, FL	208	+21.6	Kankakee, IL	98	−4.9
Galveston-Texas City, TX	210	+7.1	Kansas City, MO-KS	1,575	+9.9
			Kenosha, WI	123	0
Gary-Hammond, IN	612	−4.8	Killeen-Temple, TX	240	+11.6
Glens Falls, NY	116	+5.5	Knoxville, TN	600	+6.0
Grand Forks, ND	70	+6.0	Kokomo, IN	99	−4.8
Grand Rapids, MI	685	+13.8	La Crosse, WI	96	+5.5
Great Falls, MT	78	−3.7	Lafayette, LA	210	+10.5
Greeley, CO	136	+10.6	Lafayette-West		
Green Bay, WI	191	+9.1	Lafayette, IN	125	+3.3
Greensboro–Winston-Salem–High Point, NC	925	+8.6	Lake Charles, LA	172	+3.0
			Lake County, IL	495	+12.5
Greenville-Spartanburg, SC	621	+9.1	Lakeland-Winter Haven, FL	396	+23.0
Hagerstown, MD	118	+4.4	Lancaster, PA	414	+14.4
Hamilton-Middletown, OH	280	+8.1	Lansing-East Lansing, MI	428	+1.9
			Laredo, TX	129	+30.3
Harrisburg-Lebanon-Carlisle, PA	591	+6.5	Las Cruces, NM	132	+37.5
			Las Vegas, NV	631	+36.3
Hartford, CT	755	+5.4	Lawrence, KS	76	+11.8
Hickory, NC	222	+9.4	Lawrence-Haverhill, MA-NH	381	+12.4
Honolulu, HI	838	+9.8			
Houma-Thibodaux, LA	183	+3.4	Lawton, OK	119	+6.3
			Lewiston-Auburn, ME	87	+2.4
Houston, TX	3,247	+18.7	Lexington-Fayette, KY	348	+9.4
Huntington-Ashland, WV-KY-OH	322	−4.2	Lima, OH	157	+1.3
Huntsville, AL	237	+20.3	Lincoln, NE	212	+9.8
Indianapolis, IN	1,237	+6.0	Little Rock-North Little Rock, AR	513	+8.2
Iowa City, IA	87	+6.1			
Jackson, MI	149	−1.3	Longview-Marshall, TX	167	+9.9
Jackson, MS	396	+9.4	Lorain-Elyria, OH	270	−1.5
Jackson, TN	78	+4.0	Los Angeles-Long Beach, CA	8,588	+14.8
Jacksonville, FL	898	+24.4			
Jacksonville, NC	126	+11.5	Louisville, KY-IN	967	+1.0
Jamestown-Dunkirk, NY	141	•	Lowell, MA-NH	262	+7.8
Janesville-Beloit, WI	136	−2.2	Lubbock, TX	227	+7.1
Jersey City, NJ	542	−2.7	Lynchburg, VA	145	+2.8
Johnson City-Kingsport-Bristol, TN-VA	442	+1.8	Macon-Warner Robins, GA	287	+8.7
			Madison, WI	353	+9.0
Johnstown, PA	251	−5.3	Manchester, NH	150	+16.3
Joliet, IL	379	+6.8	Mansfield, OH	129	−1.5
Joplin, MO	136	+6.2	McAllen-Edinburg-Mission, TX	388	+37.1
Kalamazoo, MI	218	+2.8			

(continued)

TABLE 5-1   (continued)

Metropolitan Statistical Area	1988 Population (1,000)	Percentage Change 1980–88	Metropolitan Statistical Area	1988 Population (1,000)	Percentage Change 1980–88
Medford, OR	146	+10.6	Panama City, FL	125	+27.6
Melbourne-Titusville-Palm Bay, FL	388	+42.1	Parkersburg-Marietta, WV-OH	154	−2.5
Memphis, TN-AR-MS	979	+7.2	Pascagoula, MS	128	+8.5
Merced, CA	170	+25.9	Pawtucket-Woonsocket-Attleboro, RI-MA	325	+5.9
Miami-Hialeah, FL	1,814	+11.6			
Middlesex-Somerset-Hunterdon, FL	978	+10.4	Pensacola, FL	350	+20.7
Middletown, CT	86	+4.9	Peoria, IL	340	−7.1
Midland, TX	107	+28.9	Philadelphia, PA-NJ	4,920	+4.3
Milwaukee, WI	1,398	+0.1	Phoenix, AZ	2,030	+34.5
Minneapolis-St. Paul, MN-WI	2,388	+11.7	Pine Bluff, AR	91	0
			Pittsburgh, PA	2,094	−5.4
Mobile, AL	486	+9.5	Pittsfield, MA	79	−4.8
Modesto, CA	341	+29.3	Portland, ME	212	+9.3
Monmouth-Ocean, NJ	969	+14.1	Portland, OR	1,188	+7.4
Monroe, LA	144	+3.6	Portsmouth-Dover-Rochester, NH-ME	220	+15.8
Montgomery, AL	301	+10.3			
Muncie, IN	120	−7.0	Poughkeepsie, NY	262	+6.9
Muskegon, MI	161	+1.9	Providence, RI	647	+4.5
Naples, FL	139	+61.2	Provo-Orem, UT	243	+11.5
Nashua, NH	177	+23.8	Pueblo, CO	128	+1.6
Nashville, TN	972	+14.2	Racine, WI	174	+0.6
Nassau-Suffolk, NY	2,639	+1.3	Raleigh-Durham, NC	683	+21.7
New Bedford, MA	168	+0.6	Rapid City, SD	82	+17.1
New Britain, CT	148	+4.2	Reading, PA	329	+5.1
New Haven-Meriden, CT	524	+4.8	Redding, CA	140	+20.7
			Reno, NV	240	+23.7
New London-Norwich, CT-RI	259	+3.2	Richland-Kennewick-Pasco, WA	146	+1.4
New Orleans, LA	1,307	+4.0	Richmond-Petersburg, VA	844	+10.9
New York, NY	8,567	+3.5			
Newark, NJ	1,886	+0.4	Riverside-San Bernardino, CA	2,278	+46.2
Niagara Falls, NY	217	−4.4	Roanoke, VA	222	+0.9
Norfolk-Virginia Beach-Newport News, VA	1,380	+19.0	Rochester, MN	101	+9.8
			Rochester, NY	980	+0.9
Norwalk, CT	126	−0.1	Rockford, IL	282	+0.7
Oakland, CA	2,006	+19.6	Sacramento, CA	1,385	+25.9
Ocala, FL	190	+55.7	Saginaw-Bay City-Midland, MI	406	−3.8
Odessa, TX	125	+8.7			
Oklahoma City, OK	964	+12.0	St. Cloud, MN	181	+11.0
Olympia, WA	157	+26.6	St. Joseph, MO	85	−3.4
Omaha, NE-IA	622	+6.3	St. Louis, MO-IL	2,467	+3.8
Orange County, NY	294	+13.1	Salem, OR	270	+8.0
Orlando, FL	971	+38.7	Salem-Gloucester, MA	259	+0.4
Owensboro, KY	88	+2.3	Salinas-Seaside-Monterey, CA	349	+20.3
Oxnard-Ventura, CA	647	+22.3			

TABLE 5-1   (continued)

Metropolitan Statistical Area	1988 Population (1,000)	Percentage Change 1980–88	Metropolitan Statistical Area	1988 Population (1,000)	Percentage Change 1980–88
Salt Lake City-Ogden, UT	1,065	+17.0	Terre Haute, IN	133	−2.9
San Angelo, TX	99	+16.5	Texarkana, TX-Texarkana, AR	119	+5.3
San Antonio, TX	1,323	+23.4	Toledo, OH	616	0
San Diego, CA	2,370	+27.3	Topeka, KS	165	+6.5
San Francisco, CA	1,590	+6.8	Trenton, NJ	331	+7.5
San Jose, CA	1,432	+10.6	Tucson, AZ	636	+19.8
Santa Barbara-Santa Maria-Lompoc, CA	343	+14.7	Tulsa, OK	728	+10.8
Santa Cruz, CA	227	+20.7	Tuscaloosa, AL	145	+5.1
Santa Fe, NM	112	+20.4	Tyler, TX	153	+19.5
Santa Rosa-Petaluma, CA	366	+22.0	Utica-Rome, NY	313	−2.2
Sarasota, FL	261	+29.2	Vallejo-Fairfield-Napa, CA	421	+26.0
Savannah, GA	244	+10.4	Vancouver, WA	226	+17.7
Scranton–Wilkes-Barre, PA	737	+1.1	Victoria, TX	74	+7.2
Seattle, WA	1,862	+15.9	Vineland-Millville-Bridgeton, NJ	138	+3.8
Sharon, PA	122	−4.7	Visalia-Tulare-Porterfield, CA	298	+21.1
Sheboygan, WI	103	+2.0	Waco, TX	188	+9.9
Sherman-Denison, TX	98	+8.8	Washington, DC-MD-VA	3,734	+14.9
Shreveport, LA	359	+7.8	Waterbury, CT	216	+5.4
Sioux City, IA-NE	116	−0.9	Waterloo-Cedar Falls, IA	148	−9.2
Sioux Falls, SD	126	+15.6	Wausau, WI	113	+1.8
South Bend-Mishawaka, IN	244	+0.8	West Palm Beach-Boca Raton-Delray Beach, FL	818	+41.8
Spokane, WA	256	+4.0			
Springfield, IL	192	+2.1			
Springfield, MA	523	+1.6	Wheeling, WV-OH	172	−7.5
Springfield, MO	234	+12.5	Wichita, KS	483	+9.3
Stamford, CT	192	−3.5	Wichita Falls, TX	125	+3.3
State College, PA	116	+2.7	Williamsport, PA	118	0
Steubenville-Weirton, OH-WV	148	−9.2	Wilmington, DE-NJ-MD	573	+9.6
Stockton, CA	456	+31.4	Wilmington, NC	117	+13.6
Syracuse, NY	650	+1.1	Worcester, MA	416	+3.5
Tacoma, WA	559	+15.0	Yakima, WA	186	+7.5
Tallahassee, FL	229	+20.5	York, PA	410	+7.6
Tampa-St. Petersburg-Clearwater, FL	1,995	+23.6	Youngstown-Warren, OH	502	−5.5
			Yuba City, CA	118	+15.7

*Data not available

Note: Counties or parts of counties were added to or removed from some metro areas between 1980 and 1988. Direct comparisons in land area have been made in these cases. Where new metro areas have been created since 1980, comparisons have been made between 1980 data of the Office of Management and Budget and 1988 data of the Census Bureau's 1990 *Statistical Abstract*.

Adapted from: *Statistical Abstract of the United States,* 1990 (p. 911–917), Bureau of the Census, U.S. Department of Commerce.

The Rating Guide to Life in America's Small Cities (Thomas, 1990) also contains detailed geographical information. It reports on 219 "micropolitan" areas that consist of central cities of at least 15,000 residents in a county of at least 40,000 residents or other population arrangements of surrounding territories. No micropolitan area is part of an officially designated metropolitan area, except in one case. In contrast to the metropolitan areas, the 219 "micro" areas share the following characteristics: a greater proportion of young people, friendliness, lack of stress, generally less education, less racial diversity, lower incomes, closeness to nature, and closeness to metropolitan areas. Ratings are given on climate/environment, diversions, economics, education, sophistication, health care, housing, public safety, transportation, and urban proximity.

Table 5-2, which completes the chapter, presents the population in 1988 by state and shows each state's change in population from 1980.

TABLE 5-2   *Population by state in 1988 and changes from 1980*

State	1988 Population (1,000)	1988 Rank	Change from 1980 (Percent)	State	1988 Population (1,000)	1988 Rank	Change from 1980 (Percent)
Alabama	4,118	22	+5.8	Nebraska	1,611	36	+2.6
Alaska	527	49	+31.1	Nevada	1,111	40	+38.9
Arizona	3,556	24	+30.8	New			
Arkansas	2,406	33	+5.2	Hampshire	1,107	41	+20.2
California	29,063	1	+22.8	New Jersey	7,736	9	+5.0
Colorado	3,317	26	+14.8	Mew Mexico	1,528	37	+17.3
Connecticut	3,239	27	+4.2	New York	17,950	2	+2.2
Delaware	673	46	+13.3	North Carolina	6,571	10	+11.7
District of				North Dakota	660	47	+1.1
Columbia	604	*	−5.3	Ohio	10,907	7	+1.0
Florida	12,671	4	+30.0	Oklahoma	3,224	28	+6.6
Georgia	6,436	11	+17.8	Oregon	2,820	30	+7.1
Hawaii	1,112	39	+15.2	Pennsylvania	12,040	5	+1.5
Idaho	1,014	42	+7.4	Rhode Island	998	43	+5.4
Illinois	11,658	6	+2.0	South Carolina	3,512	25	+12.5
Indiana	5,593	14	+1.9	South Dakota	715	45	+3.5
Iowa	2,840	29	−2.5	Tennessee	4,940	16	+7.6
Kansas	2,513	32	+6.3	Texas	16,991	3	+19.4
Kentucky	3,727	23	+1.8	Utah	1,707	35	+16.8
Louisiana	4,382	20	+4.2	Vermont	567	48	+11.0
Maine	1,222	38	+8.6	Virginia	6,098	12	+14.0
Maryland	4,694	19	+11.3	Washington	4,761	18	+15.2
Massachusetts	5,913	13	+3.1	West Virginia	1,857	34	−4.8
Michigan	9,273	8	+0.1	Wisconsin	4,867	17	+3.4
Minnesota	4,353	21	+6.8	Wyoming	475	50	+1.1
Mississippi	2,621	31	+4.0				
Missouri	5,159	15	+4.9	United States	248,239	*	+9.6
Montana	806	44	+2.4				

*Not applicable

SOURCE: *Statistical Abstract of the United States 1990* (p. xii), Bureau of the Census, U.S. Department of Commerce.

Summary

1. Factors to consider about a geographical area that interests you include climate and terrain, housing, health and environment, crime rate, transportation, education, culture and the arts, recreation, economics and employment, density of population, churches or synagogues, utility services and rates, libraries, and local government.

2. Information about geographical areas can be obtained from the local chamber of commerce, the local newspaper, government offices, the Yellow Pages of the telephone book, a city directory, libraries, business and industrial directories, local companies, and your personal contacts. If you are researching a distant location, you need to visit the area before making a commitment to move there.

References

Boyer, R., & Savageau, D. (1989). *Places rated almanac: Your guide to finding the best places to live in America.* New York: Prentice-Hall Travel.

Bureau of the Census (1990). *Statistical Abstract of the United States.* Washington, D.C.: Department of Commerce.

Thomas, G. S. (1990). *The rating guide to life in America's small cities.* Buffalo, NY: Prometheus Books.

6

Using Your Research Skills to Get a Job: Work Organizations

Continuing with our study of the role of research in the job search, we turn now to investigating companies, firms, corporations, businesses, and institutions—we'll call them "work organizations"—groups of people who work together to provide products and services to their customers and clients and to earn profits and rewards for themselves. All career counselors and job-hunting experts recommend researching the work organization *before* you attend a job interview there—and no piece of advice is more often neglected than this one. Ignorance of the company will in all likelihood cost you the possibility of a job offer if it becomes evident to the employer that you know nothing about that organization.

Consider the material in this chapter as essential to your job search. When you present your skills and qualifications to an employer, you know what you can *give to* the organization. What do you *want from* an organization, besides pay and benefits? Job-seekers will, when hired, devote much time and energy to a company; therefore, it is important to discover and know about qualities of work environments that are significant to you. Satisfaction and fulfillment in work depends as much on your selection of a workplace as on your selection of an occupation.

You can identify various characteristics of specific companies by examining the companies' organizational charts, corporate cultures, annual reports, and other literature. You can also learn about companies by finding out what others say and write about them. Obtaining this information is a tall order, but you can do it. In fact, you *must* do it if you want to greatly increase your chances of landing an appropriate job and achieving satisfaction in your work. Gathering information about workplaces is something you can do even before you begin actively to look for a job, which is a project that will require you to do a thousand other things when the time comes.

An organization is a social structure designed for a purpose that a person cannot achieve alone. Civilization depends upon organization. Society is organized into economic, political, geographic, and social units, which are themselves subdivided into still smaller units. Thus, some organizations exist within larger organizations (Schein, 1980). The purpose of work organizations is to manufacture products or provide services. One principle of company organization is the logical division of work. Similar functions are grouped together, bringing people into divisions or departments such as sales, accounting, personnel, or production units. As the organization grows larger, more responsibility and authority must be delegated, for one person cannot do it all; then, clear lines of organizational authority need to be established. You should know to whom you are responsible—from whom you take orders and to whom you report. Such lines of authority are most clearly indicated in a company's organizational chart, which is a good starting point for an investigation of a work organization. It shows the lines of authority that connect people, job positions, departments, and divisions. An organizational chart cannot show everything, however; an unwritten network of alliances, coalitions, and exchanges of favors develops within any human organization. Informal rules and internal politics confer more authority to certain people and departments than to others. Informal procedures can undermine policies. Over time, decision-making practices move toward centralization or decentralization and become more autocratic or more democratic. Not much of this is likely to appear on a company's organizational chart.

Qualities of Excellence in Companies

What are you looking for in an organization? A study of 62 highly regarded companies, which served as the foundation for the best-selling book, *In Search of Excellence* (Peters & Waterman, 1982), identified eight attributes that distinguish excellent, innovative companies:

1. Displaying a preference for action; being willing to experiment rather than allowing overwhelming analysis to paralyze a decision-making process

2. Staying close to the customer; learning from people the company serves, and providing things that work and last

3. Fostering autonomy and entrepreneurship; encouraging practical risk-taking and tolerating failure

4. Developing productivity through people; respecting the individual by demonstrating trust and adult treatment

5. Adhering to a ''hands-on, value-driven'' philosophy; being clear on those values the company stands for; maintaining a belief in being ''the best''; emphasizing the importance of the details of doing the job well

6. Being able to ''stick to the knitting''—that is, staying reasonably close to the business the company knows and understands

7. Maintaining a simple form of organization, with a lean staff, in which everyone knows how the organization works and who reports to whom

8. Having simultaneous ''loose-tight properties,'' a coexistence of firm central direction and maximum individual autonomy; encouraging an atmosphere of solid devotion to the core values of the company combined with independence and innovation from top management to the shop floor

Peters and Waterman's eight traits may strike you as rather obvious, but unfortunately, they are all too rare in all too many organizations. Managers can pay lip service to these ideas, particularly in the area of employee relationships, but not really believe in them. This attitude then spreads throughout the entire organization. Excellent companies live their commitment to action, customers, autonomy, risk-taking, workers, and their values. In visits to the companies they were investigating, Peters and Waterman could ''feel'' the intensity of the organization's strongly held beliefs in the expressions of the people who worked there.

Another book that describes the characteristics of first-rate organizations is *The 100 Best Companies to Work For in America* by Levering, Mosko-witz, and Katz (1984). One of the authors, Robert Levering, returned to the 20 highest rated companies—"the best of the best"—to continue his inves-tigation into the making of good companies and to gather material for a new book, *A Great Place to Work* (Levering, 1988). More important than any specific policy, Levering found, was the *quality of the relationship* between the company and its workers. The following factors are essential to build a positive relationship:

1. *Continuous two-way communication* between employers and employ-ees, not secrecy and one-way decision-making directed from the top downward
2. A *friendly, informal atmosphere* where people *trust* each other, instead of a rigid social hierarchy and lack of respect
3. Authentic *teamwork,* not destructive internal politicking
4. *Fair treatment,* instead of favoritism, bias, intimidation, and abuse
5. *Work designed to give purpose and meaning,* not an "it's just a job" attitude
6. A belief that the *company cares about and is committed to its employ-ees,* instead of settling for an indifferent, transient relationship

A good workplace offers a genuine sense of community in a society where people have become increasingly isolated from one another. In other words, you look for a workplace in which you trust the people you work for, have pride in what you do, and enjoy the people you work with (Levering, 1988).

Beyond the nature of the relationship between employer and employees, "great" workplaces have all or most of the following attributes:

1. Wages and benefits that are considered fair and equitable
2. Job security, meaning no layoffs or that the organization tries not to lay off people without making an effort to place them in other jobs, either within the company or elsewhere
3. Commitment to a safe, healthy, and attractive work environment
4. Procedures to provide workers with ways of taking on increasing re-sponsibility for their own work
5. Flexible working hours such as "flextime," in which employees on eight-hour shifts can arrive at work from 7:00 to 9:00 A.M. and leave between 3:00 and 5:00 P.M.
6. Opportunities for growth through promoting from within, in-house training programs, and tolerating mistakes as a part of learning
7. Reduction of the social distance between managers and workers
8. Rights of due process, meaning procedures exist by which decisions that employees consider unfair can be appealed
9. Access to full and accurate information, not a whitewashed company line; limits, however, might include other employees' personnel rec-ords and plans that could be used by competitors
10. Right of free speech without fear of retribution

11. Right to confront those in authority
12. Right for a worker doing a good job to retain individual autonomy and not be socially pressured into conforming to a company image
13. Sharing in the company's profits and rewards that result from the improved work of employees
14. A share in the ownership of the company, such as employee stock ownership plans
15. Recognition of work efforts; acknowledgement of a worker's contributions to the organization (Levering, 1988)

What should you watch out for and try to avoid in a workplace? Many answers are possible; we'll mention five.

1. Arbitrary rule-making by an authoritarian management.
2. Abusive supervision that creates a master-slave relationship unless it is checked.
3. Disregard for employee health, safety, and well-being. Work-related illnesses are often symptoms of the effects of a bad workplace on its employees.
4. Higher priority for machines and systems than for people. The stereotyped image of a rigid, mechanical approach to work is the factory assembly line of the industrial age, with its counterpart now firmly entrenched in the modern office. Jobs in this environment are likely to be monotonous, boring, repetitious, mindless, deadening, and dehumanizing. As a result, workers feel as though they are appendages to a machine, robots, or cogs in an endlessly revolving wheel.
5. Manipulative methods of control over workers. One such technique is the "divide and conquer" strategy that pits workers against each other for political benefits gained by management. Another method of control is the subtle use of benefits and gifts to create a feeling of gratitude and indebtedness on the part of the worker toward the employer. Here, the gift is a bribe to secure influence over an employee. This contrasts starkly with the employer who gives rewards as a way of acknowledging and recognizing the employee's gift of work—something that makes the benefits possible. The motivation for the award makes all the difference (Levering, 1988).

Organizational Charts

Workplaces are organized around functions. As a company grows, it develops more functions, and the organizational chart becomes more complex. Typical functions are management, manufacturing or providing a service, marketing, maintenance of the physical plant, personnel, and accounting. In a one-person business, one person handles all functions, whereas in large companies hundreds of people can work on one function.

The growth of an organization creates additional jobs because the divisions of work become smaller and functions performed within the company expand. Management can hire an outside firm to handle some of the company's functions, but at some point the owners of the business may decide that having the company's own people perform all the functions is more efficient and profitable. Engineers, researchers, technicians, and production workers are hired to design and make the product. Professionals, paraprofessionals, aides, and service workers are employed to perform the service the organization provides to the public. Advertising workers, salespeople, market researchers, and public-relations staff are engaged to promote and sell the product or service. Personnel workers are needed to interview, hire, and train employees, and a maintenance crew is required to keep the plant and offices operating efficiently. Management controls and coordinates the efforts of the entire organization.

If you intend to work in an organization of any size, where will you fit in? Before you apply and interview at a company, examine its organizational chart and try to determine the division, department, or unit responsible for the work functions you can do and are interested in doing. Once you have identified your most appropriate workplace on the organizational chart, you can focus your attention on it and center your research around it. Doing your homework on an organization means reading whatever you can about it and talking with people who work within the department you have targeted.

The organizational chart shows the formal structure of the company. The oldest and simplest structure is the *line organizational structure,* where clear lines of authority are drawn, and each person is directly responsible to one supervisor. Figure 6-1 illustrates the higher levels of a line structure. As an organization grows in size and diversity, a *line-and-staff organizational structure* emerges as line managers require the services of staff specialists to perform the increasingly complex functions of their departments. Line authority involves supervision, discretion, and disciplinary action if needed. Staff authority does not have these responsibilities; rather, it involves assistance, advice, information, and expertise. Whatever authority a staff person or department possesses comes from the power of knowledge, persuasion, and reputation. A more interactive form of structure is the *matrix organization,* which has both vertical and horizontal lines of authority that serve to coordinate functions between departments and require teamwork and compromise in management. Finally, the *committee form of organization* (see Figure 6-2) is adopted to further employee participation, communication, and decision-making. Committees can give workers a sense of partnership with the organization, implying a more democratic style of management, but they can be counterproductive if they require too much compromise for strong decisions, are perceived as wasting time, or continue to exist after their objective has been reached (Chruden & Sherman, 1980).

Organizations other than businesses and corporations also have organizational charts. Figure 6-3 is a diagram of the structure of an educational institution.

FIGURE 6-1   *Organizational chart of a company*

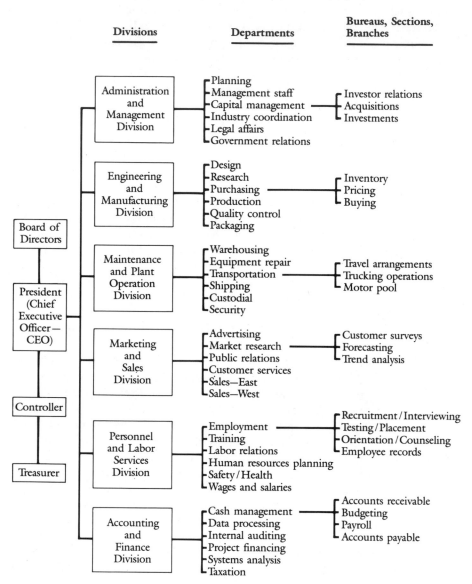

When you have studied the official structure, your inquiry should turn to the informal social, political, and communication patterns that exist in the company. These are not revealed on an organizational chart. They are a set of invisible qualities, a way of getting things done, a leadership style—an "organizational culture"—that may be more influential than any formal system mapped out on paper.

FIGURE 6-2   *The committee form of organization*

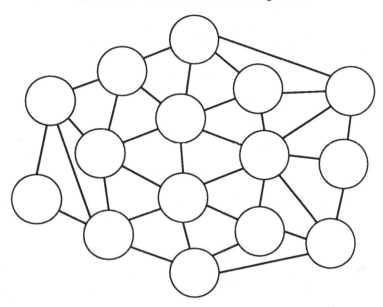

Organizational Cultures

Every organization creates, maintains, and changes its culture and passes it on to succeeding generations. Companies develop their own assortment of values, beliefs, traditions, heroes, ceremonies, and histories, just as nations do. The success of the Japanese in international business can be linked to their strong, cohesive culture and their ability to expand the idea of corporate culture to a national scale. The values of the Japanese model would not fit the American culture any more than the American political system would fit all countries throughout the world, but these models have been effective in individual cases. Strong corporate cultures create a set of informal rules that guide behavior, make people more productive, and enable employees to feel better about the work they do. They have provided the social energy for the successes of many American organizations.

In your research of organizations, you should become knowledgeable about their cultures. Some of this information may not be readily apparent until you have read some material and talked with a number of people. Even then, you may not be certain of what factors make the company tick. Corporate personalities are no less mysterious than individual human personalities. At times, you may wonder if acquiring an elementary understanding of the organization's culture is worth all the effort. If you are dedicated to finding the work organization that matches your personality and will advance your career goals, you will persist in your investigations despite periods of difficulty. This is particularly true when you examine such an indefinite subject as

FIGURE 6-3   *Organizational chart of an educational institution*

Vice Presidents	Directors and Deans

Board of Trustees

President

Vice President for Administration
- Business services
- Financial analysis
- Personnel
- Public relations
- Purchasing
- Data processing

Vice President for Academic Affairs
- Arts and sciences
- Occupational education
- Community services
- Library services
- Research facilities
- Developmental education

Department heads

Faculty, adjunct faculty

Vice President for Student Services
- Admissions
- Counseling
- Career planning and placement
- Financial aid
- Registration and records
- Athletic programs
- Alumni relations

Vice President for Facilities
- Maintenance technicians
- Custodial services
- Buildings and grounds
- Security

corporate culture. Stick with your research; this is where you get close to the essential character and vital spirit of an organization.

What, exactly, is meant by *organizational culture?* The term differs in meaning, depending upon who is using it. In an attempt to make the concept clearer in the midst of semantic confusion, Schein (1985) reviews the current usages and advances his own thoughts. Organizational cultures are perceived as observed behavioral regularities; norms that evolve in work groups (such as "a fair day's work for a fair day's pay"); the dominant values expressed by an organization; a philosophy that guides policy toward employees and customers; the rules of the game for getting along (the ropes a newcomer must learn to become accepted); and the feeling communicated by the physical layout and the way in which members of the organization interact with customers and other outsiders. Schein's own concept of organizational culture is a deeper level of assumptions and beliefs that the members of an organization share, that operate unconsciously, and that define in a "taken-for-granted" fashion an organization's view of itself and its environment. Because these assumptions and beliefs have worked repeatedly, they are likely to be uncritically accepted and to have receded from awareness. Without learning the underlying assumptions on which an organization is based, most behavior observed cannot be understood. For example, workers may have intense conflict with authority figures while, at the same time, feeling intense loyalty to the organization. In this case, the underlying assumption could be "we are one family who will take care of each other" (Schein, 1985).

Deal and Kennedy (1982) also specify several key elements of corporate culture. First are the *core values,* which form the bedrock of a company's philosophy for achieving success. These values are held by managers and employees alike. Shared values explain the fundamental character of the company. To outsiders, company values may appear to be platitudes, but to people within the organization they represent qualities that distinguish their company from all others. Values create a sense of identity for people in the organization, making them feel special. When a company proclaims "24-hour parts service anywhere in the world" or "productivity through people," these phrases aren't simply advertising slogans, they are words people belonging to the organization deeply believe in. Your research should identify the shared values and beliefs of the company and the rewards and recognitions that reinforce them. You should then ask yourself: Are these my values? Or, at least, are my values similar to theirs?

One way to discover the values of an organization, say Deal and Kennedy, is to examine the organization's heroes, rituals, and ceremonies. *Heroes* represent the company's values and become models for workers to imitate. *Rituals* offer security to workers, for they are procedures by which the job gets done. While rituals are commonplace, *ceremonies* become exceptional events by which the organization bestows awards and recognitions. All heroes, rituals, and ceremonies possess great symbolic worth in upholding the values and philosophy of the organization.

Other elements of the corporate culture are the *communications network* and the *business environment.* Storytellers, gossips, spies, and interpreters of events form the hidden system for circulating information. Often called the *grapevine,* such word-of-mouth communication is the primary means of exchanging information within the company. Your research will be greatly enhanced if you can tap into this informal communications network. The greatest single influence that shapes a corporate culture is its business environment: the company's products, competitors, customers, and technologies and the marketplace and government regulations within which it operates. The business environment shapes what the company must do to achieve success. In their quest for success, companies create several types of corporate culture.

Types of Corporate Culture

Deal and Kennedy (1982) propose four generic cultures: the "tough-guy, macho" culture, the "work hard/play hard" or "action" culture, the "bet your company" culture, and the "process" culture. None of these types pre-cisely describes a single company. A mix of all four cultures can be found in separate parts of an organization. Marketing divisions often breed a "tough-guy" culture of high risks and quick feedback on performance. Sales and manufacturing departments work hard and play hard in an active atmo-sphere of rapid feedback (either you make a sale or you don't), but of lower risks (no one product or sale is going to make or break you). Research and development people operate in an environment of high risk and slow feed-back, in which the company bets its future on a new product, but it takes a long time to find out whether or not the product is a success. Accounting is process-oriented and fits into a bureaucratic mold of low risk and low feed-back. Figure 6-4 graphically summarizes the four corporate cultures in terms of risk and feedback.

The most nerve-wracking of all business cultures is the tough-guy, macho culture of high risks and high feedback. Construction, management consult-ing, venture capital, advertising, sports, and the entertainment industries fall into this category. Financial stakes are high. Advertising campaigns, expen-sive construction projects, the Super Bowl, and multimillion dollar movies are typical enterprises of this culture. Their all-or-nothing nature makes for a fast-paced tempo rather than for endurance or persistence. Decisions must be made quickly, and the risk of failure dictates a tough attitude (at least on the surface) in order to survive in this "macho" culture.

The work hard/play hard or action culture can be seen in the hyperactivity

FIGURE 6-4   *Risk and feedback in four corporate cultures*

Risk

		High	Low
Feedback	High	Tough-guy, macho culture (marketing)	Work hard/play hard or action culture (sales, manufacturing)
	Low	Bet-your-company culture (research and development)	Process or bureaucratic culture (accounting)

of most sales organizations in real estate, computers, automobiles, door-to-door operations, fast-food franchises, office equipment manufacturers, and retail stores. The primary values of this culture center on the needs of the customer. Success does not necessarily result from making and selling better products, but rather from creating a high volume of business. A team, not an individual, produces the volume. An action orientation permeates the culture; the worst thing you can do is stand still. "Try it, fix it, do it" is the prevailing ethic. Managers tell their workers that the race is to the swift. Develop initiative, they say, get moving, and stay in the race. The action culture is better than any other type at providing the mass-produced goods people want.

In the bet-your-company culture, a project takes years to develop before the organization knows whether it will succeed or not. Deal and Kennedy (1982) place capital-goods companies, mining and smelting companies, large-systems businesses, oil companies, investment banks, architectural firms, computer-design companies, and the actuarial part of insurance companies in this category. The values of this culture concentrate on investing in the future. People must develop the stamina to tolerate uncertainty, with no feedback over long periods. In this culture, careers, products, and profits are not developed quickly, but they last a long time when success is finally achieved.

The process culture includes banks, insurance companies, financial services, many government agencies, utilities, and heavily regulated industries such as pharmaceuticals. No one transaction is likely to bring boom or bust to the company. When feedback comes, attention often takes the form of blame. Government workers, for example, may receive recognition only when someone accuses them of violation of the public trust, inefficiency, or corruption. These workers learn to be cautious and protect themselves as best as they can. Process culture workers are seldom able to measure the results of their work, so they concentrate on how the job is done. The central values of this culture are attention to detail and systematic procedures. Readers who want more complete descriptions of the elements and types of organizational culture are referred to Deal and Kennedy's *Corporate Cultures*.

The preceding classification of corporate culture may seem most applicable to business firms; you might want to try other ways of classifying organizational cultures. The six types of work environments proposed by Holland (1985) come to mind. A *Realistic* work environment is practical and mechanical, *Investigative* is scientific and intellectual, *Artistic* is expressive and intuitive, *Social* is helpful and cooperative, *Enterprising* is dynamic and competitive, and *Conventional* is orderly and systematic. At least, that's the way people see their work environments. Refer to Chapter 4 of the first volume of the Career Planning Guide series for more complete descriptions of these types. No one type exists exclusively throughout entire organizations or even departments; a combination of cultures exists within structures. Production, maintenance, and custodial departments usually exhibit predominately Realistic qualities. Research and engineering divisions are likely to be Investigative; advertising, Artistic; public relations and personnel, Social; executives, managers, and salespeople, Enterprising; and accountants, data processing, and clerical staff, Conventional. You can look for an appropriate match between your own personality and the cultural characteristics of a division within an organization.

Haberman (1983) writes of six cultures that define teacher and student roles in urban school settings. As in the case of Holland's types, each setting involves a combination of types, with the dominant type given as the title of the culture. In a *therapeutic* setting, teachers act as therapists, viewing their students as clients and helping them to overcome handicaps. The therapeutic culture influences people to adjust and cope in their environment. Teachers in a *compensatory* setting see students as learners who haven't learned as much as they should have. They aim to correct deficiencies with a test-teach-retest process. The teacher is coach, cheerleader, mentor, and instructor. This culture shapes people to strive and persist in their environment. In a *business* setting, where school behavior is thought to be transferable to work behavior, people are influenced to produce. Schedules of production evaluate students. People are shaped to set goals and compete with others. The pursuit of ideas is the primary goal in an *intellectual* setting. Thoughtful analysis, reflection about the world, and basic insights are valued more than are their applications to the world. Teachers model the scholar and researcher; students follow in their footsteps on a more elementary level. The teaching process in this setting is one of hypothesizing, testing, thinking, and forming new hypotheses. An *advocacy* setting brings the realities of direct life experiences into the school culture. The school is the society in miniature; teachers present real-life problems, conduct further discussion on them, and prod students to create solutions. This culture motivates people to become involved in a problem-solving process, take action, and promote change. A *creative* setting encourages practice and mastery of skills considered essential to performing an art or a discipline. Once this is accomplished, people are free to express those skills. The teacher is judgmental in the learning phase but becomes almost entirely nonjudgmental and noninterfering in the creative stage.

You have probably experienced several or all of these school settings as a student. Which did you find most compatible with your personality? Study this classification of school and classroom cultures again. Transfer your school cultures to work environments and recast the teacher/student relationship of the school setting in the supervisor/worker relationship or an organizational culture. Which would you prefer for yourself? Why?

There is one more classification scheme you can use to analyze organizational cultures. Your introduction to it will involve taking an inventory, the Work Organization Environment Survey (WOES) in Exercise 6-1. In this exercise, you will rate each characteristic in terms of its importance to you for your ideal work organization. If you are now working, you can rate your current workplace on the same characteristics. Types of organizational cultures will be identified for you after scoring so you can compare your ideal with your real work organization.

EXERCISE 6-1   *Work Organization Environment Survey*

Please read the instructions and complete the following survey before you read further. Photocopy the survey if you want several copies of it.

For each item in the survey, do the following: in the *left column,* circle the number that indicates the importance of the characteristic in your *ideal* work organization, according to this scale: 0 = not important at all, 1 = somewhat important, 2 = important, 3 = very important. If you are now working in an organization, circle in the *right column* the number that most accurately describes your *current* work organization, according to the same scale you used for your ideal work organization.

My Ideal Work Organization	Key: 0 = Not Important, 1 = Somewhat Important 2 = Important, 3 = Very Important	My Current Work Organization
0 1 2 3	Has specific written procedures to follow	0 1 2 3
0 1 2 3	Promotes individual creativity and expression	0 1 2 3
0 1 2 3	Encourages close working relationships	0 1 2 3
0 1 2 3	Emphasizes systematic, efficient operation	0 1 2 3
0 1 2 3	Has spirited, active, dynamic people	0 1 2 3
0 1 2 3	Has friendly, warm, sociable people	0 1 2 3
0 1 2 3	Has clear lines of authority and responsibility	0 1 2 3
0 1 2 3	Develops a competitive, challenging environment	0 1 2 3
0 1 2 3	Has people that trust and help one another	0 1 2 3
0 1 2 3	Has rules that closely control people's behavior	0 1 2 3
0 1 2 3	Drives people toward excellence and success	0 1 2 3
0 1 2 3	Fosters cooperative behavior between people	0 1 2 3
0 1 2 3	Is well established, with a solid reputation	0 1 2 3
0 1 2 3	Is enterprising, adventurous, and entrepreneurial	0 1 2 3
0 1 2 3	Is safe, comfortable, and secure	0 1 2 3
0 1 2 3	Has a cautious, stable management style	0 1 2 3
0 1 2 3	Is forward-looking with a sense of optimism	0 1 2 3
0 1 2 3	Has supervisors who give encouragement and praise	0 1 2 3
0 1 2 3	Stresses position, titles, rank, and status	0 1 2 3
0 1 2 3	Encourages risk-taking and high expectations	0 1 2 3
0 1 2 3	Emphasizes fair and equal treatment	0 1 2 3
0 1 2 3	Develops work roles that are well structured	0 1 2 3
0 1 2 3	Has an energized, stimulating work atmosphere	0 1 2 3
0 1 2 3	Has easygoing, harmonious work relationships	0 1 2 3
0 1 2 3	Is organized and businesslike in its performance	0 1 2 3
0 1 2 3	Puts pressure on people to get things done	0 1 2 3
0 1 2 3	Has a team or "family" approach toward everything	0 1 2 3
0 1 2 3	Has values oriented toward power and using influence	0 1 2 3
0 1 2 3	Is primarily concerned with results and goals	0 1 2 3
0 1 2 3	Cares about human and social relationships	0 1 2 3

Scoring.   In each group of three characteristics, place a B for the first, an I for the second, and an S for the third characteristic. Add all the B numbers for a total B-score, the I numbers for an I-score, and the S numbers for the S-score. Scores for each type can range between 0 and 30.

The items in this survey will help you examine the degree to which you favor a *bureaucratic* (B-score), an *innovative* (I-score), or a *supportive* (S-score) organizational culture. These dimensions come from the Organizational Style Index developed by Margerison (1979). If you are associated with any organization, record the second set of scores and compare your current organization with your ideal. Departments within organizations are likely to develop subcultures of their own. Therefore, you can photocopy the Work Organization Environment Survey and go through the 30 items as many times as you want. To analyze your ratings, record your raw scores and percentile ranks from Table 6-1 (on page 140) in the appropriate spaces of the following chart.

	Ideal Organizational Culture		Current Organizational Culture		Departmental Subculture		Departmental Subculture		Departmental Subculture	
	Score	%ile	Score	%ile	Score	%ile	Score	%ile	Score	%ile
Bureaucratic Score										
Innovative Score										
Supportive Score										

Of course, after you have researched any organization's culture, you can rate it on the 30 items and record your results on the following chart for purposes of comparison.

	Name of Organization		Name of Organization		Name of Organization		Name of Organization		Name of Organization	
	Score	%ile	Score	%ile	Score	%ile	Score	%ile	Score	%ile
Bureaucratic Score										
Innovative Score										
Supportive Score										

No organizational culture is good or bad in itself. A culture is good or effective if it carries out the purposes the organization intends to accomplish (Wallach, 1983). The organizational culture may be good or bad for you, depending upon your goals and what is appropriate to the situation (Margerison, 1979).

Table 6-1 provides percentile ranks and median scores for the bureaucratic, innovative, and supportive dimensions of organizations as measured by the WOES. (These dimensions will be explained in the paragraphs following this one.) The comparative median scores are interesting to analyze. Note that the median scores for all three measures of an *ideal* work organization are *higher* than the same three that workers experience in their current or *real* work organizations, a finding that one would expect. The distance between scores for ideal and actual supportive (7.3) and innovative (5.7) environments is *greater* than the distance between the scores for the ideal and actual bureaucratic environments (1.5). Overall, people place a *higher priority* on their ideal work organization scale on the collection of characteristics designated "supportive" in their organizations than on those labelled "bureaucratic" and "innovative." If the survey results are an accurate representation, organizations do fulfill a considerable portion of those hopes and expectations. Further, while the word *bureaucratic* is in itself a neutral descriptive term, it has become a negative word in our popular culture. As the survey shows, however, people want to find at least some bureaucratic qualities in their work organizations. The word *innovative* is used more positively, but people are less likely to experience innovative attributes than to experience bureaucratic ones in typical work settings, according to the survey, despite the emphasis normally placed on dynamic change and exciting new challenges.

Bureaucratic cultures are structured, ordered, impersonal, systematic, cautious, stable, and power-oriented. They rely heavily on written rules and procedures. Behavior is carefully regulated. The organization is hierarchical, with clear lines of authority and responsibility drawn on the organizational chart. Bureaucratic organizations see themselves as mature and well established, with a solid, substantial standing in the business or governmental community. They resemble somewhat the process and bet-your-company cultures; the compensatory, business, and advocacy settings; and the Realistic and Conventional types described in other classifications. Bureaucratic structures may be more appropriate for larger companies when the market for their products is stable and they have a large share of a particular market, a well-trained staff, and a strong organization. Creative and entrepreneurial people, however, may find this atmosphere stultifying and be frustrated in it. Tension and conflict can develop in a changing or growing organization when a bureaucratic department tries to maintain order and stability as sales managers develop new orders and researchers introduce new ideas. American Telephone and Telegraph, for example, appropriately developed a bureaucratic culture, bringing "universal service at a reason-

TABLE 6-1 Percentile ranks for the Work Organization Environment Survey

Raw Score	My Ideal Work Organization (N = 393)			Raw Score	My Current Work Organization (N = 272)			Raw Score
	Bur*	Inn*	Sup*		Bur*	Inn*	Sup*	
30	99	99	96	30	99	99	99	30
29	99	99	88	29	99	99	97	29
28	97	96	79	28	98	99	93	28
27	96	92	70	27	97	98	90	27
26	93	87	61	26	95	97	87	26
25	90	81	51	25	92	95	83	25
24	83	74	43	24	87	94	78	24
23	80	67	36	23	81	92	74	23
22	73	60	30	22	76	89	69	22
21	66	53	25	21	72	85	65	21
20	59	46	19	20	66	80	62	20
19	52	39	14	19	61	74	57	19
18	45	33	11	18	55	69	52	18
17	37	26	8	17	49	64	48	17
16	31	20	7	16	44	57	44	16
15	25	16	6	15	37	51	40	15
14	20	12	5	14	32	42	36	14
13	16	9	5	13	27	38	32	13
12	13	8	4	12	21	32	28	12
11	11	6	3	11	16	27	24	11
10	9	5	3	10	13	22	21	10
9	8	3	2	9	10	18	17	9
8	7	2	2	8	9	15	14	8
7	6	2	2	7	8	12	12	7
6	5	1	1	6	7	9	8	6
5	4	1	1	5	5	7	5	5
4	3	1	1	4	4	5	4	4
3	2	1	1	3	3	3	3	3
2	1	1	1	2	1	2	1	2
0–1	1	1	1	0–1	1	1	1	0–1

*Bur = Bureaucratic; Inn = Innovative; Sup = Supportive

Median Scores					
Ideal:	Bureaucratic	18.7	*Current:*	Bureaucratic	17.2
	Innovative	20.5		Innovative	14.8
	Supportive	24.9		Supportive	17.6

able cost" as a regulated monopoly for 60 years. Then came deregulation and the breakup of the company. No longer a monopoly, AT&T had to compete with rivals and adapt to new communication technologies. The old bureaucratic culture didn't operate as well in the new situation. Strong marketing and sales activities became essential to the company's survival and success. A change in AT&T's perspective was critical to future effectiveness and profitability (Wallach, 1983).

Innovative cultures are spirited, challenging, creative, adventurous, competitive, enterprising, and achievement-oriented. People look ahead with optimism and are motivated to accomplish goals. People in innovative work cultures are willing to take risks and set high expectations for themselves. They are individualistic, ambitious, and driving. Hierarchy and lines of authority do not mean as much to people in innovative cultures as they mean to people in bureaucratic cultures. Innovative cultures correspond somewhat to the tough-guy, work hard/play hard, intellectual, creative, Investigative, Artistic, and Enterprising cultures of other classifications. Innovative qualities are often more appropriate in smaller organizations, which can respond to market situations faster. There is an air of excitement and stimulation about them. However, such an atmosphere is intense, pressurized, and stressful. Some people leave or avoid an innovative culture because their personal lifestyle doesn't fit the frantic pace demanded by the organization. Innovative and bureaucratic cultures appear to be at opposite poles, but organizations can blend certain aspects of both into a creative, reasonably stable system.

Supportive cultures emphasize the values of harmony, trust, equality, security, warmth, and safety. People are more sociable, friendly, cooperative, encouraging of others, and relationship-oriented than in other cultures. The organization is seen as a humanistic and psychologically healthful place to work. Supportive cultures are similar to the therapeutic and Social environments of other classifications. A supportive culture provides an easier place in which to work, but there is little evidence that satisfaction with one's work environment makes for higher productivity (Margerison, 1979). Bureaucratic and innovative cultures can either exhibit or lack supportiveness. Managers can further a supportive atmosphere through their own personal relationships with workers. Managers cannot usually exert much influence on the amount of bureaucracy or innovation in an organizational culture, but they can affect its degree of supportiveness.

Bureaucratic, innovative, and supportive cultures exist in varying degrees in all organizations. We have seen how production, engineering, advertising, personnel, managerial, and clerical departments can each create distinct subcultures, all within the same company. In the overall culture of a college, you might detect a bureaucratic subculture in the administration, an innovative subculture in the faculty, and a supportive subculture within the clerical and maintenance staff. A strong leadership might impress its own style on all elements of an organization; a more decentralized political style might allow each unit to develop its separate subculture without interference from a central authority.

These three types of organizational cultures resemble three major social motivators researched extensively by David McClelland: the need for power, achievement, and affiliation. People with a high *need for power* are motivated to influence others and actively seek positions more for the sake of prestige and leadership than for doing things well (achievement) or making friendships (affiliation). Many people will not admit or do not like to be told they have a high power motivation, yet power itself is neutral and can be an instrument for either good or bad (McClelland, 1972). Chapter 5 of the first book in this Career Planning Guide series explored the *achievement motive.* A person with a dominant achievement motive feels a need to complete tasks that are challenging and moderately difficult and to accomplish his or her goals with excellence, rather than to seek influence (power) or new companions (affiliation). Those with a high *need for affiliation* strongly desire to form work relationships and friendships, which are more important to them than attaining a leadership position (power) or completing a task with distinction (achievement). The strongest motive in your personality should be compatible with a corresponding organizational culture. If your principal motive is power, a bureaucratic culture would most likely suit your nature. A preeminent achievement motive would be most productive in an innovative culture. A predominant affiliative motive would most likely thrive in a supportive environment.

If you currently work in an organization, ask yourself how well its culture fits your personality. If there is considerable agreement, you are probably happy in your work environment. If there is a mismatch, the three options you have are (1) to adapt to your organizational culture, (2) to change or modify it, or (3) to withdraw from it. If you are embarking on an investigation of several organizations, you can now begin to appreciate the importance of researching and finding suitable organizational cultures in which to work.

The measurement and evaluation of organizational culture presented here is a modest attempt to analyze a complex subject. Perhaps you can use some of the items on the Work Organization Environment Survey as a basis for questions in informational interviews. Some organizations volunteer information about their company culture while you are researching them or during an orientation session if you are a new employee. If their self-analysis is accurate (you need to validate it), this is valuable information; beginning workers spend as much as six to nine months learning the way things are done in their new environment.

Sources of Information About Work Organizations

The two main sources of data about organizations are your personal contacts and written material. Inside information is usually more valuable than printed material. To obtain information, you can talk with people both inside and outside the organization. You may not know a soul inside an organization that interests you, which means you will need to start with your contacts outside, first of all those who know something about the company you want to investigate. The key question to ask these people is the referral question: "Do you know the names of any people working within the organization who would be willing to talk with me?" If so, get their names and contact them for an informational interview (covered in the next chapter), or have your personal contact refer you by telephone or write a letter of introduction for you. Who do you try to talk with on the inside? The president of the company? Well, maybe. After all, this is the highest authority. Remember, however, that the boss and other top executives often put the best possible face on everything about the organization. It might be better to start with secretaries, receptionists, middle managers, production workers, supervisors, custodians, or floor sweepers and move on to department heads, directors, and executive vice presidents at a later time.

If the company, institution, or business is very small and doesn't publish anything about itself, personal contacts may comprise 100 percent of your information sources. Keep in mind, however, that even the smallest organization will have its name listed somewhere—in a business directory, telephone book, chamber of commerce publication, or city directory—and the listing may also contain the organization's address and telephone number and the names of owners, top officials, and even a few employees. Before you start talking with people inside the target organization, however, read as much as you can about it. You will sound more serious and better informed when you do talk with people, and they won't feel that you are acting on a sudden whim or that they are wasting their time with you. In this phase of the job search, you are looking only for information, not a job, although you have your eyes open in case an attractive job opportunity develops. Your interviews can be conducted in a conversational manner with people you know. As you gain more skill in your conversational interviews, interviewees may not realize you are actually interviewing them. You can informally obtain a lot of information about jobs and work organizations; people talk about these subjects all the time.

Written sources of information about organizations can be found in most public and college libraries, career resource centers, state employment agencies, chamber of commerce offices, government bureaus, and the organizations themselves. You can discover companies you never knew existed, names and titles of officers, locations, products manufactured and services provided, and the financial health of organizations. It bears repeating that you must investigate the company before you are hired. For example, consider the subject of financial status; you don't want to be hired by a company that is about to go bankrupt.

You will find many of the following directories and sources in the reference section of libraries.

• Annual reports from companies, corporations, hospitals, foundations, and the like. Call or write their personnel or public relations department for a copy.

• Better Business Bureau (BBB) reports on your target companies. Contact the local BBB office or write to the Council of Better Business Bureaus, Inc., 4200 Wilson Blvd., Suite 800, Arlington, VA 22203. The BBB can tell you how honest and dependable the company has been or if it is having legal problems. Local bureaus handle over 9 million public contacts annually without charge.

• Business periodicals such as *Barron's, Business Week, Dun's Review, Financial World, Forbes, Fortune, Inc.,* and the *Wall Street Journal;* the business pages of your local newspaper; and business sections in trade journals and popular news magazines such as *Time, Newsweek,* and *U.S. News and World Report* have articles on work organizations. The *Reader's Guide to Periodical Literature* in your library may help you find magazine articles that feature information on organizations.

• *Business Periodicals Index* (New York: H.W. Wilson Company). Published monthly, this is a subject index of magazine articles from over a hundred business publications.

• Chamber of commerce reports on local businesses. Contact the local chamber.

• *College Placement Annual* (Bethlehem, PA: College Placement Council, Inc.). This four-volume publication lists companies by name, gives addresses and names of officials, and indicates the types of college majors the company is interested in hiring. Volume I is a guide to career planning; Volume II covers administration, business, and other nontechnical options; Volume III deals with engineering, science, computers, and technical options; and Volume IV is concerned with medical, nursing, and allied health careers. The *Annual* should be in most college career planning and placement offices.

• Dun and Bradstreet's *Million Dollar Directory* (New York: Dun and Bradstreet). It lists over 100,000 U.S. businesses whose net worth is at least $500,000; arranges them alphabetically, geographically, and by industry; and includes company names, addresses, telephone numbers, annual sales, divisions and the names of those who manage them, and numbers of employees. Dun and Bradstreet also publishes a *Middle Market Directory.*

• Dun and Bradstreet's *Reference Book of Corporate Managements* (New York: Dun and Bradstreet). This reference lists about 2400 companies in alphabetical order and gives brief biographies of their directors and officers. (Dun and Bradstreet also publishes a *Canadian Key Business Directory* and a *Key British Enterprises* publication.)

• *Encyclopedia of Associations* (Detroit: Gale Research Company). It lists over 13,000 government, scientific, educational, health, religious, public affairs, business, legal, and other types of organizations. Association names, sizes of membership, names of executive secretaries, addresses and phone numbers, division names, publications, and annual conventions are among the information given in the three volumes.

• *Encyclopedia of Business Information Sources* (Detroit: Gale Research Company). One of the first places to look for what is available on companies and industries before selecting materials to read, this encyclopedia lists source books, periodicals, organizations, handbooks, and directories, organized by category, topic, and location.

• *Everybody's Business: A Field Guide to the 400 Leading Companies in America* (Milton Moskowitz, Robert Levering, and Michael Katz; New York: Doubleday, 1990). This book profiles companies in many industries, including food, clothing, shelter, health, automobile, and so on.

• *Finding Facts Fast* (Alden Todd, Berkeley, CA: Ten Speed Press). Techniques of research covered in this book are based on methods used by reference librarians, university scholars, investigative reporters, and detectives.

• *Guide to American Directories* (Coral Gables, FL: B. Klein Publications, Inc.). This directory of specialized directories lists over 5200 directories, arranged by type of business or professional association. An alphabetical index appears at the end. This is also a helpful book to consult early in your research.

• *Moody's Complete Corporate Index* (New York: Moody's Investor's Services). This periodical, published three times a year, indexes over 20,000 corporations and organizations found in Moody's other business references.

• *Moody's Industrial Manual* (New York: Moody's Investor's Services). Detailed information is presented on corporations, divisions, financial condition, officers, profit margin, stocks and bonds outstanding, and corporate history. Other Moody's manuals cover bank and finance, international, public utilities, and transportation.

• *National Directory of State Agencies* (Washington, DC: Cambridge Information Group, 1989). This directory gives names, addresses, and telephone numbers of government agencies in every state. The first part of the book lists agencies by state, the second part by function.

• *National Trade and Professional Associations of the United States* (Washington, DC: Columbia Books, Inc.). Associations are indexed by organization, title, subject, and location.

• *Occupational Outlook Handbook* (Washington, DC: U.S. Bureau of Labor Statistics or Superintendent of Documents, U.S. Government Printing Office). This excellent reference covers future trends in about 250 broad occupational groups, the nature of the work in these occupations, training and other qualifications needed, earnings, and employment prospects.

• *Standard and Poor's Register of Corporations, Directors, and Executives* (New York: Standard and Poor's). Volume I lists alphabetically about 40,000 corporations, with addresses, telephone numbers, names of directors and officers, names of divisions, products made, sales volume, and numbers of employees. Volume II provides names of directors and officers alphabetically, their residences, dates and places of birth, and colleges attended. Volume III gives industry cross-indexes, geographical indexes, and new additions.

- 10-K forms. Each company must file an official annual report with the Securities and Exchange Commission. The report includes audited financial statements and descriptions of company policies and operations. They are available from the SEC (free) or from National Investment, Inc., 80 Wall Street, New York, NY 10005 (fee charged).

- *Thomas Register of American Manufacturers* (New York: Thomas Publishing Company). This is a thorough alphabetical listing of manufacturers, indexed by products made. It covers company names, branch offices, and telephone numbers.

- *U.S. Industrial Outlook* (Washington, DC: U.S. Department of Commerce). This annual gives reviews and forecasts for over 350 manufacturing and service industries.

- *Who's Who in Finance and Industry* (Chicago: Marquis' Who's Who, Inc.). Over 20,000 business leaders are listed by name, their company name, title, and biographical data. Other volumes in this series include *Who's Who in America, Who's Who in American Politics,* and *Who's Who in American College and University Administration.*

Only a sampling of reference books and directories can be presented here; these are some of the most commonly used ones normally found in the reference section of your library. Other resources about companies are more specialized and are usually found in sections other than the reference section. Here are just a few examples:

- *Doing Well by Doing Good* (T. W. McAdam, New York: Penguin Books, 1988). Information on nonprofit work, ideological characteristics and values of this type of work, and the reality of work in this sector. This book lists the largest nonprofit agencies in the United States.

- *Good Works: A Guide to Social Change* (J. Anzalone, New York: Dembner Books, 1985). A book that could help you connect your idealism with employment opportunities. This book lists 600 social-change groups throughout the United States. The groups listed deal with problems in energy, health care, poverty, scarcity of minority opportunities, pollution, taxes, corporate lawlessness, and citizen powerlessness. These organizations aim to educate the public, empower citizens, change institutional behavior, and develop alternative institutions.

- *Guide to Careers in World Affairs* (New York: Foreign Policy Association, 1987). Over 250 sources of employment are covered in fields such as journalism, law, finance, and international business. The book provides descriptions of organizations that offer employment in world affairs.

- *Rating America's Corporate Conscience: A Provocative Guide to the Companies Behind the Products You Buy Every Day* (S. D. Lydenberg with A. T. Marlin & S. O. Strub, Reading, MA: Addison-Wesley, 1987). The title says it all; this is a rating of major companies on their corporate social responsibilities.

- *The 100 Best Companies to Work For in America* (R. Levering, M. Moskowitz, & M. Katz, Reading, MA: Addison-Wesley, 1984). Profiles work organizations that offer something more than good pay and fringe benefits—namely, an atmosphere of trust, open communication, sharing of rewards, pleasant working environments, training programs, flexible work-time arrangements, and so on—in other words, a quality work experience not often found in other companies.

Annual Reports

Try to obtain copies of a company's annual reports over the past four or five years. You can then make comparisons to learn about trends in growth and decline of sales, assets, liabilities, net worth, working capital, and numbers of employees and stockholders. Annual reports present financial highlights, the chief executive officer's letter to stockholders, an analysis of operations, an income statement, the balance sheet, the financial position of the company, a financial summary, notes to the financial statements, and the auditor's report. Let us consider each section of an annual report in that order.

Financial highlights. This section gives you a quick look at the financial health of the company. It usually appears a page or two ahead of the chief executive officer's letter and tells you at a glance how the company has performed financially over the past year. Listings include the total amount of money received by each division of the company, the total expenses of each division, and the net change of both compared to the preceding year. Also included are the number of stockholders, the number of shares they hold, the earnings per share of stock, the dividends per share, and the total number of employees working for the company.

Letter to the stockholders from the chief executive officer. In this letter, the president gives information about the objectives of the company, developments during the past year, what went well and why, difficulties that were encountered, and how management is dealing with those problems. There is a natural tendency to describe operations in optimistic terms and gloss over setbacks. Financial goals, the condition of each division, and insights into the company's future are usually found in the letter. Watch for qualifying words such as "except" or "despite"; these are clues to problem areas. Qualifiers in annual reports often mention the rate of inflation or new government regulations.

Analysis of operations. This section usually begins with an evaluation of the strengths and weaknesses of the company, documented by statistics. The company presents its reasons for changes in sales, income, expenses, and taxes. You may also find the reasoning for its pricing actions, marketing strategies, relations with competitors, and handling of government policies.

Income statement.   Now you get into the world of numbers. The income statement shows the amount of money the company made or lost over the past year, which product lines were profitable, the amount of tax paid, and whether there were unusual earnings or expenses that are unlikely to be repeated, such as selling off a losing business or paying off an unexpected expenditure. A crucial number in the income statement is net sales. Are sales increasing at a faster rate than before or going up faster than the rate of inflation? If sales are decreasing or the rate of sales increases is lower than before, the company might be headed for trouble. Growing sales increases are usually a sign of financial strength.

Balance sheet.   Everything the company owns, its *assets,* appear on the left side of the balance sheet. Anything that can be quickly converted into cash is a *current asset. Liabilities* are everything the company owes; these are shown on the right. *Current liabilities* are debts that are due in one year. They are paid from current assets. *Net working capital* is the difference between current assets and current liabilities. This is a figure to watch from year to year, as well as in quarterly reports. The balance sheet lists cash on hand, value of inventories, where cash reserves are invested, long-term and short-term debts, and *stockholders' equity,* which is liabilities subtracted from assets.

Financial position.   This section explains how the company earned its money over the past year and how the money was spent. A new stock issue might be one way in which the company made its money. The company could also have borrowed money to stimulate its growth. If sales grow and if the company has enough cash on hand to meet its payments, it can perform well on borrowed money. If sales fall, problems could lie ahead. If the company becomes liable for too much debt over several years, future profits could be affected, and it might be in trouble.

Financial summary.   Income, expenses, profits, and dividends are compared over a span of five or more years. The financial summary gives you a long-term overview of the company's performance. It can provide information on whether sales have steadily increased, how well expenses have been controlled, changes in the number of shares of stock that have been held, and whether dividend payments have increased, remained the same, or decreased.

Notes to financial statements.   The footnotes usually contain the most detailed information about a company's operations. Many people have problems with this section because technical language is often used. The footnotes may deal with deferred costs, changes in accounting practices, retirement plans, lawsuits, lease obligations, and other technical matters.

Auditor's report.   This is a letter indicating whether the certified public accounting firm's examination of the company's accounts and financial statements found them to be satisfactory. Some accountants suggest counting the number of paragraphs in this section. Two paragraphs usually are a sign of a clean bill of health. More than three paragraphs indicate that a close reading of the footnotes is advisable. Professional investors start with the auditor's letter when they read an annual report. The auditor will immediately tell you if the company's annual report is in agreement with "generally accepted accounting principles." If problems are lurking in the figures, the auditor is expected to include them in the report.

You can usually obtain a company's annual report by writing to the company and asking for one. The library often has on file the annual reports of local companies and some national or large companies. The career resource center may keep annual reports in its company file. Combining the data gained from an annual report with information written about a company in business magazines will give you valuable insights into the operation and financial condition of a company.

Types and Names of Work Organizations

As you begin your research of work organizations, the question you should first try to answer is: In what *types* of organizations would I enjoy doing the work I want to do? As a practical exercise, check the types of work organizations listed below that attract you.

EXERCISE 6-2   *Types and Names of Work Organizations*

Would I want to work in

_____ a manufacturing company office?

_____ a business firm or office?

_____ a factory (large _____ or small _____)?

_____ a corporation?

_____ a hospital or nursing home?

_____ an airport/bus or train station?

_____ an airplane/bus/train/taxi?

_____ an educational institution?

_____ a retail store?

_____ a business of my own?

_____ an information retrieval service?

_____ a state or national government office?

_____ a government agency or bureau?

_____ a private home?

___ a bank or financial institution?

___ a church/religious organization?

___ the outdoors (most of the time)?

___ a building construction company?

___ a museum/art gallery?

___ a hotel or motel?

___ a police or fire station?

___ a professional association?

___ an advertising/public relations firm?

___ a day nursery?

___ an animal care hospital?

___ a retirement community?

___ a garden/farm?

___ a women's resource center?

___ a boat/freighter/marina?

___ a pharmacy store (or department)?

___ an architectural firm?

___ a funeral home?

___ a lumberyard?

___ a long-distance truck?

___ a short-distance route truck?

___ a supermarket?

___ a youth or children's center?

___ an employment agency?

___ a machine and tool company?

___ a consumer cooperative?

___ a counseling/family service office?

___ a fast-food restaurant?

___ other: _____

___ a library or bookstore?

___ a research laboratory?

___ a department store?

___ a theater/TV or radio station?

___ a newspaper/magazine office?

___ a political organization?

___ a recreational center?

___ a restaurant?

___ a military organization?

___ a doctor's or dentist's office?

___ an automotive service station?

___ a law office?

___ a beauty salon/barbershop?

___ a clothing store?

___ a publishing/printing office?

___ a dairy or dairy store?

___ a community action agency?

___ an insurance/real estate office?

___ a bakery?

___ an appliance store?

___ a hardware store?

___ a machine repair shop?

___ a private or public foundation?

___ a travel agency or bureau?

___ an auto dealership or garage?

___ an engineering or design department?

___ an amusement park?

___ an industrial supply firm?

___ a management consulting office?

___ a city or county government office?

___ other: _____

This list of work organization types was drawn largely from the Yellow Pages of the telephone book. It concentrates on types, not on specific names or organizations.

After you have identified one or several types of work organizations that attract you, it will be easier to determine the names of specific work organizations you should investigate. The Yellow Pages of the telephone book is one place to start. You can also consult the *College Placement Annual* (published yearly and found in a career resource center or college career planning and placement office). Look at a local city directory or an employer directory in your public library or chamber of commerce office or at city hall. Resources covered in the previous sections may give you some leads. In the following spaces, list your potential places of employment.

Name of Work Organization	Name of Contact Person	Address/Telephone
1.		
2.		
3.		
4.		
5.		
6.		
7.		
8.		
9.		
10.		
11.		
12.		

Things You Need to Know About a Work Organization

In addition to the organization's structure and culture, there are many other aspects on which you should focus your research. The investigation can focus on an entire organization, if the organization is not too large. When the size of the unit goes beyond 100 people, consider limiting yourself to a department within the organization or to a subunit within a department, if necessary. Keep the object of your investigation to a manageable size, with reasonable numbers of people involved. All the items in this section of the chapter can be turned into questions to ask while you read and interview for information.

1. Structure of the organization, division, department, or subunit.   You want the names, addresses, telephone numbers, physical locations, and numbers of employees in the organization. Secure a copy of the organization chart, if one is available, and determine your target department on the chart. This is where your investigation should concentrate, unless the organization is too small to have departments. Locate the industrial category into which the organization fits. Is it food growing or distribution, clothing, wood products, electronics, automotive, home construction, office equipment, chemicals, crude-oil production, rubber or plastic products, education, financial services, paper products, aerospace, photographic equipment, pharmaceuticals, industrial or farm equipment, mining, petroleum refining, appliances, cosmetics, metal manufacturing, health care, social services, or some other category? Locate the person or committee with hiring authority in the target organization or department. If it is an individual, obtain that person's name and title. If it is a committee, get its name and the names of the people on it.

2. Products made or services provided by the organization or department. Why is the organization in business? Discover what it does to stay in business and make profits (or to keep appropriations coming, if it is a government agency). What is its volume of business and its market share in a certain area or in the country? This information might be available in the company's annual report, promotional material, or employment guide. Are the products or services good or inferior? Find out the opinions of the customers and general public. Always know what the company does before you interview there for a job. Ignorance of an organization's products and services is a real knockout factor in the minds of almost all personnel managers and employers.

3. The organizational culture or departmental subculture. An organization's or department's culture, or work environment, is expressed in its values, beliefs, assumptions, customs, procedures, leadership styles, and goals. Is the organizational culture bureaucratic, innovative, or supportive? Would you call it "tough-guy," "work hard/play hard," "bet your company," or "process"? Is it Realistic, Investigative, Artistic, Social, Enterprising, or Conventional? You can ask questions about this subject in an interview. If you do, you may need to explain the meaning of the term *organizational culture*. You may also need to define the words, such as *bureaucratic* and *innovative*, that are used to describe different organizational cultures. Try out your assessment of the company atmosphere in nonjudgmental terms during an interview and ask the person whether he or she agrees with your interpretation of the organization.

The values and beliefs of an organization or department are often indicated in the way people dress on the job, the physical setting, your first impressions, subjects highlighted in communication and publications, and the general appearance of the workplace. Do people dress formally or casually? The manner in which they use clothing says something about the organization. The physical environment of buildings, offices, and grounds reveals information about the organizational climate. Are buildings and offices functional, decorated artistically, or extravagant and lavish? Are the grounds attractively maintained? The physical characteristics of the reception areas and the degree of warmth with which you are received make up your first impressions of a workplace. Examine the organization's publications, such as a newsletter or annual report. These communications can give you an idea of which subjects an organization considers important. Do the places where people work appear clean and neat or sloppy and dirty? Are they standardized or personalized? These factors give clues to the characteristics of the corporate culture. Are the values and goals of the organization compatible with your personality pattern?

4. Types of people employed by the organization or in the department.   What kind of people work there? Who gets ahead? Who are the "heroes"? Is there a predominant type of personality, almost to the exclusion of other types? Is there a mix of personalities? You could analyze a work environment using Holland's personality types. Try to estimate the percentage of Realistic, Investigative, Artistic, Social, Enterprising, and Conventional types within the organization. Is your personality pattern compatible with the dominant types?

5. Needs and problems of the organization or department.   If you cannot obtain information about the needs and problems of an organization from your personal contacts and people working on the inside, you may need to interview people in similar departments of organizations in the same field. Look for reasons why an organization is experiencing a problem or need. Typical causes of problems are declines or losses of sales; slow growth, no growth, or too much growth; low morale among staff; destructive political infighting; labor/management strife; high staff turnover; poor image in the community; obsolete equipment; stagnation; unnecessary expense; lack of communication; materials shortages; failure to find enough skilled people; questionable decision-making practices; unfavorable market forces; absenteeism; threats from competitors; lack of coordination between different segments of the overall organization; focusing inward when the perspective should be expanding; clashes between value systems; mediocre products or services; and inconsistent treatment of employees. Can your abilities help the organization solve its problems and provide for its needs? If so, a person with hiring authority may be willing to create a job that you would love to tackle because of the challenge it represents, the values that are expressed, and the skills you would use.

6. Decision-making patterns.   What is the structure of the organization's decision-making authority? Is it centralized into the hands of one or a few, or is it decentralized, requiring the participation of many? Under what circumstances does the organization make its decisions? Some decisions may be made autocratically out of necessity and other decisions made more slowly, allowing a democratic process to take place. Leadership can be authoritarian, democratic, or laissez-faire. In some companies, the conventional wisdom is to give all authority to a top official and get out of that person's way. In other organizations, that practice could cause an insurrection. Do you want to be a part of an organization's decision-making process? Decisions take time: information must be gathered; committees meet and assign work; consensus is often slow to develop; leaders can reject the advice of an advisory group. These are the costs of a more democratic style, and you might become impatient with it. Authoritarian decision-makers take the burden of decisions from you, but you suffer a corresponding loss of freedom. Determine your own decision-making preferences and find out what the organization practices when it makes decisions.

7. Advancement and promotion opportunities.   Find out how long it takes to move to a more desirable position. You expect to "pay your dues" in terms of time spent in an entry-level job, but you probably do not want to stay forever in the same job. What are the typical career ladders in an organization? Does a person or a committee make the decisions on promotions or increases of responsibility? Would you make your request for advancement through an interview, or is there an application process? Try to discover the kinds of people the organization is most likely to promote. A seniority principle may govern, or management may find a way to get around it. You can ask employees about the fairness of advancement policies, but be careful about the way you ask—it could be a sensitive area of inquiry. You could set in motion a lengthy account of past injustices, real or imagined, which would have to be confirmed or denied by others. Does the organization favor those who are the most productive, innovative, cooperative, enterprising, creative, cautious, or willing to take risks? Dissecting the organizational culture can go a long way in explaining why some people move fast and others slowly on their career paths.

8. Wage structure and salary range.   Look for beginning, average, and top wages and salaries offered by the organization in your chosen field of work. If the top pay rate is only 10 or 15 percent higher than the starting wage, this is not a good situation. Top pay rates should be at least twice as high as the beginning pay figures. A little research on this subject can put you in a stronger negotiating position if you decide to apply for a job with the organization. Obviously, you will compare this factor with the earnings offered by other organizations you investigate. Include fringe benefits in your research: bonuses, paid vacations, pensions and retirement programs, medical and dental benefits, sick days, personal days, stock purchase and profit-sharing plans, reimbursement of moving expenses, and conference and travel expenses.

9. Future prospects for the organization or department.   What are the projections for the growth or decline of the entire organization or a separate division?

What is the anticipated rate of change? Is the company stagnating? Learn the reasons for its expected progress or its downward course. Naturally, you want to associate with a growing company, but do not automatically reject an organization in trouble. Perhaps your abilities could help solve or lessen its problems and enable you to become one of its "heroes." Be alert for expansion plans or possible cutbacks. Where will they occur within the organization? Watch for new products and services that are being developed. Can you get in on the ground floor of these plans? There is always the hazard of products, services, and activities being phased out. Is there a current function to avoid because it may not exist in a few months or years?

10. History and past performance.   An organization, like a nation, has a history. When did it start? Discover the significant past events and the names of leaders who affected its history. What have been its ups and downs over the years? Knowledge of the organization's past will score points for you in any interview situation.

11. Standing or rank in the industry, field, profession, or region.   Who are the competitors within the same industry or field? How does the organization rank in comparison with its competition? What perceptions do people have of the organization's image or reputation? (This subject is similar to people's "rankings" of colleges and universities.) What factors affect the reasoning and judgments that go into the ranking of an organization or one of its divisions? You may choose strictly quantitative criteria, dealing only with numbers and attempting to be completely objective. Sometimes, however, this kind of evaluation is too superficial and doesn't get to the heart of the matter. Many people make qualitative judgments that have more to do with character, nature, degree of excellence, and other subjective elements.

12. Staff morale.   Do the workers consider their organization to be a pleasant or disagreeable place in which to work? Why? This has to do with working conditions and employee feelings. Workers motivated by the values and beliefs of the organization are enthusiastic about working there. Do the people you talk with see their workplace as beneficial to them, or is it just a place to make a living? Employees will not usually tell you that a company is a terrible place in which to work, but indifference and detachment could be a clue that all is not well. Check the turnover rate of the organization or your target department. Some turnover of staff is natural, but if the rate is high (one third or more per year), it is a sign of trouble. A large proportion of people leaving a company should signal excessive stress, anxiety, and discontent. The organization's health and safety record may offer further indications of the disposition of employees. Good health and a low accident rate is often a sign of good morale; many illnesses and casualties could mean poor morale. Another feature to check is the manner in which rewards and recognition are given. Do they exist? When do they happen? How are they received?

13. Education and training opportunities.   Does the organization encourage its employees to further their education or training by offering to pay all or part of tuition and other educational expenses? Some companies provide educational facilities of their own, even multimillion dollar campuses, to educate their workers. Check on the in-service and on-the-job training programs the organization offers. Are there workshops, conferences, and seminars you can attend? Does the company have a staff development fund set aside for the benefit of employees? Your ability to upgrade your skills will be a significant factor in staying employed and advancing on the job in the future.

14. Political environment within the organization or department.   Office politics is an important part of corporate culture and an integral feature of every organization. Most people feel that politics is a nasty business and want no part of it; if it is ignored, maybe it will go away. However, ignorance of and indifference to politics will more likely make you a victim of some political struggle within the organization. Studying the political climate helps you make informed decisions about which organization to choose and how to survive when you get there. From interviews with over 1000 people who have experienced job failures, Kennedy (1980) discovered that the great majority (75 percent) failed because they were unskilled in office politics. They possessed the technical skills but were unable to get along with their bosses, adjust to their co-workers, or be loyal to the values of the company.

Your political analysis should deal as much with your work associates as with your managers and administrators. You'll have to limit your analysis of management in large organizations, but you should reach at least two levels above and below where you would be on the organizational chart. Kennedy (1980) suggests several questions to answer in obtaining information for political analysis. To whom does each person report, and what is that person's position? Regarding managers, what is their leadership style (by default, dictatorial, somewhere in between)? Are there any major differences in style from that of others at the same level or above? Who reviews each person's decisions, and who has the power to veto their decisions? How much do each person's decisions affect the organization? Do they have line or staff positions? What has been each person's promotion record? How many and what kinds of people report to each person? Which people, and how many of them, consult with each person on their decisions? With whom does each person socialize? How astute is each one politically? What is each person's educational and socioeconomic background? Your personal contacts inside the organization must help you obtain this information; you cannot do it adequately by yourself from the outside. After answering these questions, rank these people in their order of importance, disregarding the titles they hold. Look for alliances and coalitions, if you can detect them during your research.

15. Special requirements.   Would you have to meet any special qualifications or standards in order to join the organization or department? Some companies or institutions require that you obtain a license or certificate. You might need to provide your own tools or equipment in some organizations. Membership in a labor union is required in a closed shop; it might be desirable in some companies even though the employment contract does not require you to join. Similarly, some professional associations operate as if they were a closed shop.

16. Impact of employment in the organization on your family.   How would the acceptance of a job in a new location affect the lifestyle of your spouse, children, or other relatives to whom you have responsibilities? What sacrifices would be necessary because of the working conditions of the organization? What benefits would result? Any change will have an emotional impact on your family and friends; this should be assessed. What cost-of-living increases or decreases would there be in housing, food, clothing, education, transportation, and cultural and recreational activities?

17. Other possible considerations.   One example would be the stability of the company. In general, larger organizations tend to be more stable in their economic development. Public employment tends to be more secure than private jobs, if only for the reason that it is generally harder to terminate a governmental employee. All things being equal, an older company is usually safer than a newer one.

EXERCISE 6-3   *Work Organization Research Worksheet*

Choose an organization in your local area where you could conceivably seek a job in an occupation ranked high among your prospects. Your research could focus on an entire company or institution, if it is small (say, under 50 or 100 employees). In the case of a large organization, you should concentrate on a division or department. In other words, limit the size of the unit you research. Otherwise, your investigation will be too general and the scope too broad. *Refer to the previous section for information on the subjects to research. This worksheet follows the format used in that section.* Photocopy this worksheet if you intend to investigate more than one work organization.

1. Name of organization _____

   Address _____ Telephone _____

   Other locations _____
   Approximate   Industrial
   number of employees _____ category _____

   Sources of information about the organization:

   Titles of written sources: _____

   _____

   _____

People Contacted
(Names)   Address/Telephone   Dates
                                                            Contacted   Interview

_____   _____   _____   _____

_____   _____   _____   _____

_____   _____   _____   _____

Thank-you letters sent:

Yes _____ When? _____ Will send _____ When? _____

Name of person with hiring authority _____

Divisions/departments within organization _____

_____

(Obtain or make an organizational chart. Indicate where you would fit in.)

In which department would I work? _____

What could I do for this organization? _____

2. Goods produced/services provided _____

Volume of business and share of market in area _____

3. Organizational culture or departmental subculture—type(s): _____

_____

Values/beliefs _____

Customs/rituals/ceremonies _____

Clothing worn on the job _____

Physical setting _____

First impressions _____

Subjects highlighted in communications _____

General appearance of workplace _____

Are the values of the organization compatible with my personality? _____

Why? _____

_____

4. Types of people in the organization _____

Compatible with my personality? Why? _____

_____

5. Needs/problems identified _____

_____

Could my skills help solve or reduce the problems or provide for needs?

How? _____

_____

6. Decision-making patterns (describe them): How are decisions made? _____

_____

7. Advancement opportunities _____

_____

Next highest position on career ladder _____

8. Wage/salary structure: Pay in my intended job (starting, average, top) _____

_____

Fringe benefits available _____

9. Organizational growth prospects: Rapid? Slow? None? Decline? _____

Why? _____

_____

10. History: How old? _____ Significant events: _____

Past leaders: _____

11. Rank or image in industrial category _____

Names of competitors _____

12. Staff morale (good, bad, indifferent?) Why? _____

_____

13. Educational/training opportunities _____

_____

14. Political environment within organization: _____

_____

Names of people (in rank order) studied in political analysis _____

_____

15. Special requirements to be hired _____

_____

16. Impact of employment in organization on my family _____

_____

17. Other: _____

_____

_____

Summary

1. Characteristics of quality organizations are written about and dis-cussed all the time. Four books that could help you identify the features you are looking for in an organization are Peters and Waterman's *In Search of Excellence* (1982); Levering's *A Great Place to Work* (1988); Levering, Moskowitz, and Katz's *The 100 Best Companies to Work For in America* (1984); and Deal and Kennedy's *Corporate Cultures* (1982).

2. Obtain a copy of an organizational chart when you research a com-pany. It will give you an overview of the entire operation and help you locate the division or department that could best use your talents. Small businesses with few employees may not publish an organizational chart; in such cases, try to make one yourself.

3. Organizations develop their own unique sets of values, beliefs, cus-toms, practices, rituals, ceremonies, heroes, communications networks, and ways of doing things. A company operates in an environment to which it must adapt if it is to achieve success. You should study the culture of an organization because you want your personality to be compatible with the atmosphere in which you work.

4. Several classifications of organizational cultures can help you analyze your attempt to match your characteristics with those of the organization. Deal and Kennedy (1982) classify corporate cultures into the tough-guy, work hard/play hard, bet-your-company, and process types. Holland's Real-istic, Investigative, Artistic, Social, Enterprising, and Conventional types could be used to assess work environments. Haberman (1983) describes educational environments as therapeutic, compensatory, business, intellec-tual, advocacy, and creative settings. Margerison (1979) and Wallach (1983) analyze organizations in terms of their bureaucratic, innovative, and supportive cultures. This last classification can be linked to McClelland's (1972) power, achievement, and affiliation motives.

5. Information about work organizations can come from written re-sources and from interviewing personal contacts. Use a combination of both. Unless absolutely no written material on an organization exists, start your investigation by consulting annual reports, business sections of newspapers and trade journals, business magazines, the *College Placement Annual,* and the many encyclopedic volumes on companies and their officials such as

Dun and Bradstreet's, Moody's, Standard and Poor's, the Thomas *Register,* and *Who's Who* books.

6. Annual reports are a gold mine of information. They contain statistical data, some of which are difficult to comprehend without help. A company's annual report usually includes the following sections: financial highlights, a letter to the stockholders, analysis of operations, income statement, balance sheet, financial position, financial summary, notes to financial statements, and the auditor's report.

7. Exercise 6-2 can help you identify types of workplaces that attract you and specific work organizations you could investigate.

8. After listing the names of a few places where you could conceivably work, you need to know a number of things about each organization in order to make a wise choice. Suggested features to investigate are (1) structure, (2) products made or services provided, (3) organizational culture or department subculture, (4) types of people, (5) needs and problems, (6) decision-making patterns, (7) advancement and promotion policies, (8) wage structure and salary range, (9) future prospects, (10) past history, (11) standing among competitors in the industry, (12) staff morale, (13) educational and training opportunities, (14) political environment, (15) special requirements, and (16) impact on your family. You should research all these factors for whatever work organizations you are seriously considering. Do it now; get in the habit of researching this subject all the time. When it comes to actively searching for a job, you may be too pressed for time to learn how to do it well.

References

Chruden, H. J., & Sherman, A. W., Jr. (1980). *Personnel management: The utilization of human resources* (6th ed.). Cincinnati, OH: South-Western.

Deal, T. E., & Kennedy, A. A. (1982). *Corporate cultures: The rites and rituals of corporate life.* Reading, MA: Addison-Wesley.

Haberman, M. (1983). Organizational cultures in school settings. *Education Digest, 49,* 47–49.

Holland, J. L. (1985). *Making vocational choices: A theory of vocational personalities and work environments* (2nd ed.). Englewood Cliffs, NJ: Prentice-Hall.

Kennedy, M. M. (1980). *Office politics: Seizing power, wielding clout.* Chicago: Follett.

Levering, R. (1988). *A great place to work: What makes some employers so good (and most so bad).* New York: Random House.

Levering, R., Moskowitz, M., & Katz, M. (1984). *The 100 best companies to work for in America.* Reading, MA: Addison-Wesley.

Margerison, C. J. (1979). *How to assess your managerial style.* New York: AMACOM (a division of American Management Association).

McClelland, D. C. (1972). The two faces of power. In D. C. McClelland & R. S. Steele (Eds.), *Human motivation: A book of readings* (pp. 300–316). Morristown, NJ: General Learning Press.

Peters, T. J., & Waterman, R. H. (1982). *In search of excellence: Lessons from America's best-run companies.* New York: Harper & Row.

Schein, E. H. (1980). *Organizational psychology* (3rd ed.). Englewood Cliffs, NJ: Prentice-Hall.

Schein, E. H. (1985). *Organizational culture and leadership.* San Francisco: Jossey-Bass.

Wallach, E. J. (1983). Individual and organization: The cultural match. *Training and Development Journal, 37*(2), 29–36.

7

Using Your Speaking Skills to Get a Job: Interviewing for Information

Interviewing is a subject that strikes terror into the hearts of job-seekers everywhere. Writing résumés and researching companies, while time-consuming, are parts of the job search that can be done in a relatively leisurely, relaxed manner. But interviewing is something else. An interview is over almost in a flash, and a lot can transpire in a short amount of time. The interviewer will ask you many questions, some of which you may not anticipate. You may be unsure whether you responded competently. Your voice may become shaky and unsteady, indicating your lack of composure. Your hands may be clammy when you first meet the interviewer; both of you will know how tense you are. You will probably be afraid that your mind won't work fast enough. You might trip over some words, again revealing your nervousness and lack of confidence. You know the interview is at the very center of the job search process, and this make-it-or-break-it atmosphere is what produces the strain of the situation. Interviewing is an activity you may have participated in only a few times every so often, or it may be something you know you will have to do sometime to get a job but you've never done it before. Thus, most job-hunters approach the interview with a sense of fear and apprehension.

Because of the tension surrounding the job interview, career counselors conceived the idea of using interviewing first as a means of obtaining information rather than a job. In doing this, a job-seeker could practice interview techniques with all kinds of people and obtain essential facts and knowledge at the same time. What could be better? If you made mistakes during the interview, disaster would not strike because a job offer was not riding on the outcome. The risk of rejection was removed from the situation, and the pressure was considerably lightened. The people job-seekers talked with would benefit, too. They could have the pleasure of reflecting on their work experiences and sharing their insights with another person who valued their knowledge. They could feel the satisfaction of helping someone else get started and possibly playing some part in their success.

Perhaps inevitably, some problems developed with the use of interviewing for information. Some job-hunters abused the ethics of this kind of interview when they found they could manipulate it into a way of getting around the screening devices of the personnel department and moving directly into the office of a person with hiring authority. The more those people with the power to hire were exposed to clever sales pitches for jobs rather than honest inquiries for new perceptions and understanding, the more suspicious they became of those who wanted to interview "for information only." Consequently, with some employers, you may need to overcome an initial doubt concerning your motives. The practice of interviewing for information must be done sincerely and genuinely.

Informational interviewing is a powerful instrument in the job search. Used correctly and for the proper reasons, it can give you all kinds of new knowledge and widen your network of personal contacts. The "nonjob survey"—another name for the informational interview—will help you discover features about occupations, jobs, companies, and employers you cannot find any other way. And, the more you interview for information, the more you become accustomed to interviewing itself. You begin to lose the anxieties and terrors you once felt about interviews, and you become better equipped to handle the worries and pressures of job interviews when they arise.

Purposes and Advantages of Informational Interviewing

An informational interview is just what the name suggests: an interview for information. This type of interview precedes job interviewing. Informational interviewing is also called the "nonjob interview survey approach" (Billingsley, 1978), because it involves making a survey of a company but not asking the employer for a job. Bolles (1986) has called it "researching your ideal job," because some people took advantage of the practice of informational interviewing. In the first volume of this series, *Taking Charge of Your Career Direction,* you interviewed for information to obtain knowledge about occupations that interested you. Now you must add the purpose of gaining knowledge about work organizations and how they employ particular occupations of interest to you.

There are a number of advantages to using the informational interview technique, beyond the value of furthering your knowledge about occupations and organizations. Informational interviewing gives you the freedom to conduct more of the interview in your own style (you are asking the questions) and to evaluate employers and their companies for yourself. There is less pressure or stress in this type of interview, because you are not discussing a specific job opening. Acceptance or rejection is not an issue; no such decision must be made. If you are talking with a person who has the power to hire, that person doesn't have the pressure of such a decision either. You can relax more in the interview, for you are screening the employer and the organization. You can focus on your needs instead of the needs of the employer. The information you obtain is more likely to be up to date than the printed material you read. By asking the referral question, you may add more personal contacts to your network of people who could help you later in the job search.

Once in a while, the informational interview becomes an indirect route to a job offer. If you are talking with a person who has hiring authority, there is always the possibility you might impress that person enough to arouse his or her interest in offering you a job. Remember, however, that the first step that changes the informational interview into a job interview must come from the employer. For the job-seeker to switch an informational interview into a request for a job is dishonest and intrudes on the employer's territory under false pretenses.

You may find that the greatest benefit of the informational interview technique is the loss of fear of, and anxiety over, talking with people you do not know. This has been the experience of many of my students, particularly homemakers returning to school. The people you interview are generally very cordial when you ask them for facts and advice; in fact, they feel complimented. Students may approach an informational interview exercise with self-doubt and misgivings, only to emerge from it in high spirits, elated at their success, more knowledgeable, having made another contact or a friend, and ready to continue the process.

One cautionary note needs to be made, however. All information, particularly from interviewing, should be evaluated and verified. No one person represents everyone in the organization or the occupation. Find out whether the perceptions of the person you have interviewed are accurate, up to date, and objective. They should be relatively consistent with the data you obtain from other informational interviews and the material you read.

Informational Interview Procedures

A typical sequence of activities in setting up and carrying out an informational interview goes as follows: (1) identify and investigate a target organization, (2) identify a person within the organization with whom to talk, (3) understand and ethically use the informational interview approach, (4) make an appointment by letter or telephone, (5) prepare questions for the interview, (6) conduct the informational interview, and (7) write a thank-you letter.

Step 1 *Identify and investigate a target organization* in which you are, or will be, interested when you seek a job in one of your major occupational choices. For ideas on setting this beginning step in motion, refer to the previous chapter on researching work organizations.

Step 2 *Identify people within the organization whom you would like to interview for information.* They can be people who are working in a major occupational choice of yours and have the authority to hire. Those with hiring authority can be important decision-makers in the organization: a department head, a section chief, an administrative aide, a company president, or an executive vice president. A middle manager, a staff worker, or a second-in-command in a department could also be appropriate, since these people may serve on hiring committees. Include all kinds of workers—secretaries, production workers, custodians, and so on. They know a lot about what goes on in an organization, even if they are not in a position to hire. Select a person to ask for an interview. There should be others to see, but concentrate on the first interview for now. This person could be someone you already know or to whom you have been referred by a personal contact.

Researching an organization will help you identify people with whom you would like to talk. This second step builds on the first.

Step 3 *Understand the purpose of the informational interview and use it properly.* If you have already decided to apply for a job at a workplace, you have gone beyond the needs and purposes of the informational interview. The interview described here is not a job interview; that comes later in the job search. This is an interview for information and advice only.

Informational interviewing is like shopping before you buy a product. Shopping and buying are two separate activities. Shopping is gathering information that provides the basis for a later purchase. When you gather information about occupations and organizations from reading material and interviewing people, you are shopping for jobs (Greco, 1980).

Job-seekers and people with hiring authority are analogous to salespeople and buyers, respectively. Sellers believe their product may meet some need of the buyer's company. The seller proposes a survey to gather enough information to find out whether this is true or not. Then, both buyer and seller are in a better position to discuss a possible sale. The job-seeker, in effect, makes a similar proposal to an employer, asking for information in order to make a decision about whether to pursue a job with the organization (Billingsley, 1978).

Any talk about a job offer comes later, possibly as a result of the informational interview or at the discretion of the employer during the interview. The informational interview is simply a way of getting to talk with knowledgeable people, some of whom may be influential, important, and empowered to hire. This method can be used ethically and with integrity. Unfortunately, however, it has been used deceptively by a few as a way to maneuver around a company's usual hiring procedures so as to speak directly with a person who has hiring authority. Understandably, some employers may be suspicious of informational interviews, having been tricked by a job-seeker posing as an information-gatherer who suddenly puts the bite on them for a job, a "wolf in sheep's clothing," so to speak. Informational interviews can lay the foundation for future job offers, but they were not designed to ask employers for jobs.

Step 4 *Write or telephone for an appointment with the person you would like to interview for information.* Have a definite purpose in mind for the interview. If you are in a career planning class, you can say you are asking for an informational interview because you are working on a project to help you learn more about occupations, organizations, and jobs. Reassure the person that your purpose is not to ask for a job. The worst thing that can happen to you is that this person will say, "I'm too busy"—but keep in mind that most people are delighted when someone asks them for help and advice. One way to ask for an interview is to write a letter of introduction. For a sample letter, see Figure 7-1. This type of letter is different from a cover letter or letter of

FIGURE 7-1   *Sample letter of introduction*

91919 S. Jefferson Avenue
Anyville, Anystate 00000

April 30, 0000

Mr. John Doe
Vice President for Sales
XYZ Corporation
19191 N. Lincoln Street
Anytown, Anystate 00000

Dear Mr. Doe:

1 am currently a member of a class (or group) at_____
and have been assigned a career planning project to complete. The
project concerns an investigation of various occupations and
organizations that are of interest to me. Would you be willing to
talk with me about a career in selling and business management in a
company such as yours?

Sales and business management are the two occupational fields that
interest me most at the present time. Interest inventories and work
experiences indicate that I should seriously consider sales or
management. Right now, I need to talk with a person who is actually
working in these fields in order to gather information on which to
base a decision about my occupational future.

I will contact your secretary next Monday in the hope that I can
set up an interview with you. Please be assured I am not using this
request for an interview as a way to ask you for a job. I need your
advice and more education before I start to seek a job. I will be
most appreciative of receiving any information I can from you.

Respectfully,

Mary H. Dataseeker

Mary H. Dataseeker

application. The purpose of the cover letter is to obtain a job interview, whereas the letter of introduction lets the employer know he or she will not have to make uncomfortable decisions about a job applicant. All you are asking is an opportunity to obtain more information for a career planning project. No employment demands will be made. The sample letter of introduction should not be copied word for word; use it as a guide. If you have learned about the person you want to interview through a personal contact, you could start your letter by mentioning that your mutual friend or acquaintance suggested talking with him or her. Always request permission before using a person's name. You could begin your telephone request in the same way. Over the phone, you can explain that you are working on a career planning project and need to talk with a person who is currently working in an organization or an occupation that interests you. Ask for about 20 minutes of time so that you can get some questions answered and get some advice. You can also ask if the person could suggest any written sources of information for you to read before you come to the interview. You want to give the impression that you will not be wasting their time. Figure 7-2 offers an idea for starting the telephone conversation. Resist the suggestion of interviewing over the telephone if the opportunity is offered.

Try to hold the interview where the person works so you can see the work environment for yourself. Another way to obtain an informational interview is to appear directly at the organization without having made a formal appointment. You may not be able to conduct an interview right then and there, but you could schedule an appointment for a later time. Sometimes you can simply create an opportunity to interview for information on the spur of the moment. It can develop anytime or anywhere. You don't have to be in an office to hold an informational interview.

Step 5 *Prepare questions for the informational interview.* Ask how the person became interested in the occupation and the organization and how that person got there. Ask about the responsibilities of the job, the abilities and preparation needed, and what features of the work give them personal satisfaction. Ask how he or she views the future of the job and workplace and what changes seem forthcoming. Avoid asking for information you could obtain elsewhere. A list of possible questions to ask in an informational interview follows in the next section. The last question to ask is crucial, for it can expand your network of personal contacts. The *referral question* should be asked before leaving the interview.

Step 6 *Conduct the informational interview.* Bring your written questions with you and use them as a framework for conducting the interview. Do the same things you would for a job interview: dress properly, have a neat appearance, be punctual, know the name and title of the person you are interviewing, know some things about the company, show you are prepared from the questions you ask, listen carefully, practice good eye contact, and so on. Refer to the chapter on job interviews for more details. Have a clear purpose for your interview session. Limit yourself to goals that are achieva-

FIGURE 7-2 *Sample opening of a telephone request for an interview*

Hello, Mr. Doe. My name is _____ from _____

_____ . I am working on a career planning

project that involves some research about ___(name of occupation and/or organization)___ .

I'd like to meet with you for about 20 minutes to ask you a few questions. May I suggest

next _____ at _____ as a time for the interview? (If

your request is accepted, make sure you know where and when the interview is to take place.)

ble in the short amount of interview time you have. Have note paper and a pen or pencil with you so you can write responses to your questions in the form of notes or shorthand during the interview. Complete the answers from the words or phrases in your notes afterward. A tape recorder allows you to maintain better eye contact, but always ask permission of the person you are interviewing before you use one. Be sure to thank the person interviewed for the time he or she spent with you. If the interview has gone well, it's OK to leave copies of your résumé with the person you have interviewed, as long as you make it clear you are not asking for a job at this time. Just say that if he or she meets anyone who is looking for a job applicant with your career interests, abilities, and preparation, you would greatly appreciate it if your résumé were passed on to that person. You will have expanded your opportunity to connect with employers who have jobs to offer.

Step 7   *Write a thank-you letter after the interview.* Express your gratitude for the time, attention, and help given you. You should send the thank-you note to the person interviewed no later than two or three days after the interview. Your thoughtfulness marks you as a courteous person and serves to activate the memory of the person you interviewed. If you did not leave your résumé after the interview, you could send several copies of it with your thank-you letter, with the explanation that you would be grateful if the possibility arose to give it to an employer who is looking for a person such as yourself. A separate thank-you note should go to the secretary, if you arranged the appointment through one.

Suggested Questions for the Informational Interview

Use the following list of questions as a guide. Compose questions of your own to fit the circumstances of the occupation or organization you are investigating. Where you read "this occupation/organization" below, substitute the name of the actual occupation or organization in your question. Reaffirm your purpose for the interview or that you are working on a career planning assignment. Make sure again you have permission to ask questions about the person's occupation and work organization. In the following format, the topic of the question is stated first, followed by a number of questions you could use to open the subject you want to discuss.

1. *Job search techniques used.* How did you get into this occupation/ organization? What steps did you take to get where you are now? What methods did you use to find work in the occupation you are in now?
2. *Occupational/organizational interests.* How did you become interested in this occupation/organization? What attracted you to this particular occupation/organization?
3. *Getting started in the occupation.* What entry-level jobs might qualify

a person for this occupational field? What is the progression of jobs, from the beginning to the top?

4. *Responsibilities in the work.* What does the company expect you to do on the job? What responsibilities and duties do you have in your work? What characteristics should a person look for in a job such as the one you have?

5. *Products, services, customers, competition.* What products are manufactured (or what services are provided) by the organization? (This question would be a mistake in a job interview!) Who are your customers? Who are your competitors? What is your rank or standing compared with your competitors in the industry?

6. *Abilities and qualifications required.* What skills, aptitudes, or personal qualifications does a person need for this occupation (or to work in this organization)? What essential abilities are needed to do your job well?

7. *Preparation and background needed.* What preparation, education, training, or background is required for entrance into this field of work? Are particular degrees or licenses required to enter this occupation?

8. *Values and personal satisfaction.* What aspects of this occupation/ organization give you personal satisfaction? What values are expressed by this occupation/organization?

9. *The organizational culture.* What basic assumptions and beliefs are shared and supported by most people in your division or organization? What practices and ceremonies mean a lot to those working here and to the organization? Who are the heroes or exemplary figures in this organization, and what do they stand for? What is the guiding philosophy of the organization?

10. *Personality characteristics.* What personal traits, values, and interests are necessary or helpful to succeed and advance in this occupation/ organization? What personal qualities do administrators and supervisors look for in their employees here?

11. *Causes of dissatisfaction.* What are the major frustrations, annoyances, or sources of dissatisfaction in the occupation/organization? What problems, both internal and external, cause dissatisfaction in the job or workplace?

12. *Unique qualities or strengths.* What strengths set this occupation/organization apart from others? What are the best things you can say about this occupation/organization?

13. *Working conditions.* How much time do you spend at work? Is the amount of time you spend on the job due more to the nature of the occupation or to the nature of the particular organization? Does your working time affect the amount of time you can spend with your family? How do people dress for work here? Is the work mostly indoors or outdoors? What is the noise level? Does the physical layout of the building(s) make the organization's work environment pleasant? Describe

the morale of the people who work for the organization and give some reasons for their attitude.

14. *Salary ranges.* What are the beginning, average, and top salaries or wages in this occupation? How does your organization pay in comparison to other organizations in the same industry? What fringe benefits are offered? (*Do not ask:* What is your salary?)

15. *Decision-making patterns.* How would you describe the decision-making style of this organization? Who makes the decisions on how the work will be done in your department?

16. *Organization of the organization.* What are the lines of authority in your company? (Ask for an organizational chart.) To whom do you report? Whom do you supervise?

17. *Advancement opportunities.* What opportunities exist for advancement, promotion, or change of jobs within the organization? Where could I expect to be in this organization after five years with a good work record?

18. *Typical day at work.* Describe a typical day at work in your occupation and in this organization. Can you leave your job behind after work, or is it the kind of job you take home with you? Explain.

19. *Related occupations.* What other occupations are closely related to this one? Would one need the same skills and aptitudes for them? Are any related occupations represented in this organization?

20. *Temporary work and courses to take while in college.* Could you suggest any temporary, part-time, or summer work experience that would help a person prepare for your occupation? What courses in school or college were especially helpful to you in preparing for this occupation?

21. *Future projections.* What do you see in the future for this occupation/ organization? Will there be a continued demand for it? Is the number of workers in the occupation/organization growing or declining? How secure will employment be in this occupation/organization?

22. *Changes.* What changes do you think are coming for this occupation/ organization over the next few years? How can a person prepare for those changes? What are the latest developments in your field?

23. *Special problems and concerns.* Are there any special problems, concerns, situations, circumstances, or challenges of which a person should be aware when considering this occupation/organization? How would you try to solve these problems or face these challenges?

24. *Other information or advice.* What other advice or information can you give a person considering, preparing for, or entering this occupation or organization? Because you know this occupation/organization better than I do, what other questions should I be asking about it?

25. *The return visit.* Is it all right to contact you for another interview if I need more information and advice in the future? In case I need more advice and information in the future, could I make another appointment to talk with you?

26. *The referral question.* (Never conclude an informational interview without trying to obtain referrals to other people in the same or similar occupations/organizations.) Could you suggest the names of other people with whom I could talk in this occupation/organization? May I mention your name as the person who referred me? Would you be able to write a letter of introduction for me (or make an introduction for me over the telephone)?

You can also get ideas for questions from the 30 items of the Work Organization Environment Survey and the section entitled, "Things You Need to Know About a Work Organization" in Chapter 6.

If a Job Offer Is Made . . .

Suppose you go to an informational interview sincerely and honestly for the sole purpose of seeking new knowledge, and the employer becomes so impressed with your competence and good intentions that he or she decides to ask whether you would consider employment at the company. You have a decision to make on the spur of the moment, right in the middle of the interview. The employer is suggesting that the interview for information be changed into an interview for a job. This switch is perfectly legitimate, because the idea comes from the employer. What are your options?

One alternative is to continue interviewing for information. You could say, "I am very honored by your proposal; however, I need more time to think about it. I have a few more companies that I want to look into before I decide which ones I am most serious about." (Then, if it is true, "I can assure you that I am greatly impressed by what I have seen here and I will be back to talk with you.") The second option is to begin discussing the details of the job being offered and move right into the subject that constitutes the next chapter of this book.

EXERCISE 7-1   *Informational Interview Exercise*

The directions for this exercise consist of following the seven steps of the informational interview technique outlined in the section entitled, "Informational Interview Procedures." For people in a career planning group or class, there is an eighth step of preparing a report for an instructor, counselor, or group to evaluate. You may also be asked to give a short account of your experience to your group or class. The informational interview report has three basic parts.

1. *Identification material:* your name, the name and title of the person you interviewed, the organization that person works for, where the interview was held, and the date of the interview.
2. *Questions asked:* your written list of questions composed before the informational interview took place.

3. *Summary of subjects discussed and information obtained:* a short review of the topics covered and the knowledge gained from the interview.

These are working papers, so a polished report is not a primary concern in this exercise. If you make a tape, include it. The purpose of the exercise is to experience the techniques of informational interviewing and to appreciate the potential benefits of this job search activity.

EXERCISE 7-2   *First Impressions Exercise*

First impressions, rightly or wrongly, carry a lot of weight when interviewers and employers evaluate you. Naturally, you want to create a positive first impression by displaying attractive personal characteristics and appearing properly dressed, poised, and in control. Do you impress other people as you think you do? One way to find out is to conduct an experiment.

First phase.   In the following list, circle the five words that describe the impression you would most like to make when you meet another person for the first time. The word in parentheses after each item has the same or a similar meaning to the first word. If it expresses more clearly the impression you want, circle it instead.

Adventurous (daring)	Intelligent (bright)
Alert (observant)	Knowledgeable (well-informed)
Ambitious (aspiring)	Mature (grownup)
Assertive (strong-willed)	Mild (placid)
Businesslike (efficient)	Modest (humble)
Capable (competent)	Optimistic (positive)
Caring (concerned)	Organized (disciplined)
Cautious (careful)	Outgoing (sociable)
Charming (appealing)	Pleasant (agreeable)
Cheerful (good-natured)	Polite (gracious)
Confident (self-assured)	Practical (down-to-earth)
Considerate (kind)	Progressive (forward-looking)
Decisive (firm)	Quiet (reticent)
Delicate (refined)	Radiant (sparkling)
Dominating (masterful)	Reliable (trustworthy)
Easygoing (relaxed)	Reserved (self-controlled)
Enterprising (energetic)	Sensitive (perceptive)
Enthusiastic (responsive)	Serious (resolute)
Forceful (aggressive)	Stylish (fashionable)
Friendly (amiable)	Tolerant (permissive)
Fun (playful)	Traditional (conservative)
Genuine (sincere)	Trusting (accepting)
Graceful (agile)	Unconventional (eccentric)
Hard-working (industrious)	Vivacious (lively)
Humorous (witty)	Warm (compassionate)

Next, have a conversation with someone you do not know. Talk for at least five minutes. The same list of words is printed below. Ask the person with whom you have talked to look at the list of unmarked words that follows and select the five words that he or she believes best describe you. If you are in a class, exchange lists with another person. Make sure you do not know each other. This is a test of *first* impressions.

When you receive the other person's perceptions (or first impressions) of you, ask yourself whether this is the impression you want to make on other people. If so, congratulate yourself. If not, what changes can you make?

Second phase.   To the person who has been just given this list of words: Please circle the *five* words you believe best describe the person with whom you have just talked. The word in parentheses has the same meaning as, or a similar meaning to, the first word. If it expresses more clearly the impression you want to describe, circle it instead.

Adventurous (daring)   Intelligent (bright)
Alert (observant)   Knowledgeable (well-informed)
Ambitious (aspiring)   Mature (grownup)
Assertive (strong-willed)   Mild (placid)
Businesslike (efficient)   Modest (humble)
Capable (competent)   Optimistic (positive)
Caring (concerned)   Organized (disciplined)
Cautious (careful)   Outgoing (sociable)
Charming (appealing)   Pleasant (agreeable)
Cheerful (good-natured)   Polite (gracious)
Confident (self-assured)   Practical (down-to-earth)
Considerate (kind)   Progressive (forward-looking)
Decisive (firm)   Quiet (reticent)
Delicate (refined)   Radiant (sparkling)
Dominating (masterful)   Reliable (trustworthy)
Easygoing (relaxed)   Reserved (self-controlled)
Enterprising (energetic)   Sensitive (perceptive)
Enthusiastic (responsive)   Serious (resolute)
Forceful (aggressive)   Stylish (fashionable)
Friendly (amiable)   Tolerant (permissive)
Fun (playful)   Traditional (conservative)
Genuine (sincere)   Trusting (accepting)
Graceful (agile)   Unconventional (eccentric)
Hard-working (industrious)   Vivacious (lively)
Humorous (witty)   Warm (compassionate)

Summary

1. Two broad categories of interviews are informational and job interviews. You never ask for a job in an informational interview; you request this

type of interview to obtain facts and to evaluate the company and employer so as to determine whether you would want to return for a job interview at a later time.

2. Informational interviews have several advantages. You can hold this kind of interview without the stress and worry of rejection. You can screen employers; they must pass your selection test. You can concentrate on your needs rather than those of the employer. Occasionally, an employer may be impressed enough with your potential to offer you a job on the spot. The initiative for changing an informational interview into a job interview must always come from the employer. It is unethical to interview an employer on the pretense of a request for information when you are actually planning to ask for a job.

3. The steps in conducting an informational interview are: (1) identify and research target organizations, (2) identify people who have hiring authority or are working in a major occupational prospect of yours, (3) understand the ethical issue that the request for information is not another way to put the bite on an employer for a job, (4) make the interview appointment, (5) prepare questions, (6) hold the interview, and (7) write a thank-you note expressing your appreciation for the time the person you interviewed spent with you.

References

Billingsley, E. (1978). *Career planning and job hunting for today's student: The nonjob interview approach.* Santa Monica, CA: Goodyear.

Bolles, R. N. (1986). *What color is your parachute?* Berkeley, CA: Ten Speed Press.

Greco, B. (1980). *How to get the job that's right for you.* Homewood, IL: Dow Jones-Irwin.

8

Using Your Speaking Skills to Get a Job: Interviewing for Jobs

"This is it," you say to yourself. All your hard work in preparing a résumé and a cover letter, talking with personal contacts, registering at the placement office, filling out application forms, scanning the newspaper want ads, researching companies, and talking to workers and employers comes down to this—going face to face with an interviewer for a job. Tension and anxiety mount as the time approaches. Your whole life, you think, is going to be decided in the short span of 30 minutes. Everything seems to depend on the interview.

Some job-seekers worry themselves frantic. If you must torment yourself with anguish, Hellman (1986) suggests that you imagine the worst. Really get into it. You walk into the interviewer's dimly lit office, which is painted dark gray and has narrow slits for windows. The interviewer, a beetle-like, spindly-legged creature, looks up and shrieks, "You dare come in here?" He proceeds to chase you around the room with a switchblade. You are rejected on the spot and told, "We went out of business a year ago, but we still wouldn't hire you even if you were the last person on earth." Television cameras zoom in to record your moment of humiliation. You go to pieces and babble incoherently. Wire services pick up the story; it is front-page news all over the world. People point at you as you walk down the street. An "R" for Rejected is emblazoned on your chest. You are renounced by family and friends. You wander aimlessly through life, a victim of the job interview!

When your worst-case scenario is complete, come back to reality. Yes, the interview is important. It is where job offers are made, the culmination of your efforts to land a job. But, no, the world doesn't end if you are not offered a position. The important thing is to keep going, for many more job possibilities are out there. The more you work at interviewing, the easier it becomes.

Preparation and practice are the keys to effective performance in the job interview. Being prepared lessens the tension that can otherwise build up before such an occasion. Don't just wait for the interview to happen; do things to make it happen better. Research the company and its people. Thoroughly digest the ideas of Chapter 6, the chapter on work organizations. Look presentable, be well groomed, and wear appropriate clothing to make a good impression. The way people dress for the job is among the data you collect in your visit before the interview. For practice, interview for information (the subject of the previous chapter) before you interview for a job. Also, before the job interview, have a friend, parent, or spouse help you rehearse answering anticipated questions. Questions interviewers typically ask are included in this chapter. Prepare several questions you can ask; write them on a card or piece of paper if you think you might forget them. Find out the interviewer's name so you can use it in your greeting. Figure out what you can do for the organization, what your value to it would be. Contact references for their permission in case you are asked to furnish names of people who will vouch for you. Choose your references carefully, making sure they know your work and will recommend you with sincere enthusiasm. Know the location of your appointment and how to get there, and plan to arrive a few minutes early. These ways of actively preparing and practicing for your job interview will help you approach it in a good spirit and with faith in yourself.

EXERCISE 8-1   *Job Interview Self-Test*

Suppose you are seeking employment in your Number One occupational choice. You will need to identify your occupational goal, the specific position you are seeking, and where the interview is taking place. At the top of a sheet of paper, write down your major occupational choice, the specific position you are seeking, and the type (or actual name) of the work organization. The employer or personnel manager asks several questions, which are shown in the box that follows this paragraph. How would you answer these questions? Assume you have the necessary qualifications and preparation, and, on the sheet of paper you just headed with your occupational goal, write down for each interview question the first thoughts that come to your mind. Either write the actual words you would use to respond, or indicate the substance of your response.

Job Interview Self-Test

1. Why do you want to enter this occupation as a career?
2. Why are you interested in working for our company (or organization)?
3. Why should we hire you? What can you do for us?
4. What kind of people do you want to work with?
5. What salary range would you consider appropriate for this job?
6. What do you want to know about our organization? Do you have any questions you want to ask us?

After you have written your responses, review them and ask, "If I were the employer, would I hire myself? Why?"

These six basic questions will probably appear in one form or another in most job interviews. Our comments about each question will center on how you could respond, where you could find the information, and why employers ask the question.

1. *Why do you want to enter this occupation as a career?* Talk about your career interests, work values, and occupational goals. (Chapter 4 of *Taking Charge of Your Career Direction* identifies occupational interest areas, Chapter 7 prioritizes work values, and Chapter 9 helps you establish career goals.) Answering this question with a statement about your occupational goals and objectives and the values expressed in those goals demon-

strates your motivation to achieve in your work. Employers like to hear that a job candidate is interested in a job being offered and values it because there are qualities about the job that make it important. A motivated employee simply makes a greater commitment to the job.

2. *Why are you interested in working for our company (or organization)?* Indicate that you have taken the time and made the effort to investigate the organization and have found some features about it that interest and appeal to you. (Chapter 6 of this book contains information on researching work organizations.) Employers are interested in finding out what you know about them. The fact that you have spent time researching the organization is a real compliment. Most employers will appreciate and be impressed with your knowledge of their company.

3. *Why should we hire you? What can you do for us?* This is the place to discuss your skills, aptitudes, and job-related achievement experiences. Emphasize how your abilities and background will fit the needs of the organization and the particular job you are seeking in it. (Chapters 5 and 6 of *Taking Charge of Your Career Direction* cover these subjects.) Always support your claim that you possess an ability or skill with an achievement experience that proves it. Ability to substantiate your strengths is a powerful tool that clearly separates you from your competition and is one of the most important concepts in the job search process (LaFevre, 1989). The employer has tasks to accomplish and wants to know how your skills and experience will help. Some job search experts consider this question to be the most fundamental of all.

4. *What kind of people do you want to work with?* This question may be another way of asking, "What kind of a person are you?" You could think of a set of words that illustrate people, such as the ones you find in Holland's six basic personality types. You can find descriptions of the Realistic, Investigative, Artistic, Social, Enterprising, and Conventional types in Holland (1985) or in Chapter 4 of *Taking Charge of Your Career Direction*. Reviewing this material will help you find words that will most accurately describe you. You can explain that you are looking for a work environment that has these kinds of people. You want to be compatible with your fellow workers in the organization, and you hope your personality fits reasonably well with theirs. Who could argue with these sentiments? The employer has the same hope that you will fit in well. Neither of you wants to contend with personality clashes that are irritating, difficult, and frustrating. The material about organizational cultures in Chapter 6 can also help you respond.

5. *What salary range would you consider appropriate for this job?* If no other reason can convince you to explore companies before the job interview, the discussion of salary should. Employers often ask for salary figures because they want to know how much you may cost them and to gather data on which to screen candidates. Not doing your homework for this question can cost you money and even the job itself. Try to learn the salaries of the positions just above and below your target position on the organizational

chart. You can begin salary negotiations at the top of this range without pricing yourself out of the market. You can also avoid underselling yourself and discovering later you could have settled for a higher figure. Quoting a salary figure that is too high could make you seem unreasonable and unrealistic. A low figure may give the impression that you lack a proper sense of self-worth. In other words, don't appear greedy or needy. If you cannot find the salary information you want from printed materials, perhaps your personal contacts can provide it. Competing companies might furnish their pay scale for comparable positions, or you could look at average pay rates in such books as the *Occupational Outlook Handbook* or *The American Almanac of Jobs and Salaries* (Wright, 1990). The College Placement Council (62 Highland Ave., Bethlehem, PA 18017) publishes beginning salaries earned by new college graduates. Remember that salaries differ from region to region of the country. In some organizations, salary schedules are published and become public knowledge. These wage figures are set by collective bargaining agreements between management and unions or associations. The salary question here is cut and dried; management must stick to the terms of the agreement. In some cases, however, the administration may have more flexibility; additional pay may be gained through supplemental job responsibilities. Keep fringe benefits in mind. After you add fringe benefits, a lower salary figure may be worth more than a higher figure. What should you do if you cannot find definite salary numbers at all? If possible, do not give a dollar figure in the interview. You could state that, while your naturally desire a decent wage, your primary concern is to do the work you want to do. Ask for more time to think about salary. All things considered, it is better to delay salary negotiations until you have decided you want the job and the organization has decided it wants you; this usually takes more than one interview.

6. *What do you want to know about our organization? Do you have any questions you want to ask us?* As you investigate an organization, more questions will arise about it. These questions become more specific and detailed with your increasing knowledge, thereby revealing the fact you have researched the company. Your questions should go beyond pay, fringe benefits, vacations, and number of sick days. It is all right to ask about these matters, but combine them with other concerns such as responsibilities you would have on the job, working conditions, the growth potential of the organization, the nature of the work in the position you are seeking, or how the organization employs your chosen occupation. Telephone or write to the personnel office before your interview and ask them to send you pamphlets and brochures about the organization's products, services, and employee benefits. Ask for the company's annual report. Check with career resource centers, college placement offices, and chambers of commerce for this kind of information. Employers often ask for your questions to find out whether you are curious about the organization and are motivated to learn more about it. Failure to ask questions may leave the impression that you are not

all that interested in the company, a factor that will work against you in a job interview.

Interviewers

There are all kinds of interviewers. Good ones are able to turn a formal interview into a cordial discussion, make you feel at ease, and bring out a lot of information all at the same time. However, you cannot assume that all interviewers will be proficient or professional in their work. Interviewing is a demanding job, far more difficult than job-seekers realize. It is a real art, requiring extensive verbal and social skills. Some supervisors have been trained to do a different job but still wind up talking to job applicants. They may want to get the interview over as quickly as possible, creating the feeling you are wasting their time. Other interviewers are pushed into talking with candidates because no one else is available to do the job. Many employers hire others to do the interviewing for them because they find it so burdensome. There are even a very few interviewers who probe where they shouldn't, deliberately create unnecessary stress, or don't take their responsibilities seriously. My students, returning from practice interviews, can often describe the mistakes the interviewer has made.

Despite this, most interviewers will be competent and experienced. They will display warmth, respect, and empathy for you, and they will be pleasant, practiced, and polite. They will ask you open-ended questions, giving you the opportunity to explain a subject such as a qualification or an experience. Open-ended questions allow a wide range of possible responses (Ivey, 1980). For example, which question would you prefer to answer: "What are some things you would like to tell me about your present job?" or "Do you like your current job?" The first question is open; it invites you to select any quality about your job that comes to mind. The second question is closed in that it calls for a yes-or-no response. Unless a follow-up question is asked or you are given a chance to volunteer an explanation, you may not be able to clarify your likes or dislikes. Not all closed questions are wrong. If a job-seeker talks too much, an interviewer may use a closed question to limit the length of the response.

Because questions often put people on the defensive, capable interviewers create opportunities for job candidates to expand and elaborate on topics under discussion. Simple expressions such as "That's interesting," "I see," "Tell me more," or even "Uh-huh" or nods of the head indicate the interviewer accepts your statements and encourages you to continue. Suppose you say, "I start rather slowly when I learn a new job, but when I know my work, I can do it without help from anyone else." The interviewer responds, "It takes a while for you to acquire new skills, but once you have, they stay with you for good." You feel accepted, listened to, and understood because the interviewer restated or paraphrased your thoughts using slightly different words. Suppose you describe an experience on a previous job by saying, "I appreciated my boss allowing me to try a new idea even though I did not foresee all the difficulties I would have." The interviewer replies, "You were grateful for your employer's support, particularly when the going got tough." Your emotional experience of gratitude is picked up and labeled by the interviewer, making you feel that you were heard, acknowledged, and interpreted correctly.

In a comfortable atmosphere, you may need to practice restraining yourself from giving too much information. Interviews are not confessionals; you can control how much information you want to reveal. Most interviewers are not trying to trick you into making painful or embarrassing disclosures. They want to help you communicate, obtain certain facts about your abilities and preparation, determine your motivation and personality characteristics, stimulate your interest in their organization, and then close the interview courteously and efficiently.

Types of Job Interviews

All job interviews involve evaluation of the applicant, but beyond this, they can be divided into several types. There are screening, structured, unstructured, group, board, stress, serial, and secondary interviews. Two or more types are often combined in a single interview. Analyzing each kind of job interview separately can give you a greater appreciation of this complex form of interaction.

Screening interview. The initial interview is often a screening device; the interviewer does not intend to select anyone for a position. The main purpose of a screening interview is to eliminate candidates who do not possess the necessary qualifications. Generally, interviews conducted in a college placement office are screening interviews. Your objective as a job candidate is to get invited to the subsequent (or selection) interview by competently presenting your abilities, preparation, and interests and by avoiding factors that can knock you out of the running. The screening interviewer will cover your qualifications and check the facts you have specified on your résumé and application form. Interviewers in this situation are under pressure. If they send unqualified job applicants to supervisors, their own competence becomes suspect, and they will be soon out of a job. You can try to determine ahead of time the factors on which you will be judged. In your informational interviewing, perhaps you can ask for a list of factors by which job candidates are evaluated. Typical rating checklists include items such as enthusiasm, initiative, maturity, leadership potential, appearance, communication skills, experience, technical skills, and education. Many personality traits are difficult to assess with any degree of accuracy. In fact, studies have indicated that there is almost no correlation between the factors rated on a checklist after an initial interview and the ratings of the same factors after a year's observation of job performance (Drake, 1982). Interviewers should evaluate only realistically observable behavior. You should find ways to avoid the screening interview, if possible. However, for most entry-level positions, there is probably no way around this type of interview.

Structured (or directed) interview.   The structured interview proceeds from a preselected list of questions that are asked of each job applicant. After all candidates have been interviewed, their answers are compared in an attempt to be as objective as possible. The interviewer makes notes about the applicant's responses or codes responses on a checklist. This type of interview can be impersonal due to its predetermined schedule of questions, but it is the type that is used most often in screening interviews. The more directed or structured an interview becomes, the more difficult it is to introduce your own information to the interviewer. You may feel as if you are caught in a lockstep procedure that allows no variation. You could politely interrupt the schedule of questions by saying, "If I could break into your pattern of questions for just a moment, I'd like to give you some additional material on this point." This statement should be carefully timed and not be said in such a way as to make the interviewer think you are trying to take control of the interview. Most interviewers, no matter how structured their procedure, will give you an opportunity to add your own comments and ask questions.

Unstructured (or nondirected) interview.   The questions in the unstructured interview are open-ended, which allows you to respond in many different ways. Open-ended questions give you the choice of how to respond; your answer is not directed by the way the question is asked. One favorite open-ended interview question is "Tell me about yourself." How do you respond? There are probably a half-million things you could say, but you must pick one of them. Even though the atmosphere is non-threatening, an unstructured interview can cause considerable anxiety. The ambiguity of the situation augments the tension, especially to unprepared job-seekers. The unstructured interview offers control of the interview to job applicants, some of whom do not want the responsibility. Interviewers may be more interested in the way you handle unstructured situations than in the content of your remarks. They use a nondirected approach because they believe it is possible to learn more about your personality characteristics this way. The more you are encouraged to talk in a job interview, the less structured the process is likely to be. Your goal, however, is no different from that in other types of interviews. You want to set forth your objectives, qualifications, and accomplishments as clearly as you can.

Group interview.   When there are many job applicants, the group interview may be used. The technique of the group interview originated in the military as a way of selecting officer candidates. A group was brought together, given a task to accomplish, and carefully watched. From individual interactions within the group, a leader would eventually emerge (Medley, 1978). In a business situation, a group of people is told to hold a discussion on a given topic. Again, the group is observed. Observers focus more on your behavior with other members of the group than on the actual words spoken. You may never experience this type of interview, but if you do, try to determine the characteristics the interviewers are looking for and direct your attention toward contributing to the functioning of the group.

Board interview.   The board interview brings in one job applicant to face many interviewers. The interviewers have rehearsed their roles before you enter. Let's say seven people are on the board. Six may ask questions, each one concentrating on his or her own area of interest, while one person watches only your nonverbal behavior. Nonverbal communication is body language, the way you express yourself without the use of words. The board interview is most likely to be used by an organization that is interviewing for a high-level position such as president or vice president. If you are ever in this interview situation, pretend you are talking to only one person, the one who is questioning you. In this way, you may forget the other eyes that are upon you and mentally convince yourself that you are in a simple one-on-one interview. By concentrating on one person at a time, you may appear more relaxed and maintain your confidence, the two important factors for this type of interview (Medley, 1978).

Stress interview.   Job interviews contain a certain amount of stress by their very nature. Some interviewers intentionally introduce stress into the interview to assess the candidate's reaction to pressure. Interviewers justify this approach when the job requires people who can cope with stress. They want to test an applicant's tolerance or resistance in high-pressure situations. The normal interview does not use artificially induced stress methods, so you are not likely to run into them. One stress technique is silence. You are answering questions, and suddenly the interviewer becomes very quiet and simply stares at you without saying a word. A few seconds can seem like hours of silence. If you start displaying nervousness and become obviously uncomfortable, you are flunking the test. To pass the test, sit quietly, look up and smile pleasantly, and keep your composure. After a reasonable time, you could ask, "Is there anything more we haven't covered?" or "Would you want me to expand on anything I've mentioned so far?" Other stress techniques include speaking in a stern voice, being unfriendly, challenging everything you say, dwelling on the same subject much longer than necessary, returning to the same issue time after time, increasing the pace of questioning, and allowing progressively less time to compose answers. Some questions involving negative or sensitive issues may be intended to provoke a stressful reaction. Consider these:

- Why aren't you earning a higher salary at your age?
- You certainly change jobs a lot. Have you had problems with them?
- In what ways do you think your supervisor could have done a better job?
- Your grades in school are rather low. Are you really suitable for the job?
- Did you know that the other job applicants have more experience than you have?

Try to imagine answering these questions when you are with friends. Request more time to answer. Reframe the question in such a way that you can introduce an ability that you can prove you have. Whatever you do, maintain your composure and keep in mind that the interviewer may be pushing you to see how you react.

Serial or successive interviews.   When you visit a company's home office for a day or two, you may be given a series of interviews with several interviewers, each one usually on a one-to-one basis. Treat each interviewer as if he or she were the first, establishing a good relationship with each one and repeating any information you may have already given with as much enthusiasm as you can muster. A final decision concerning your employment will be reached by a committee of those you met. The fact that you have gotten this far in the interviewing process indicates that you have been doing things right.

Secondary interview.   This is a follow-up interview to confirm impressions from the first interview. Any time you have more than one interview with the same person, it is important to be consistent in your responses. As with successive interviews, treat each one as if it were the first. You may grow tired of stating the same information several times, but don't let it show. Your most important interview will be with the person who would become your supervisor in the event you are hired (Rogers, 1982).

Before the Interview

1. *Learn as much as you can about the organization*—its products, its services, how large it is, its record of growth, its problems, relationships with its employees, and so on. Every professional job counselor and every piece of written material about interviewing gives this advice, but there are still many job-seekers who go into the job interview not knowing a thing about the company. If you are knowledgeable about the business and the concerns of the organization, you will be in a much better position to show how you can be of value to the employer.

Many companies prepare a fact sheet about themselves, print an annual report, and publish brochures about the kinds of job applicants they are seeking. They will send these publications to you at your request. Talk to insiders who work for the company or who know people working there. The library has business and industrial directories that give you names and data on organizations. Researching work organizations is thoroughly covered in Chapter 6 of this book.

Knowing some things about the organization will do wonders for your self-confidence as you approach the job interview. You will impress the employer or interviewer because you have taken the time to do your homework. Knowing enough about yourself to know who you are and what you want is very important, too; the interviewer could begin by inviting you to tell about yourself.

2. *Determine through your research of the organization and yourself what you can do for the employer and the organization.* Keep in mind that the employer's main interest is going to be what you can do for the organization, not what it can do for you. This is a time to review your past achievement experiences and how they translate into present skills and abilities that could be of use to the employer. Answers may come in the form of increased production, a more efficient way of doing things, a better way of getting people to work together, increased sales, or higher profits. Prepare yourself for this ahead of time; your primary job in the interview is to convince the employer that it is in the organization's best interests to hire you.

3. *Role-play mock interviews with a friend.* Rehearse what you want to say during the interview, but don't prepare a speech and memorize it. Get a friend or relative to role-play a mock interview, casting yourself as the job applicant and your friend as the job interviewer. The more practice you have, the more poise and self-confidence you will acquire for the interview. Prepare interview questions about such subjects as the content of the work, hours, and working conditions. Anticipate questions the interviewer might ask you. The interview is a two-way street in that it is a mutual exchange of information.

4. *Know exactly where you are to go for your appointment so you can arrive on time.* As simple as this sounds, you'd be surprised how many job-seekers get lost on their way to the job interview. Obtain the exact address, know how to get there, know the location of the building and room where you are supposed to appear, and allow enough time for travel to the interview site so you won't be late. Call the employer's secretary or receptionist if you are unsure of any of these details. Give yourself extra time to get there in case you encounter traffic jams, a train stops you, or you take a wrong turn. If you use public transportation, obtain the bus schedule and allow sufficient time for it. Arrive on time for your job interview; often, job-seekers come a few minutes early to take care of last-minute details.

5. *Take the following items with you to the job interview:*

    a. A pen. You may be asked to fill out an application form. You might ask if you can complete it at home, where you can take your time and respond carefully to the items.

b. Your résumé. Even though you may have already submitted one, take an extra copy of your résumé with you. The information on it is accurate and can be easily transferred to an application form.
c. A small notebook. You may not use it, but it will be there if you need to write down important information the employer gives you.
d. Your driver's license.
e. If you don't have a résumé, be sure you have on a reminder sheet your social security number, your birth record, a list of previous places of employment (including locations, dates of employment, names of supervisors or employers, and duties performed), educational record (names of schools, locations, dates of attendance, and degrees obtained), and references. Refer to the worksheet in Exercise 4-2 on pages 102–103.

6. *Learn the name and title of your interviewer.* You can ask for this information when you set up the interview. Though small, this amount of research on your part will still impress the interviewer or employer. "Nothing is more valuable to a person than his or her name." Second only to that would be a person's title.

7. *Dress appropriately for the interview.* Wear neutral, professional clothing and make sure it is clean and well pressed. Employers will assume they are seeing you at your best in terms of appearance. If you do not look your best, they will wonder, "How much worse can it get?" Your clothes say a lot about you before you open your mouth. The basic dark blue or gray business suit is preferred for most interview occasions. Casual clothing is all right for some situations, as long as it is clean and neat; but when in doubt, stay on the side of formality. Shoes must be polished and shined; black, cordovan, or dark brown are suggested colors.

Men should be shaved and have a neat haircut that conforms with current business standards. Those men with a beard or a mustache should have them neatly trimmed. The plain white shirt with a collar that fits comfortably is normally worn; a pale blue shirt is also acceptable. A good-quality tie, in colors that complement the suit and shirt, is recommended. Calf-length socks that match or complement the suit are advised; short socks that expose hairy legs detract from a job-seeker's appearance.

Women should avoid both flamboyant and ultrafeminine clothing as well as heavy makeup. If used, nail polish should be clear or lightly tinted; perfume should be minimal. Jewelry should not be overdone but suitable for business. Blouses should be simple; low-cut necklines are out. Skirts should be of moderate length. The best choice for shoes is the closed-toe pump with heels of average height. Purses should be coordinated with the outfit, and they should not be too large or overstuffed. Pants are not recommended. In the case of successive interviews with the same company, think of ways to combine your clothes for the sake of variety.

People generally look their best by dressing conservatively and being neatly groomed. Leave political buttons at home; they may get votes, but they don't get jobs. Avoid gum-chewing and smoking. Don't slouch in the chair if you have to wait a few minutes for the interviewer; you may be observed while you wait.

Some job-seekers may regard the subject of interview dress as rather ridiculous, but keep in mind that appearance is meaningful to most companies. In a survey conducted by John Molloy (1988), 93 percent of the executives in top corporations stated they would turn down people who showed up improperly dressed for a job interview on that basis alone. Since companies take their image seriously, the job interview is not the time to declare a personal statement of independence and nonconformity. It is a compliment to any organization that you thought enough of them to dress professionally. As a job-seeker you are also a product; package yourself well for the job market (LaFevre, 1989).

During the Interview

1. *Give the impression of optimism and energy when you first meet the interviewer.* Introduce yourself to the interviewer and address him or her as Mr., Ms., or Dr. and last name. Shake hands firmly, but don't crush bones or jerk the arm out of the socket. Indicate that you are pleased to meet the interviewer, but don't be gushy and come on too strong. Watch for an indication of where your are to sit. Sit down at the same time the interviewer does, not before. Be genuinely glad to meet this person; the interviewer could become a significant person in your life.

2. *Be aware of the importance of nonverbal communication.* Communication experts tell us that we transmit more information nonverbally than we do through words. In interviewing, you can adopt a posture of involvement with the interviewer. To do this, Gerard Egan (1975), a counselor-trainer, offers the acronym SOLER.

> S = Sit squarely, facing the other person, your back against the back of the chair, both feet on the floor, maintaining good posture. ("S" is not for "slouch.")
>
> O = Open position—crossed arms and crossed legs are often signs of lessened involvement. An open position is a nondefensive position.
>
> L = Lean slightly forward, at about a ten-degree angle. Again, this is a sign of involvement.
>
> E = Eye contact—look directly (but don't stare rigidly) at the interviewer most of the time. ("E" doesn't mean "evasiveness.")
>
> R = Remain relatively relaxed—which means not fidgeting nervously or engaging in exaggerated facial expressions, but rather feeling natural with your body as an instrument of communication. In-

volvement has a kind of tension about it that is balanced with being comfortable in contact with other people. Relaxation gives you the "living space" you need to listen adequately and respond fully. The SOLER rules are not commandments to be rigidly applied in all cases; rather, they are guidelines to help you establish yourself physically with the interviewer (Egan, 1975).

Eye contact is an important element of nonverbal behavior. It should be established from the very beginning of the interview. Look directly at the interviewer whenever he or she is speaking. It's all right to look away for a short time while you are talking, but bring your vision back to the interviewer as you finish answering a question or making a point. People tend to draw assumptions about eye contact or the lack of it. Looking away from a speaker indicates that you are concealing a reaction or are displeased with the interviewer. Looking away while you are talking may mean you are uncertain of yourself; looking at the listener signals confidence in what you are saying. Looking at a speaker conveys agreement with the words being expressed (Medley, 1978). However, eye contact should not be overdone, because staring at the interviewer is distracting, annoying, and unnatural. We mention these features of nonverbal communication because of its potential to undercut the impression you want to make.

3. *Learn to control nervousness through preparation, good health, and understanding that some nervousness is to be expected.* Everything you have done in your job search leads to the moment you face a person who can hire you. You realize that all can be wasted if you don't handle things properly, and this knowledge creates the high tension often associated with the job interview. You may worry about the nervousness you're likely to exhibit. Four points about controlling nervousness can be mentioned here. First, interviewers accept applicants' nervousness as normal behavior and as a sign of interest in the job position. You wouldn't be nervous if you didn't care. As the interview goes on, nervousness tends to diminish or disappear entirely. Second, the more you prepare for the interview, the more you put yourself in control of things. That is likely to reduce your nervousness about the interview itself. Preparation is the key to self-confidence in this situation. Third, remember that interviewers and employers are under pressure, too. They must discover and hire good people, or else their business suffers. Fourth, get a good night's sleep before the interview. More important than this, though, is the long-term maintenance of good health habits. Exercise every day, eat right, and average seven or eight hours of sleep per night.

4. *Be sincere, brief, and truthful in your replies to the interviewer's questions.* If you are less than honest in your answers, you begin to create a fantasy world of fabrications that may come back to haunt you later. Bluffing is easily spotted by skilled interviewers, and it will rub out your chances of getting a good job. It indicates a lack of self-confidence. Don't say you can do something when you know you cannot. Claim a skill only when you can

back it up with proof that you have used it to accomplish something. If you know yourself, you know what you can do and the kind of contribution you can make to the employer's organization. Avoid talking too much; answer questions briefly and to the point. Focus attention on strengths and past successes. You don't have to volunteer information on weaknesses, but if you are asked a question on them, indicate what you are doing to overcome any shortcomings.

5. *Ask questions about the position and the organization.* They will reflect an interest in the job you are seeking and in the organization you are hoping to join. Asking intelligent questions is one of the easiest ways of impressing an employer. Some of your questions can relate to salaries and fringe benefits, but be sure to balance these concerns with other questions about the nature and content of the work itself and the responsibilities you will be expected to assume. That way you'll avoid the impression that you're interested only in what you take from the organization rather than what you can give. Suggestions for questions you could ask an employer will appear later in this chapter.

6. *Anticipate a discussion about desired salary.* You are well into the job interview and the employer seems interested in you, but no discussion about pay has taken place. In this situation, you have every right to inquire about what salary to expect and to determine whether the amount of money offered for the job is satisfactory. However, a discussion of salary is likely to occur without your bringing up the subject. How would you handle the question, "What salary do you expect"? This can be a scary question. If you state a figure that is too high, you may price yourself out of a job you want because the employer thinks you are unreasonable. If you state a figure that is on the low end of the employer's range, it might be accepted and, later, you'll discover that you have cost yourself some money through your ignorance. A little research could have informed you about the high side of the employer's salary range. If you haven't done your homework on the organization, you'll have to say, "I'll take the going rate," and then hope for the best. That lackadaisical approach could cost you a considerable amount of money, when you think of the cumulative effects of starting at a lower salary.

7. *A few "don'ts" for the job interview:*

    a. Avoid the overly smooth, ultracool, "no sweat" impression; interviewers don't appreciate con artists.

    b. Don't criticize or come down hard on previous employers or work associates. If you can't say anything good about them, say nothing. Employers may wonder if you'll give them the same treatment later on.

    c. Avoid running yourself down. Don't volunteer weaknesses or liabilities, but be prepared to discuss them if asked. Focus on your past accomplishments.

d. Don't discuss controversial subjects; the job interview isn't the place for them.

e. Avoid giving flat "yes" or "no" answers. Direct the conversation toward your goals, strengths, and achievements.

f. Don't overdo your need for a new job. Anxiety may be interpreted as desperation.

g. Don't be pressured into taking a job at a lower level than you want. Two weeks later, you may be looking for another job.

h. Don't overstay your welcome. The interviewer will probably give you some cues when it's time to leave. Better to leave a couple of things unsaid than to put the interviewer seriously behind schedule. Thank the interviewer for the time spent with you. Reassure him or her that you really want the job.

After the Interview

1. *Evaluate the interview as soon as you can.* Before your impressions of the interview fade from memory, critically examine the process you have just experienced. Try to review your performance immediately after the interview, if possible. There are several factors to judge.

- *First impressions.* Did you greet the interviewer or employer with a sense of energy and a feeling of optimism? Were you dressed appropriately? Did you establish eye contact immediately? How relaxed did you feel?
- *Preparation.* Were you adequately prepared for the interview? Did you know enough about the organization? Did you know the name and title of the interviewer? Were you able to anticipate some of the questions that were asked? Had you rehearsed answers to these questions?
- *Communication.* Did you fail to communicate any information you wanted to get across to the employer? Did you communicate your job objective, why you want the job, and your work values and abilities? Did you discover the nature of the work you would be expected to perform?
- *Questions.* What questions did you ask? Did you leave out anything you wanted to ask?
- *Responses.* Which questions from the employer did you answer well? With which questions did you have difficulty? How well did you handle questions that probed weaknesses or desired salary? Were you able to neutralize weaknesses or turn limitations into positive statements?
- *Other impressions.* What kind of an impression did you make on or leave with the employer? Identify the parts of the interview in which you believe you made your strongest impressions. When do you think you may have given negative impressions? Did you thank the employer for the interview?
- *Next steps.* Did you find out what happens next? How soon will the employer contact you? Is there anything you should do in the meantime?

- *Improvement.* What would you do differently if you could hold the interview again? How can you improve your interview style and presentation?

2. *Write a thank-you letter within three days after the interview,* regardless of the outcome of your application. State your appreciation for the interviewer's interest and time spent. This courtesy will lead the employer to think of you as a thoughtful and conscientious person. Restate your interest in the position and the organization. Remind the employer of the job for which you interviewed and the date and location of the interview. Clarify anything from the interview that will help persuade the employer of your worth. Add a new point of information about yourself if it is revelant or needed. Keep the thank-you letter brief; three or four lines is sufficient. Refer to Figure 3-10 in Chapter 3 for an example of a thank-you letter.

3. *Follow up.* As the need for a thank-you letter indicates, your campaign for a job with a particular organization does not end with the employment interview. Probably, the employer or personnel manager has promised to get in touch with you. It's easy to think: "I've done all I can do about the job opening, so now I'll wait and hope I get a job offer." Meanwhile, the employer is talking with other candidates and screening other résumés and applications. The hiring function is probably sandwiched in with a dozen other activities that make up the employer's working day. As the hours and days tick away, the memory of your interview recedes further in the employer's consciousness. Anything you can do to reinforce the favorable image of things that went right or to correct any mistaken impressions will bring you back into awareness, if only for a moment. When you haven't heard anything within the time frame established at the interview, you can get in contact with the employer by telephone, drop-in visit, or follow-up letter. Don't ask whether a decision has been made yet; offer a new insight into a problem the employer is facing or ask two or three more questions that have come to mind since the interview. If you are truly interested in the organization, you will continue to learn about it, and your follow-up insights and questions to the employer will demonstrate this. Of course, no follow-up technique is a foolproof guarantee of a job offer. The employer might not have made a decision yet, or you could be turned down. However, you have strengthened your relationship with the employer and increased your chances of being offered a job. Persist without being a pest. A good follow-up strategy will increase your chances of receiving a job offer by 30 percent or more (Jackson, 1991).

4. *Acceptance of a job offer.* If the job is offered to you, notify the employer as soon as you have decided to accept. Assume that you don't have an offer until you get one in writing. Some offers contain a time limit for acceptance, after which the offer will be withdrawn. If no time limit is given, one or two weeks is usually considered sufficient time to decide whether to accept or reject an offer. If you can't make up your mind, ask the employer for an extension of time and state why you need more time to make a decision.

Your acceptance letter constitutes an employment agreement. Confirm the details of the job offer. Inform the employer when you intend to report for work, unless that date has already been established, and express your pleasure and enthusiasm for the opportunity. Refer to Figure 3-12 for an example of an acceptance letter. Also, write a thank-you letter to those people who agreed to act as references for you.

5. *Declining a job offer.* If you decide not to accept a job offer, write a courteous letter informing the employer of your decision. Express appreciation of the employer's consideration, and give the reasons for your decision. You may want to apply to the same employer at some future date, so you will want to be remembered favorably. Should you accept another job position before hearing from the employer, you should immediately inform the employer as well as the person who referred you. Refer to Figure 3-13 for an example of a letter declining a job offer.

6. *If you did not get the job,* think through your interview and try to discover what you could have done better. Most job-seekers experience plenty of rejections, so don't become discouraged. Stay open to all the techniques of the job search. The important thing is to keep trying.

Questions Frequently Asked in Job Interviews

How would you answer the following questions in a job interview? Rehearse your responses with a friend. Assume you have the necessary qualifications and preparation.

Questions About Personal Characteristics and Opinions of Yourself

- Tell me about yourself. Describe yourself as a person.
- What kind of people do you prefer to work with? Why?
- What type of people are the most difficult for you to work with? Why?
- What basic qualities of work motivate you most? Why?
- What aspects of work and life give you the greatest satisfaction? Why?
- What kinds of activities do you feel most confident in doing? Why?
- Describe an obstacle, either inside or outside yourself, that you have had to overcome. How did you do it?
- Describe an incident or a situation in which you fought or would fight for something you deeply believed and valued.
- How would a person who knows you well describe you?
- What motivates you to put forth your greatest effort? Illustrate your response using an occasion in which this happened.
- Which characteristics of yours do you think need to be strengthened? Why?
- Describe your greatest achievement.

- What two or three accomplishments have given you the greatest satisfaction? Why?
- Which historical or public figures do you admire most? Why?
- Which magazines do you read regularly? What do you like about them?
- Name a book you have read in the past year. Why did you read it?

Questions About Decisions, Goals, and the Future

- What motivated you to choose the career field for which you are preparing?
- Describe your long-term career goals and how you are preparing to achieve them.
- What do you see yourself doing five years from now?
- If you had complete freedom, you would choose a different occupation from the one you have chosen. What would it be? Why?
- What goals outside your career have you established for yourself?
- What would be your next step if we were to hire you for this job?
- What salary range would you consider appropriate for the job?
- What are your salary requirements or expectations?
- What do you expect to be earning in five years?
- Which is more important to you: the money or the nature of the work on the job?
- What would you really most like to do with your life?

Questions About Abilities, Qualifications, and Skills

- Why should I hire you? What can you do for us?
- Tell me about any natural talents you have that other people, such as teachers, parents, relatives, or friends, have talked about.
- What do you believe are your strongest skills and aptitudes? How would they help you on the job you are seeking?
- In what ways do you think you can make a contribution to our company?
- How do your qualifications and preparation fit the requirements for this job?
- If you were hiring a person for this job, what qualities would you look for?
- What are the reasons for the successes you have experienced in your occupation?
- Describe a situation in which you worked under a lot of pressure.
- What kinds of activities or assignments have you felt most confident doing?
- What qualities or strengths do you have that would be helpful to our organization?
- Give the names of three people with whom we can check as references for you.

Questions About Education and Training Experiences

- What is the most important thing you have learned in your education?
- Tell me about any experiences in school or college of which you are particularly proud.
- How difficult was school/college for you? Which subjects were the easiest/hardest and why?
- Do your grades in school reflect your true ability? Why or why not?
- If you had an opportunity to live your school or college years again, what would you do differently? Why?
- What was your college major? Why did you choose it?
- What have you learned from your school or college experiences that will help you in your working or adult life?
- Describe your plans for continued study, degrees, or efforts to improve your skills.
- What did you learn from your extracurricular activities that you could carry over into your adult life?
- Do you believe your school and college experience has prepared you for your career? Why or why not?

Questions About Work Experiences

- Which full-time, part-time, or summer jobs have held the greatest interest for you? Why?
- Describe the biggest crisis in your work experience. How did you deal with it?
- What were the major difficulties and drawbacks in your last job?
- What kind of people do you prefer to work with? What is there about these people that makes them easy to work with?
- What have you done in your previous jobs to become better accepted by your work associates?
- What accomplishments in your previous work experience were recognized by your supervisors or managers?
- Give an example of a problem you encountered when working and explain what you did about it.
- What are the most significant qualities you are looking for in an employer?
- What has been the most (or least) promising job you have ever held? How did it turn out? Explain your feelings about it.
- What were some aspects of your job performance that a supervisor believed you could improve upon?
- (If you are now working): Why are you considering leaving your present job?
- What is there about this job that appears better than your current (or previous) job(s)?

Questions About Work Organizations, Job Positions, and Geographical Areas

- Why are you interested in joining our organization?
- What would you like to ask me about the organization?
- Will you relocate? Are you willing to go wherever the company sends you?
- Would you accept a temporary job with the company? Why?
- We are not able to pay you the salary you should have. Will you accept a lower pay rate and work up to the figure you believe you should have?
- Describe your ideal job.
- What would you do to improve the quality of work in this company?
- What kind of working conditions/atmosphere/culture/environment do you prefer? Why?
- When can you start work?
- How long do you plan to stay with our organization?
- I've asked you a lot of questions. Do you have any questions for me?

More Responses to Interview Questions

Answers to six basic interview questions were discussed at the beginning of the Job Interview section of this chapter. Here are six more questions, with ideas for responding to these inquiries should they be asked during your job interview.

Tell me about yourself.   What would you say? Do you talk about your favorite person, the weather, or pet cockatoo? Before your interview, think about how you would respond to open-ended questions such as this one. If you lack preparation, they can throw you off balance. The interviewer is directing you to say something, but the subject is not specified. Of the thousands of topics you could bring up, the one you choose is assumed to be of great importance to you. One strategy is to ask the interviewer to be more specific. You might ask, "What part of my background is of greatest interest to you?" If the interviewer still gives you nothing on which to focus, talk about a strength or qualification for the job. You can bring up an outstanding achievement experience, a list of skills you can deliver to the job, or how well your preparation fits the needs of the organization. You could communicate your desire and enthusiasm for the work or how your values will motivate you to perform with excellence on the job. This question gives you a tremendous opportunity to steer the interview toward subjects you want to emphasize, so you definitely should prepare for it.

What are your weaknesses?   There is no reason for you to volunteer negative points about yourself, but if you are asked to list any, accept responsibility for them, explain what you have learned from them, and indicate what you are trying to do about them. Do not dwell on excuses for a weakness; they will never help your performance in a job interview. Turn any weakness into a statement an employer or interviewer could identify with. "I sometimes get impatient with others when I am trying to get a job done." What employer hasn't felt the same way? "I usually show up at work when I have a bad cold and should have stayed at home." While others would rather not share your cold, what employer is going to consider your dedication to work a negative trait? If you must discuss a weakness, explain the steps you are taking to overcome it. "When I get frustrated by the lack of progress on a job, I remind myself to exercise patience with others so we can pull together and get the work done." If the interviewer keeps pressing for more limitations, you can say that every person has some weaknesses and you are no exception, but they are not so important that they get in the way of your performance on the job.

How did you get along with your former supervisor or boss? How did you respond to any criticism of your work made by a supervisor or employer?   Such questions may be the interviewer's way of trying to discover faults or weaknesses, or how thin-skinned or teachable you are. Indicate that you listened carefully to the criticism, evaluated it, and resisted any temptation to defend yourself at the time. If the advice was constructive and reasonably presented, you could say that you appreciated the helpful concern of your supervisor. Emphasize your willingness to learn from your mistakes and to cooperate with your employer in doing your job better. Do not berate or jump all over a former employer, even when you believe you have just cause. Employers have a tendency to see eye to eye with other employers. While you are raking a previous boss over the coals and think you are scoring points with your righteous indignation, the interviewer may be thinking, "If you can say this about a former employer, you could do the same thing to us later." People who complain about previous work organizations are more likely to be perceived as potential troublemakers. Just mention that you respected your former boss as a professional and you appreciated your former supervisor's guidance, and let it go at that.

Why did you leave your last job (or any previous jobs)?   An interviewer often probes with this type of question to find out whether you had any problem with a company or caused any trouble. There are plausible reasons for leaving a job. For example, another job offered a greater challenge, a higher salary, a more convenient location if the previous commute was too time-consuming, or an opportunity more in line with your career goals. Other believable reasons to leave a job are to raise a family or return to school. Perhaps there was no possibility of further advancement; as long as you stayed in the old job, you weren't going anywhere. Your position might have been eliminated, or you might have been laid off due to the nature of the local economy, or perhaps the company was not generating new work. Basically, you want to reassure the interviewer that you left a job to improve yourself, to be happier, or to be more effective in your work—not because of something horrible that happened.

Have you ever been fired from a job? If you haven't been fired, your answer is obviously "no." If this has happened to you, don't lie. It is an established fact, so stick to the truth. Cold, hard facts can be easily checked. Being fired is a rather common experience, and your interviewer might silently commiserate with you. Instead of using the words "I was fired," say "I was let go," which means essentially the same thing but lessens the impact. If losing your job was your fault, be strong enough to admit it. Then, immediately indicate that you have matured and learned from your mistakes. You have taken steps to correct whatever the problem was, so the reason you were let go is no longer a concern. If you feel you were unfairly treated, refrain from telling your interviewer what a louse your ex-boss was. You could say that you were interested in making some improvements or being more efficient on the old job, but not everyone saw it that way. The interviewer is likely to respect you for not bad-mouthing a previous employer with whom you have a grievance. If your company was bought out by another organization, perhaps you could explain that the new owners had completely different ideas on how to do things (Hellman, 1986).

What kind of job are you seeking? What do you want to be doing five years from now? The interviewer wants to know whether you are just drifting aimlessly from one job to another or whether the job opening is a logical part of a larger career pattern. Your answer should demonstrate that you have definite career objectives and have well-planned long-term and short-term goals. Stating your career goals and objectives implies your desire to achieve and perform with excellence on the job. Employers are always looking for motivated employees. Emphasize your commitment to your occupational choice and your willingness to stay with the organization. One of the worst answers to this question is "anything." Most employers interpret this as a sign of indecision, indifference, and instability.

There are no final or perfect answers to suggest because each interviewer and interview is unique. Many of your responses will be prompted by your research on the company and the people who work in it. Any questions about your private life are considered out of bounds. Some interviewers try to justify the invasion of your personal life on the grounds that they want to make sure your private life will not interfere with your work life. Your answer can indicate that you are applying for the job because it is work you want to do, and your personal life will not get in the way of your occupational life. Speak evenly, without getting angry. If the interviewer keeps asking personal questions, reconsider whether you are interested in working for the organization.

Suggested Questions You Can Ask as a Job Applicant

Even though you are being screened and evaluated in the job interview, you should still make it an exchange of information. There is no reason to stop assessing the organization. Always be on the lookout for factors that would make the company a poor choice for you. In a structured interview, you may be asked to wait until the end to ask your questions. Specific inquiries should vary from one organization to another. Prepare some questions ahead of time; more will certainly come to mind during the interview. Focus your questions on the job and the nature of the work at first. The interviewer may feel you are rather narrow-minded and self-serving if you ask only about pay, benefits, and vacations.

A "starter list" of questions is printed below. Of course, you should add your own concerns to these suggested questions.

1. What are the characteristics of the people your organization or department usually hires?
2. What is the growth potential for the company? What new products or services are being planned?
3. Is there a job description of the available position? If so, may I see it? What are typical assignments or responsibilities in this job?
4. Is the job a new position? If not, who was the person on this job before he or she left and what is that person doing now?
5. What traits are you looking for in a person you expect to hire for this position?
6. What is management's policy or practice regarding promoting people from within the organization?
7. How will (the economy, a recent governmental action, a strike, the weather, a materials shortage, and so on) affect the operation of the organization (or department)?
8. What efforts are being made to improve (a situation you know about in production, construction, inventory, supply, accounting, management, technical details, and so on)?
9. How much responsibility would I have in (planning, budgeting, decision-making, and so on)?
10. Will I be required to travel extensively on the job? How much time would I spend away from the home location?
11. How would you describe working conditions here? (Specific items could be hours, overtime, noise factor, work setting, company policies, and the like.)
12. Do you have an organizational chart for the company (or department)? Where would I fit in?
13. Who would be my immediate supervisor? Will I have an opportunity to speak with that person before a hiring decision is made?

14. What kind of formal training program does the organization operate? (If one exists, ask about its length and type.)
15. What is the schedule of salary increases in the company, assuming job performance is satisfactory?
16. How would my performance on the job be evaluated? How often are performance reviews given?
17. Where do people who work for the company live? What housing arrangements exist in the community?
18. When could I expect you to contact me? (If a job offer is made:) May I let you know by (date)?

Keep going. Other questions can be asked at appropriate times. You should not ask: "Do I get the job?" Questions like this one put interviewers on the spot, and you will only hear that they have other job candidates to talk with. You will have made yourself look overly anxious and gained nothing in the process.

Interview Knockout Factors: Reasons Job Applicants Are Rejected

- Job goals and objectives not well defined; lack of career planning
- Achievement motivation not evident; no record of achievement experiences to support the skills claimed
- Not prepared for the interview; failure to research the organization
- No real interest in the job vacancy or in the work organization
- Interested only in the money and benefits; unrealistic salary demands
- Inadequate knowledge of the job position or the occupation
- Little or no social poise; inability to communicate clearly
- Disrespectful, rude, coarse; lack of tact, courtesy, and civility
- Poor personal appearance; poor posture; lack of eye contact
- No sense of humor; lack of enthusiasm; indifference, passive attitude
- Not able to take constructive or well-meant criticism
- No evidence of handling responsibility, leadership, or initiative
- Belittles and disparages previous employers and supervisors
- Expects too much too soon; job expectations are unrealistic
- Makes excuses for unfavorable comments on records, such as poor work habits
- Education or previous work experience has no relevance to job being sought
- Asks no questions or poor questions about the job or the organization
- Late to interview without plausible reason
- Attitude of "What can you do for me?"

These characteristics must be turned around for the interview to be successful.

EXERCISE 8-2   *Role-Played Job Interview*

Work in groups of three. One person will be the job applicant, another person will be the interviewer or employer, and the third person will be the observer, who evaluates the interview on a rating form. The job interview in this role-playing exercise will probably last about ten minutes. Then take about five minutes for the applicant and interviewer to discuss the interview and for the observer to evaluate it. When this process is completed, change roles and continue with the next two interviews.

Directions to the Job Applicant

1. You are applying for a job. Make it a job in your Number One occupational prospect at the present time. Assume you have the necessary training and qualifications for the position you are seeking. Give the interviewer your completed résumé and/or job application form from Chapters 3 and 4.

2. Answer questions asked by the interviewer honestly and sincerely. Say what needs to be said, but avoid talking too much. Think of reasons for the employer to hire you or for the interviewer to recommend you for another interview.

3. Ask questions of the interviewer. Determine the information you need to know about the organization and the position you are seeking.

Directions to the Interviewer

1. Determine the position the applicant is seeking and the name or type of organization you represent. Obtain a copy of the applicant's résumé and/or job application form and ask questions about them if you wish.

2. Ask questions of the job applicant from the list of questions found in an earlier section, Questions Frequently Asked in Job Interviews. Ask at least two questions from each group; cover personal characteristics, decisions and goals, abilities and qualifications, education and training, work experiences, and work organizations and geographical areas, for a total of at least 12 questions. Feel free to improvise on these questions or to create your own questions if you prefer.

3. The job applicant should ask you some questions about the job and the organization. Since you are role-playing, simply make up your answers as best you can. Use any knowledge you have about the job or organization, or use your imagination as creatively as you can when you answer the applicant's questions.

Directions to the Observer

1. Make sure the job applicant identifies the title of the position or occupation and the name or type of organization before the interview begins. Record the names of the applicant and interviewer, as well as your own name as observer.

2. Observe the job interview. If the interview is recorded on videotape or audiotape, you will have the opportunity to replay the taped interview.

3. Evaluate the role-played job interview on one of the rating forms that follow on the next two pages. Use the rating form from the applicant's book, or use a photocopied or mimeographed rating form. Give the rating form to the job applicant at the end of your evaluation. Since the role-played interview is for practice, be critical in your evaluation. You will do no favor to the applicant if you ignore or overlook any mistakes he or she made. Now is the time to correct them. At the time of a real job interview, it will be too late to work on weak points of the job applicant's interviewing style.

Summary

1. A job interview is a different situation than an informational interview in that all parties know you are a candidate for a job opening. All kinds of questions will be asked of you: the reasons you are interested in a particular job in the particular organization, your qualifications and preparation, whether you will fit into the company's work environment, and desired salary or wages. In other words: Why are you here? What can you do for us? Will you fit in? What will you cost us? You should always ask questions of the interviewer for further information, demonstrating your interest about the organization. Of course, nothing should keep you from acquiring more information about the organization after the job interview or from continuing to evaluate that information.

2. There are many types of interviewers. Most are competent, courteous, and professional. Unfortunately, a few add needless stress to an already stressful situation. Skilled interviewers ask more *open* than *closed* questions, enabling job applicants to express themselves more freely. Capable interviewers encourage you to expand on your comments by listening carefully, rephrasing your statements, and reflecting your feelings accurately. These interview techniques aid communication, but you must be careful not to reveal more information than you intend to give.

3. There are several types of job interviews: screening, structured, unstructured, group, board, stress, serial, and subsequent interviews. Some types can be combined with other types in a single interview. Job offers are unlikely to be made in the first interview, which is typically a screening session.

4. Before the job interview, you should learn all you can about the orga-

Job Interview Rating Sheet

Name of Job
Applicant _____

Rating key for each item:

Name of
Interviewer _____

2 points = Excellent or Good on this subject;
would not be a problem in a job interview.

Name of
Observer _____

1 point = Fair, but needs improvement;
could be a problem in a job interview.

Job Position
Sought _____

0 points = Poor, needs much improvement;
will be a serious problem unless corrected.

Name or Type
of Work
Organization _____

First Impression/Dress/Clear Speech   **Points**
1. Applicant gives <u>feeling of optimism and energy</u> when first meeting
   the interviewer.   1. _____
2. Applicant has completed <u>résumé</u> or <u>job application form.</u>   2. _____
3. Applicant is <u>groomed well;</u> is neatly and <u>appropriately dressed.</u>   3. _____
4. Applicant <u>talks clearly and distinctly;</u> words are not mumbled.   4. _____

Nonverbal Behavior/Body Language
5. Applicant <u>sits squarely</u> in chair; has good posture.   5. _____
6. Applicant maintains <u>open position</u> (arms not crossed, and so on). 6. _____
7. Applicant <u>leans slightly forward</u> (about ten degrees).   7. _____
8. Applicant establishes good <u>eye contact</u> throughout interview.   8. _____
9. Applicant appears <u>relatively relaxed;</u> maintains poise.   9. _____

Content of Job Interview
10. Applicant communicates <u>job objective</u> to interviewer or employer. 10. _____
11. Applicant expresses <u>work values</u> explaining why job is wanted.   11. _____
12. Applicant makes known <u>abilities</u> relevant to job being sought.   12. _____
13. Applicant relates past <u>achievements</u> to skills used on the job.   13. _____
14. Applicant demonstrates <u>interest and enthusiasm</u> for the job.   14. _____
15. Applicant <u>answers</u> interviewer's <u>questions with confidence.</u> 15. _____
16. Applicant <u>neutralizes weaknesses</u> or turns them into positives.   16. _____
17. Applicant <u>asks questions</u> about the job and work organization.   17. _____
18. Applicant <u>avoids flat "yes" or "no" answers</u> to questions.   18. _____

Closing the Interview
19. Applicant learns when <u>interviewer will contact him or her</u>
    about hiring decision.   19. _____
20. Applicant <u>thanks interviewer</u> by name for the job interview.   20. _____

Observer: Rate each item and add the points you gave the
job applicant. Give this rating form to the applicant.   **Total Points** _____

36–40 points: You're hired!!!
30–35 points: You may get the job, but other candidates are in the running, too!!
20–29 points: Your getting the job is doubtful; you need more interview practice!
11–19 points: Not likely to get the job; much more interview practice is needed.
0–10 points: No job; you definitely need to do much more hard work on preparation and
                planning for job interviews and career planning in general.

Comments:

Job Interview Rating Sheet
(modified for classroom use)

Name of Job
Applicant _____

Rating key for each item:

Name of
Interviewer _____

2 points = Excellent or Good; this subject
would not be a problem in a job interview.

Name of
Observer _____

1 point = Fair or Average but needs improvement;
could be a problem in a job interview.

Job Position
Sought _____

0 points = Poor, needs much improvement;
will be a serious problem unless corrected.

Name or Type
of Work
Organization _____

Content of Job Interview   **Points**
   1. Applicant communicates <u>job objective</u> to interviewer.   1. _____
   2. Applicant expresses <u>work values</u> explaining why job is wanted.   2. _____
   3. Applicant makes known <u>abilities</u> relevant to job being sought.   3. _____
   4. Applicant relates past <u>achievements</u> to skills used on the job.   4. _____
   5. Applicant <u>asks questions</u> about the job and work organization.   5. _____
   6. Applicant <u>neutralizes weaknesses</u> or turns them into positives.   6. _____
   7. Applicant <u>avoids flat "yes" or "no" answers</u> to questions.   7. _____

Nonverbal Behavior/Body Language
   8. Applicant <u>sits squarely</u> in chair; has good posture.   8. _____
   9. Applicant maintains <u>open position</u> (arms not crossed, and so on).   9. _____
  10. Applicant <u>leans slightly forward</u> (about ten degrees).   10. _____
  11. Applicant establishes good <u>eye contact</u> throughout interview.   11. _____
  12. Applicant appears <u>relatively relaxed</u>; maintains poise.   12. _____

Other features of the Job Interview
  13. Applicant demonstrates <u>interest and enthusiasm</u> for the job.   13. _____
  14. Applicant <u>talks clearly and distinctly</u>; words are not mumbled.   14. _____
  15. Applicant learns when interviewer will contact him or her
       about hiring decision and thanks interviewer for the job interview.   15. _____
       (Good grooming and appropriate dress are assumed in this exercise.)

Observer: Rate each item and add the points you gave the
job applicant. Give this rating form to the applicant.   Total Points _____

26–30 points: You're hired!!!
21–25 points: You may get the job, but other candidates are in the running, too!!
16–20 points: Your getting the job is doubtful; you need more interview practice!
11–15 points: Not likely to get the job; much more interview practice is needed.
 0–10 points: No job; you definitely need to do much more hard work on preparation and
                planning for job interviews and career planning in general.

Comments:

nization, determine through your research what you can do for the employer, anticipate questions and rehearse your answers, know exactly where the interview is to be held, take pen and résumé with you, learn the name and title of the interviewer, and dress appropriately.

5. During the interview, show energy and optimism to make a good first impression, be aware of your nonverbal communication, control nervousness through proper preparation, respond to questions honestly and sincerely, ask questions, and handle salary and benefits from a base of researched information.

6. After the interview, evaluate your experience as soon as possible, write a thank-you letter, and follow up with a telephone call or drop-in visit (or a letter if you have not been notified of the decision within the time limits set up at the interview). If you don't get the job, persist in your efforts. Keep learning, and keep working to improve your job search skills.

References

Drake, J. D. (1982). *Interviewing for managers: A complete guide to employment interviewing* (rev. ed.). New York: AMACOM (a division of American Management Association).

Egan, G. (1975). *The skilled helper.* Pacific Grove, CA: Brooks/Cole.

Hellman, P. (1986). *Ready, aim, you're hired! How to job-interview successfully anytime, anywhere, and with anyone.* New York: AMACOM (a division of American Management Association).

Holland, J. L. (1985). *Making vocational choices: A theory of vocational personalities and work environments* (2nd ed.). Englewood Cliffs, NJ: Prentice-Hall.

Ivey, A. E., with Simek-Downing, L. (1980) *Counseling and psychotherapy: Skills, theories, and practice.* Englewood Cliffs, NJ: Prentice-Hall.

Jackson, T. (1991). *Guerrilla tactics in the new job market* (2nd ed.). New York: Bantam Books.

LaFevre, J. L. (1989). *How you really get hired: Straight talk for college students from a corporate recruiter.* New York: Arco.

Medley, H. A. (1978). *Sweaty palms: The neglected art of being interviewed.* Belmont, CA/North Scituate, MA: Lifetime Learning Publications.

Molloy, J. T. (1988). *John T. Molloy's new dress for success.* New York: Warner Books.

Rogers, E. J. (1982). *Getting hired: Everything you need to know about resumes, interviews, and job-hunting strategies.* Englewood Cliffs, NJ: Prentice-Hall.

Wright, J. W. (1990). *The American almanac of jobs and salaries* (rev. ed.). New York: Avon.

9

Into the Working World

You have learned a lot about job search strategies, sources of job leads, writing résumés and cover letters, completing applications, researching work organizations, and interviewing for information and jobs. What remains? In this chapter, we will answer two questions. When you have received several job offers, how do you evaluate them? When you accept an offer, how do you keep the job and cope with its problems? These questions deserve your attention. After a successful job search, some people fail to consider the equally important subjects of appraising job offers, keeping a job, and managing the problems of work. Reading this chapter will help you anticipate situations you will experience in the future and make you better prepared for them.

Evaluating Job Offers

When your job search campaign succeeds in producing offers of new job positions, you have important decisions to make. In the case of a single job offer, the question is whether or not to take the job. With two or more job offers, the question becomes which one to choose. It's a nice problem to have, but a dilemma nonetheless. This is a time to continue acquiring information about the positions being offered to you.

Several circumstances must be considered when you seek further information. For example, fringe benefits may turn a lower salary into a higher total compensation package in the long run. A lower beginning salary may be offset by more frequent salary increases in the salary schedule. A growing organization is more likely to create advancement opportunities than a company that is standing relatively still. An organization that promotes from within is better for your advancement chances than one that relies on outsiders to fill higher level positions. Consider the ages of your supervisors and co-workers; if they are close to retirement, your advancement possibilities may be enhanced. Lateral moves into related departments could hold greater opportunities for advancement. If you are thinking about job security, examine the layoff history of the company; some companies are quick to trim the number of employees during economic downturns. The important point is that you must persevere in your information-gathering activities in order to make proper evaluations of organizations that offer you jobs.

To help you evaluate job offers, two lists of factors to consider are presented, one for a single job offer and the other for two or more job offers. Examine these lists now to identify factors you should examine when you evaluate job positions. Use the lists when actual job offers come your way.

Evaluating One Job Offer

Answer each question with a *plus* when you feel positive, a *minus* when you feel negative, and a *zero* when your feelings are neutral or the question does not apply to you. No score can tell you exactly what decision to make, but avoid or beware of job offers that have a negative tally for a total score. Question and be cautious of those that total between one and ten on the plus side, and carefully consider job offers that score over ten points.

_____ 1. Will the position fit into my long-range occupational plans and career goals?
_____ 2. Does the job express my major work values and meet my basic needs in life?
_____ 3. Will my abilities and skills contribute to the progress of the organization offering the position?
_____ 4. Is the job itself intrinsically interesting and psychologically involving?
_____ 5. Is the salary for the job being offered and the company's salary schedule for future years reasonable and satisfactory?
_____ 6. Does the organization offer an attractive benefits package, including insurance, paid vacations, income supplements, and the like?
_____ 7. Is the job an advancement over what I do now, and does it offer advancement opportunities for the future?
_____ 8. Does the employer have an excellent reputation in its field or industry?
_____ 9. Is the size of the organization or the department where I would work right for me?
_____ 10. Does the organization manufacture products or provide services with which I would be proud to be associated?
_____ 11. Are the people with whom I will be most closely associated in the organization compatible with me and possible for me to get along with?
_____ 12. Do the values, philosophy, and assumptions of the organizational culture fit my personality characteristics?
_____ 13. Can I easily commute to the workplace?
_____ 14. Will the work the position requires challenge the best that is within me?
_____ 15. Is the management of the organization stable, responsible, and worthy of my respect?
_____ 16. Is my immediate supervisor a person who is competent, agreeable, and admired, with whom one can be friends?
_____ 17. Has the company experienced recent growth? Does the organization have growth potential for the future?
_____ 18. Does the company keep its employees even in hard times? Does the position have a reasonable degree of security or permanence?
_____ 19. Do the functions of the job have the support of the management of the organization?
_____ 20. Are the hours of work agreeable to me? Are other working conditions in the organization what I want them to be?

_____ 21. Is the company in an industry that is growing or that will be around for a long time?

_____ 22. Does the organization offer training programs or pay for continuing education?

_____ 23. Will the job in this particular organization allow adequate time for family and recreational interests?

_____ 24. Are desirable community, cultural, recreational, educational, social, and religious facilities available where the job is located?

_____ 25. Other (write in):

Evaluating Two or More Job Offers

A matrix is provided on page 211 for the purpose of comparing two or more positions. Completing the matrix involves six steps.

Step 1. The factors to be considered with each position are listed vertically down the left side of the matrix. If you do not want a particular factor in your list, simply cross it out and don't use it. There are spaces for additional factors at the bottom of the matrix.

Step 2. List each position and the name of the organization across the top of the matrix. There are spaces for four positions.

Step 3. Weigh each factor according to a 1-to-5 scale. Ask yourself how important each factor is to you and give it a weight number in the weight column.

5 means the factor is *very important* to you.
4 means the factor is *above average in importance* to you.
3 means the factor is of *average importance* to you.
2 means the factor is *below average in importance* to you.
1 means the factor is of *little importance* to you.

Step 4. Use a code to show whether each job and organization is positive (+), neutral (0), or negative (−) with regard to each factor you are considering. Base your judgments on the information you have obtained from your research.

+ = *Factor is expressed* in the position/organization.
0 = *Neutral*; can't determine, don't know, or doesn't apply.
− = *Factor is not expressed* in the position/organization.

Place the code in the space just to the left of the parentheses.

Step 5. Multiply the weight by the code (W × C), and enter the product inside the parentheses. For example: $4 \times + = +4$, $3 \times 0 = 0$, and $2 \times - = -2$.

Comparison of Job Offers	Position/ Organization		Position/ Organization		Position/ Organization		Position/ Organization	
Factor	Weight	Code WxC	Code WxC		Code WxC		Code WxC	
1. Job fits into career plans	___	___ (__)	___ (__)		___ (__)		___ (__)	
2. Job expresses major values	___	___ (__)	___ (__)		___ (__)		___ (__)	
3. Abilities can be used on job	___	___ (__)	___ (__)		___ (__)		___ (__)	
4. Work is interesting, involving	___	___ (__)	___ (__)		___ (__)		___ (__)	
5. Salary meets expectations	___	___ (__)	___ (__)		___ (__)		___ (__)	
6. Fringe benefits are good	___	___ (__)	___ (__)		___ (__)		___ (__)	
7. Advancement potential exists	___	___ (__)	___ (__)		___ (__)		___ (__)	
8. Company has excellent reputation	___	___ (__)	___ (__)		___ (__)		___ (__)	
9. Size of organization is right	___	___ (__)	___ (__)		___ (__)		___ (__)	
10. Pride in quality of products/services	___	___ (__)	___ (__)		___ (__)		___ (__)	
11. Work associates will be compatible	___	___ (__)	___ (__)		___ (__)		___ (__)	
12. Organizational culture fits personality	___	___ (__)	___ (__)		___ (__)		___ (__)	
13. Location of work is convenient	___	___ (__)	___ (__)		___ (__)		___ (__)	
14. Work will challenge my best efforts	___	___ (__)	___ (__)		___ (__)		___ (__)	
15. Management style is attractive	___	___ (__)	___ (__)		___ (__)		___ (__)	
16. Immediate supervisor is respected	___	___ (__)	___ (__)		___ (__)		___ (__)	
17. Company is growing/has growth potential	___	___ (__)	___ (__)		___ (__)		___ (__)	
18. Reasonable job security exists	___	___ (__)	___ (__)		___ (__)		___ (__)	
19. Job functions have management support	___	___ (__)	___ (__)		___ (__)		___ (__)	
20. Working hours/conditions are agreeable		___ (__)	___ (__)		___ (__)		___ (__)	
21. Company is in a growing industry	___	___ (__)	___ (__)		___ (__)		___ (__)	
22. Training/paid education is available	___	___ (__)	___ (__)		___ (__)		___ (__)	
23. Job allows adequate time off work	___	___ (__)	___ (__)		___ (__)		___ (__)	
24. Community is acceptable to family	___	___ (__)	___ (__)		___ (__)		___ (__)	
25. ___	___	___ (__)	___ (__)		___ (__)		___ (__)	
___	___	___ (__)	___ (__)		___ (__)		___ (__)	
___	___	___ (__)	___ (__)		___ (__)		___ (__)	
___	___	___ (__)	___ (__)		___ (__)		___ (__)	
___	___	___ (__)	___ (__)		___ (__)		___ (__)	
___	___	___ (__)	___ (__)		___ (__)		___ (__)	
Total Scores		___	___		___		___	
Rank		___	___		___		___	

Step 6. Sum the products for each position. Add the numbers of each column, subtracting where indicated. The total score gives you the place of each job among the alternatives.

Figure 9-1 is an example that applies three factors to one job.

FIGURE 9-1 *Job matrix using three factors*

Factor	Weight	Code (W × C)	
1. Job fits into career plans.	5	+	+5
2. Job expresses major values.	3	0	0
3. Abilities can be used on job.	4	−	−4

Working on the Job

The story is not over when you have landed a job. Working on the job, or job maintenance, is a whole new chapter. Many beginning workers hope to connect with a mentor who will guide them in learning the ropes in an organization and advancing on the job. A mentor might offer advice similar to the 15 guidelines for keeping a job presented later in this section. The employer has responsibilities, too, for the relationship between employer and employee is interdependent.

Mentors

A *mentor* is a trusted guide or counselor who coaches a person in the art of career maintenance, development, and advancement in an organization. "Mentoring" is not systematic, planned action; it usually happens spontaneously. The mentor offers knowledge, support, encouragement, and wise advice, guiding a protégé through difficult situations or away from dangerous pitfalls. Mentors are most often found in managerial and professional work environments, although there is no reason the same kind of relationship cannot develop in other types of work. The relationship is somewhat similar to the good parent looking out for the interests of a son or daughter. In career mentoring, however, the relationship is professional rather than parental. For example, a junior executive identifies with a top manager, or a college student becomes aligned with a respected professor.

The protégé is not the only beneficiary of the mentoring relationship. Mentors often receive assistance in return from a willing associate, enhance a reputation for helpfulness, and gain satisfaction in contributing to the careers of others and to the success of the organization. The company may benefit from greater worker loyalty and better work adjustments made by new employees.

Marilyn Moats Kennedy (1980) identifies five types of mentors. The *information mentor* tells you about customs and practices within an organization, communicating material that is not written in the company orientation manual. The *peer mentor* relates to you as an equal on subjects of mutual interest. Many companies connect you with this type of mentor after you are hired—an organizational "buddy system." The *retiree mentor,* though no longer with the organization, can still provide a wealth of information about the history of the company and perceive any "time bombs" that may affect its future. The *competitive mentor* is someone in your occupation who works for a company not on your target list. Finally, the *godfather mentor* is one who can make things happen for you. The "godfather" not only teaches and inspires but also has power and clout. The relationship between you and this person is reciprocal. You may want to use the godfather's influence; the "godfather" wants to interact with a kindred soul who could become a sympathetic supporter and admirer in the organization. The relationship is based upon a kind of chemistry that both recognize (Kennedy, 1980).

The Art of Keeping a Job

There seems to be nothing that one can say about keeping a job without sounding trite. Be on time for work; notify your employer ahead of time when you cannot avoid being absent; read the policy manual; and follow directions—these are hardly unusual or controversial admonitions. However, such simple things cost people their jobs more often than anything else. Lack of competence or ability to do the work is rarely the reason an employer fires an employee. Usually, the damage is done by some annoying habit, poor interpersonal skills, or failure to communicate. Fifteen points in the art of keeping a job are listed as follows:

1. *Punctuality: Come to work on time.* Following this simple admonition can do more for you than an acre of promises. Employers see punctuality as a sign that you are responsible and dependable, and that is worth a lot of points in their books. When you first start a new job, plan to arrive 10 or 15 minutes early. This extra margin could conceivably save you from making a negative first impression by arriving late due to unfamiliarity with the route you take to work and with the parking facilities, delays by traffic jams, or the like. When lateness becomes a pattern, check your own attitudes toward your job.

2. *Communication: Notify your employer or supervisor whenever you must be absent from work.* The company policy manual will probably contain instructions on what to do whenever you must be absent from the job. Workers sometimes need to leave work to meet doctor's appointments, take care of legal matters, or conduct other business they cannot do outside of work hours. Obtain your supervisor's permission in advance so there is no question about the legitimacy of your absence. Try to keep absence to a bare minimum. Employers want their workers to be on the job regularly in order to avoid delays or interruptions in production or service.

3. *Knowledge of procedures: Read the organization's policies,* which are usually printed in a manual or a pamphlet. Read the policies thoroughly before you start the job, or no later than the first few days of employment. Know what the policies are. You may disagree with some, and others may

not make sense to you. Inquire politely about the rationale behind the policies you don't like; they may make more sense to you when you consider a different viewpoint. Some organizations have an orientation program to discuss company policies.

4. *Listen to directions: Follow instructions, rules, and regulations.* When you start a new job, contact your supervisor and find out exactly what you are expected to do. Ask questions, and keep asking them until you understand completely where you stand and how you should proceed. Directions are usually simple to comprehend, but many people stumble on this item because they failed to listen, were daydreaming, or were not paying attention.

5. *Ethics: Do not take unfair advantage of your work organization* by extending coffee breaks, lengthening lunch periods, arriving late for work, making frequent personal calls, reading newspapers or magazines, or stopping work a half-hour before quitting time. Sooner or later, this attitude will be noticed and will create a negative impression on your supervisor or employer. Give a few minutes of your own time to finish a task. Staying a few minutes overtime to complete something can't hurt you in the eyes of the employer and may make it easier to ask for a privilege later.

6. *Stay occupied: Keep busy all the time at work.* Offer to take on more duties if you don't have enough work to do. Learn the jobs of your work associates and even that of your supervisor. If a co-worker could use some help in finishing a job after you're done with yours, volunteer your assistance. You may be repaid with interest some day.

7. *Friendliness: Become acquainted with your fellow employees.* Engage in friendly conversation with others on coffee breaks or during lunch periods. Get to know experienced employees. Your work associates can tell you of the informal procedures that operate at work. As a new employee, try to avoid becoming too closely associated with any one group, since work groups often have informal cliques. You might want to dissociate yourself from a group later, but this will be very hard to do if you are closely connected to it from your first day on.

8. *Recognize others: Give them credit when the occasion arises.* You will increase your esteem among your work associates and supervisors if you can honestly compliment them or members of their families on their accomplishments. Learn the names of your co-workers and try to remember their interests and concerns. At social occasions, try to learn the names of your colleagues' spouses and children.

9. *Anticipate accurately: Develop realistic expectations about work.* Students who spend two or four years at college frequently experience an *expectations gap*—the difference between what a recent college graduate thinks the world should be like and what the world is really like. The campus is often quite different from the world of work; this can be quite a shock for the recent graduate. One of the great values of work experience during college is the lessening of this shock through actual contact with the world of work.

10. *Teamwork: Learn to work cooperatively with your immediate supervisor and work associates.* Your supervisor will generally make work assignments, evaluate your performance, and offer constructive criticism as needed. If you believe your supervisor is not meeting these responsibilities, try to discuss the matter courteously with the supervisor or obtain assistance from an appropriate person in the personnel office or a union representative.

11. *Stay in style: Avoid extremes in dress, mannerisms, and hair styles.* It is better to remain on the conservative side in matters of lifestyle at least until you know more about the lay of the land. Even where no official dress policies exist, employers expect workers to maintain whatever standards of good taste or acceptability prevail in the organization.

12. *Contribute: Show yourself to be a planner and a problem solver.* Careful planning, combined with goal-setting and frequent analysis of your efforts, will assist you in becoming a much more valuable employee. When suggesting a solution to a problem at work, listen attentively to the ideas and suggestions offered by others. Consider why something is currently done; there may be perfectly valid reasons for it. Instead of criticizing current practice or another's suggestion, you might state that your idea could supplement or expand the value of their ideas. A positive statement doesn't run down other practices or suggestions. Positive ideas have a greater chance of being accepted because they don't encourage negative reactions on the part of others.

13. *Excellence: Concentrate on the quality of your work on the job.* You want your work to be accurate, well done, and neat. This will depend on the knowledge you have about the job and your ability to learn new responsibilities. Employers and work associates will tolerate quite a lot if a person's work carries a mark of excellence.

14. *Faithfulness: Be loyal to the employer who is (or has been) loyal to you.* This does not mean you must accept everything your employer does. When disagreements occur, bring them up with the supervisor or employer. Don't go to the outside and broadcast your complaint to the world; your employer will resent this, and it won't solve the problem. As long as you are a member of the organization, either speak well of it or don't speak of it at all.

15. *Healthy self-confidence: Project a positive self-image at work.* Acknowledge other people with good eye contact and a pleasant smile, gracefully accept compliments for a job well done, concede past mistakes but don't dwell on them, don't undersell your own ideas with phrases such as "There are probably better ways to do this, but . . . ", and avoid putting yourself down with false modesty or boasting with misleading claims.

Obligations of the Employer

Workers are obligated to meet employers' expectations in order to keep their jobs or to move up in the organization. On the other side of the coin, workers rely on employers to fulfill various obligations to them.

Communication of expectations.   Employers are responsible for letting their employees know exactly what is expected of them on the job and for giving them the instructions, training, and guidance needed to meet these expectations. New workers usually receive much of this information from their immediate supervisors. The immediate supervisor is often responsible for greeting new employees on their first day of work, introducing them to co-workers, showing them to their desks or work stations, and offering the information they need to learn their way around the workplace. In time, the supervisor is apt to explain exactly what the new worker is expected to do and to outline the work rules and procedures to be followed.

Pay.   One of the employer's major responsibilities is to pay employees for their work. Forms of pay vary widely. Some workers receive annual salaries; others are paid a fixed amount per hour, day, or week. Some are paid on a piecework basis—reimbursed according to the amount they produce. Salespeople are sometimes paid commissions, a certain proportion of the value of their sales. Commissions may either constitute a worker's total pay or supplement a fixed salary. Some workers (taxi drivers, waiters and waitresses, and cosmetologists, for example) count on customers' tips to boost regular wages or salaries.

Pay schedules vary, too. Payday may occur weekly, biweekly, on specified days (the 1st and 15th of every month), or according to some other schedule.

Regardless of how or how often workers are paid, however, they can expect their employers to withhold certain amounts from their earnings. The starting pay quoted to new workers is the *base or gross pay,* their earnings before deductions. Under the law, employers must withhold money from workers' base pay for federal income taxes. Other withholdings are generally required for state and local income taxes. The amount withheld depends on the amount a worker earns, his or her marital status, the number of persons he or she supports (dependents), and tax law specifications. To determine the amount withheld for taxes, new workers fill out tax withholding forms, indicating their marital status, address, and the number of their dependents. The amount withheld each year should come close to the worker's annual tax bill. Payroll deductions are also made for retirement and disability programs, which provide retirement income or benefits to workers who are unable to work because of sickness or injury. By law, most workers must participate in these plans. Many workers may also elect to have their employers make deductions for health and hospitalization plans, savings bonds or other types of savings programs, union dues, or shares of stock in the employing company.

The amount a worker receives after all deductions are made—called *take-home pay*—can total less than two thirds of the gross pay. New workers who are unprepared for these deductions may be disappointed that their first paycheck totals less than the amount they expected when hearing their starting pay. However, many workers actually earn more than their paychecks indicate because of their fringe benefits.

Fringe benefits may include retirement income, disability pay, unemployment insurance, hospitalization coverage, paid vacations, paid holidays, sick leave, and other similar benefits paid for partly or wholly by employers. Because such benefits can boost a worker's income by a significant amount, it is to a new worker's advantage to learn as much as possible about such plans and to participate in elective programs, such as insurance plans, that offer worthwhile benefits. A worker's immediate supervisor or a personnel office representative can usually provide detailed information about such plans.

Adherence to laws protecting the rights of workers. Workers are guaranteed the right to organize and to bargain collectively through representatives of their own choosing under the National Labor Relations Act. The Fair Labor Standards Act sets hourly minimum wages, requires some workers to be paid premium rates for overtime pay when they work over 40 hours in a week, and prohibits oppressive and unsafe child labor. Other laws require employers to treat all persons equally—regardless of race, color, religion, sex, or national origin—in all aspects of employment, including hiring, promotion, pay, firing, apprenticeship, job assignment, and training. The Occupational Safety and Health Act requires employers to provide workplaces that are free of recognized health and safety hazards. Other federal, state, and local laws that concern the rights and well-being of workers are too numerous to mention here.

Problems of Workers

No work is without its problems. In this section, we first discuss problems that appear to affect certain identifiable groups of workers more than others. Following that, the problem of job burnout is examined. Job burnout strikes many people after they have encountered repeated disappointment and discouragement at work. The process often starts with unrealistic expectations of extraordinary satisfaction on the job, followed by feelings of frustration and indifference toward the work when those expectations are not fulfilled.

Difficulties, Dilemmas, and Dissatisfactions of Selected Types of Workers

Younger workers. Many young people start work with great expectations— sometimes beyond the capacity of any job to deliver. They expect a great amount of intrinsic reward from work, features such as opportunity for self-expression, challenge, interesting work, and freedom to make decisions.

Many young workers express an entrepreneurial spirit; they strive for independence and are willing to take risks. They are attracted more to small, growing companies and less to large, bureaucratic organizations. They are bothered by authoritarianism at work and ask management to give them opportunities for self-motivation. The basic assumptions behind the old expression "a fair day's work for a fair day's pay" are being questioned. Unions have usually been concerned about setting standards for a fair day's pay, whereas employers have stressed the right to determine a fair day's work. Young workers are challenging both union and management by demanding a voice in establishing their working conditions, as the following case illustrates. Three young workers in their early twenties were hired to clean offices at night. One evening the foreman caught one of the young janitors asleep with his feet on a desk, another reading a paper, and the third doing schoolwork. The foreman gave them a written warning, and the workers filed a grievance. By really hustling, they had cleaned all the offices in five hours instead of eight so they could use the other three hours for themselves. The union steward tried to understand their point of view but felt the company was justified in expecting eight hours' work for eight hours' pay. He explained to the young workers that, if they continued to finish their work in five hours, the company would either give them more work or get rid of one of them. They slowed their pace. The union steward felt that he had settled the grievance within the understood rules and kept everyone happy, but the young workers were far from satisfied. They had wanted the union to establish the boundaries of work and the rate of pay, and then they wanted the freedom to manage their own work operations within the time frame and assignments given them (*Work in America,* 1973).

Older workers.   Age discrimination makes it more difficult for older people to keep their jobs or to find new jobs today. Two thirds of American men aged 65 or older were working in 1900; that figure is now about 2 percent. The contributions of the 55-plus age group can be easily ignored or devalued in our youth-oriented culture. The elderly are viewed as a social problem, and our approach to social problems is to reduce their visibility (Slater, 1990). Forced or encouraged retirement occurs earlier for many aging people today. Retirement is the time-honored method of taking older people out of the labor force or out of the competition for jobs. Older workers find themselves fighting the impression that aging is linked with decreasing capabilities for work and training. While a gradual slowing-down can be associated with age for many people, this slowing can be more than compensated for with the wisdom and experience an older person brings to a work organization. Unfortunately, the labor market is generally unresponsive to the needs of older workers. If they need to find new work, older people often face a serious decline in their wages compared to their previous jobs. Only two choices are usually offered concerning work: either take a full-time job or accept total retirement. Alternative work arrangements, such as job-sharing and gradual reductions in time schedules, are not options for most older workers (Rones, 1983).

Minority workers.   About one third of all minority workers are unemployed, are irregularly employed, or have given up looking for a job. Another third have full-time jobs year-round, but they work mostly in manual labor or the service trades, which frequently pay less than a living wage. Many minority people know they will hate their jobs before they take them, because they are the worst jobs society has to offer (*Work in America*, 1973). There are white-collar Black workers who find themselves in a sort of no-man's-land on the job. They have experienced the turnaround that has allowed them to enter occupations once reserved for White people, but they are still apprehensive about their security and survival in a work environment they perceive as hostile and threatening. Psychiatrists William Grier and Price Cobbs (1968) tell of a Black professional named John who competed in a training program that led to higher management positions. Although he was unnerved by the seeming confidence of his White, middle-class competitors, John performed with excellence in the classroom. His group went for specialized training in another city, staying in a sumptuous hotel. John's White colleagues easily accepted the plush carpets, spacious rooms, thick steaks, and other embellishments of an affluent lifestyle. John felt out of place, yet he was attracted by the money and extravagance he saw around him. The inner conflict produced the first downward slide in his functioning. John wanted other Blacks in lower level jobs to know that he was a "brother" and had not abandoned them even though he was in a management training program. He felt uneasy with White employees below his job level, wanting friendly relationships with them but fearing that their prejudice could somehow undermine him. The essential skill to be mastered in his training program was supervision, but John began to have difficulty being firm with both Black and White subordinates. Black subordinates would misunderstand, believing he was being tougher on them to impress the Whites. White subordinates would complain that he was abusing his position of authority and acting out anti-White feelings. John coped with this problem, but other conflicts caused periods of depression. As his effectiveness dropped, he was finally dropped from the training program. The inner strain John experienced when he had to exercise power over others sent him on a declining spiral toward failure. Anxieties such as those illustrated in this case will not change unless the social environment concerning racial matters changes as well.

Women workers.   Over half of all adult women 19 to 64 years of age are currently in the labor force, and this figure is expected to reach 60 percent between 1995 and 2000. At least nine of every ten women will work outside the home at some point in their lives, Department of Labor studies show. Home, family, and the husband's job gave women their identity in the past, but an occupation other than housekeeping is increasingly the major source of identity for women. Many half-truths exist about women and work. One is that women work just for "pin money." Actually, most women work because they must supplement an inadequate family income or support themselves or their children. Another misconception is that women miss more days at work. A public health survey showed that women lost an average of 5.3 days per year, compared to 5.1 days for men (Twaddle & Hessler, 1987). Work-life expectancy for all women is 25 years, but it averages 45 years for the single woman worker, compared to 43 years for the average man. Other myths are that women are less involved in their work than men are (studies show an equal concern with meaningful work); that women are more content than men with routine, undemanding jobs (there are no data to support this notion); and that women are less concerned than men about advancement (women want promotions as much as men do). Stereotypes such as these help employers justify work-related discrimination. As of 1990, women earned about 70 percent as much as similarly employed men. Women are more frequently consigned to lower status, less challenging jobs. At least 75 percent of the jobs in the higher-paying professional occupations are still held by men (Hoyt, 1989). Advancement is harder for women to win, and much of the work assigned to women deflates their sense of self-worth. Most low pay, low status white-collar jobs are held by women, even though they derive the same satisfaction that men do from the intrinsic rewards of work. When an occupation is composed almost entirely of one sex, this is evidence of occupational gender-typing. Women are often excluded from occupations labeled "masculine." The same limitations in some occupations can also be imposed on men. Table 9-1 provides data on certain female-dominated and male-dominated occupations. Occupational gender-typing usually has little reasoning behind it. "Men's work" in one age may become "women's work" in another; for example, telephone operating and secretarial work were once male-dominated occupations in the United States.

Blue-collar blues.   Blue-collar workers work mostly in production and maintenance occupations and are paid by the hour or according to the amount they produce. Some of their major complaints about work stem from having little or no control over work assignments and feeling locked in because of the lack of opportunity to advance. They can be suspicious of new technology, fearing that its impact will lower their status or cost them their jobs. Society as a whole often takes a negative view of manual labor, and blue-collar workers themselves tend to see white-collar employees as having more job privileges than they do.

White-collar woes.   "White-collar workers" is a term used to describe office, administrative, clerical, sales, technical, and professional employees. Much job dissatisfaction today is found among well-educated people in regi-

TABLE 9-1   *Male- and female-dominated occupations, 1987*

Female-Dominated Occupations	Percentage Female Workers	Male-Dominated Occupations	Percentage Male Workers
Child-care worker	98.6	Airplane pilot and navigator	98.1
Dental assistant	100.0	Automotive body and small-	
Licensed practical nurse	96.8	engine repairer	100.0
Preschool and kindergarten		Construction trades	
teacher	98.3	(combined)	98.4
Receptionist	98.0	Carpenter	98.9
Registered nurse	92.1	Plumber	99.5
Secretary	98.9	Fire fighter	98.1
Telephone operator	86.7	Material-moving equipment	
		operator	96.1
		Office machine repairer	100.0
		Tool and die maker	98.7
		Truck driver, heavy	98.5

Adapted from: Mellor, E. F. (1987). Weekly earnings in 1986: A look at more than 200 occupations. *Monthly Labor Review,* 110(6), 41–46.

mented, monotonous, low-paying clerical positions. Higher credentials are now demanded for such work, but the pay, the status, and the amount of challenge of the jobs have not improved. The office is seen as the white-collar counterpart of the factory and its assembly-line methods. Impersonality characterizes the system; the individuality of the worker is acknowledged only when a rule is not followed or a mistake is made. Middle managers, once pillars of company loyalty, protest that they lack influence in decision-making but are still expected to carry out company policy. They worry about being out of touch with the values of younger workers and about being less competent with new technology. Feelings of insecurity and inadequacy may lead to damaged relationships with subordinates, colleagues, and those at home. Some managers want to change their career direction but think there is too high a price to pay or feel they must wait until their children are grown.

Job Burnout

A social worker, burdened with a heavy caseload and too much paperwork, complains: "The job has become just a job. I must have 20 forms to fill out in triplicate every time I see a client." A psychiatric nurse reveals: "Lately, my first reaction to patients has been 'Now what do they want?' If things keep going this way I'll be the patient." A teacher admits: "At one time, I really cared for my kids. I've simply lost interest in them. It doesn't matter to me what they learn." A corrections officer says: "I've seen it all. Now, I just go through the motions. Every day is just another day on the job." Every kind of work has boring aspects, and everyone experiences a bad day periodically.

But when statements such as you have just read result from underlying feelings of alienation and exhaustion that persist over long periods of time, the person may well be on the road to burnout.

Burnout appears to be especially common in the helping professions, but it may affect all types of work to some extent. Although burnout has undoubtedly existed throughout human history, psychologists have only recently studied burnout seriously. Herbert Freudenberger (1980) compares a burned-out person to a burned-out building.

> What had once been a throbbing, vital structure is now deserted. Where there had been activity, there are now only crumbling reminders of energy and life. Some bricks or concrete may be left; some outlines of windows. Indeed, the outer shell may seem almost intact. Only if you venture inside will you be struck by the full force of the desolation . . . people, as well as buildings, sometimes burn-out. Under the strain of living in our complex world, their inner resources are consumed as if by fire, leaving a great emptiness inside, although their outer shells may be more or less unchanged. [p. xv]

Christina Maslach (1982) identifies burnout on the job as a type of reaction to stress. It is a response to constant emotional strain from interaction with people, particularly with troubled people. Burnout runs in a cycle of emotional exhaustion, depersonalization, and a reduced feeling of personal accomplishment. For example, people in helping professions may try to do too much, get overinvolved, or become overwhelmed by the emotional demands made by others. Such people feel drained of physical and mental resources. They lose energy, drive, and spirit until they cannot give any more of themselves to their clients. Cynicism replaces idealism. People experiencing burnout detach themselves emotionally from the needs of other people. Some detachment is necessary in order to function well on the job, but too much can lead to callous indifference. Burned-out people exhibit less caring and a negative feeling toward others. Finally, they turn their negative attitudes inward, and burnout culminates with a sense of inadequacy on the job. As self-esteem and a belief in personal competence crumble, the burnout victim turns to counseling and therapy or changes jobs to find work that doesn't involve stressful contact with people.

Some work environments seem to be breeding grounds for burnout. These are workplaces where workers feel they have little or no control over their work, no influence on decisions affecting them, no opportunity to get away from stressful situations, and arbitrary loading on of more responsibility than they can handle. There are too many demands made on them, too many people to serve, too much information to digest, and too little reward for making the effort. Workers are thrown into situations more competitive than they can bear, such as competing for bonuses, promotions, or recognition. Workers are evaluated according to the number of products made or people served rather than by the quality of their work. A counselor, for example, may be judged by the number of clients seen, not by what was done for them. Some institutional policies may be damaging to psychological health.

Workers are asked to follow procedures they don't believe in. Endless paper-work, red tape, writing reports, and filling out forms frustrate the achieve-ment of doing the job a person was hired to do. Employees complain about lack of support and inconsistent application of the rules. All workplaces are likely to have one or a few of these characteristics, but too many of them in extreme forms can precipitate burnout over time.

Some people are more vulnerable to burnout than others. They may be overachievers with unrealistic expectations; some people envision work as an everlasting adventure, filled with challenge, excitement, pleasure, and productive activity. When these expectations are not fulfilled, they are un-able to adjust to reality. They strive even harder and throw all their time and energy into the job, but this excessive devotion is rarely rewarded. After the initial period of enthusiasm wears out, stages of stagnation, frustration, and apathy are likely to follow (Edelwich, 1980). Burnout candidates are often low in self-esteem and self-confidence. They feel as though they are at the mercy of their environment and do nothing to shape or improve it, passively allowing things to happen to them. A definite factor in burnout is the need for approval. When appreciation from others is not forthcoming, burnout candidates feel betrayed and may begin to disparage and belittle those around them. People who do not have control of strong emotions such as hostility, anger, impatience, and intolerance toward others appear to run greater risks of burnout. For example, one who constantly puts others down may be using hostility to prop up a weak ego (Maslach, 1982).

The job itself may contain built-in dissatisfactions that lend themselves to burnout. Jerry Edelwich (1980) catalogs frustrations that can eventually add up to burnout.

Not enough money. As a result, people feel that their choices are limited and their life is constricted.

Too many hours. Working hours are considered excessive; others may work fewer hours, which is seen as unfair; there is little chance to get away from the job; inadequate vacation time is offered.

Career dead end. People feel blocked or caught in a rut; little or no oppor-tunity exists for advancement to a higher position.

Too much paperwork. Filling out forms and writing numerous reports rather than doing the job described at the time of hiring makes people think they are serving only the organization's needs, not those of people.

Not sufficiently trained for the job. For example, paraprofessionals may have to do the work a professional should do. Sometimes, however, the opposite is heard: "I am overtrained for this work."

Not appreciated by clients. This occurs most commonly when working with people who don't want help in the first place or demand more than a helper can give.

Not appreciated by supervisor. People feel they are not given responsibility commensurate with their skills and abilities, not consulted about decisions, overlooked by supervisors, and evaluated unfairly or according to irrelevant criteria.

No support for important decisions. A worker is held responsible for a superior's failure to support or implement recommendations.

Powerlessness. A worker experiences little or no chance to make an impact on other people or to influence decisions; recommendations made are ignored or gather dust.

System not responsive to client's needs. The organization exists for its own sake and places a low priority on meeting the needs of the clients and customers it is meant to serve.

Bad office politics. Internal power politics get nasty; polarization occurs among superiors and subordinates; too much petty infighting, jealousy, and undermining of ambitions and reputations occur.

Other frustrations. These might include instances of sexism, racism, ageism; being caught in the cross fire of bureaucratic decisions and nondecisions; too many demands made by too many people; a suspicious public constituency; lack of community awareness or support; poor personal image; disappointment with one's fellow workers.

Apathy takes the form of a progressive emotional detachment in the face of frustration. The starting point is the idealism and enthusiasm of the beginner. If one is to come out of the clouds and work effectively, some detachment is desirable and inevitable. In the burned-out person, however, the detachment that develops out of frustration is a kind of numbness. A psychiatric ward aide expressed apathy as follows:

> At the beginning, like everybody else, I was gung-ho. I'd wake up thinking, 'Here's another day. What can I get done today?' I spent a lot of time with the patients, gathered as much information as I could, and tried to work as a team with the rest of the staff. After five or six months, as I found the results I had expected not happening, I got to be indifferent. I'd wake up in the morning and not care about going to work. It was just another day, just a job. I spent less time with patients and did what was necessary only to get by. It was unpleasant having to do things that way, and I got away from it by spending time socializing with the staff instead of working with patients. [Edelwich, 1980, p. 165–166]

"Indifferent," "just another day," "just a job," "did what was necessary to get by," "going through the motions," "putting in time"—involvement and enthusiasm have turned to apathy. The worker has decided to stop trying, hoping only to avoid future letdowns.

Apathy results in alienation and estrangement not only from others, but from one's self as well. Many burnout victims feel far removed from the rest of society, unable to connect their own lives to the lives of other people. Symptoms of depression may appear; a pervasive listlessness and despair may surround one's personal life as well as life on the job. Apathy is a defense mechanism the burned-out person uses. It separates the person from the painful situation, but it also cuts off that person from things that might help: other people, meaningful work, and a feeling of belonging. For this reason, this numb, alienated stage of burnout is the most dangerous (Mangano, 1982).

What can a person do to counteract burnout? There are strategies that will help neutralize the effects of burnout or reduce its likelihood.

1. *Adjust expectations and set realistic goals.* This does not mean giving up your ideals and becoming apathetic. It does mean setting achievable goals based on an honest appraisal of your abilities and values.

2. *Do your job differently; vary your work routines.* Determine which parts of the job can be changed and which cannot. Analyze the consequences of a change in work procedures. Talking to co-workers or your supervisor or taking a workshop or seminar may give you some new ideas about doing your job. Taking action may not be easy, but constant frustration is worse.

3. *Get away from the job for a while.* Getting away can involve a time period ranging from a 15-minute coffee break or a 1-hour lunch period to a day, a week, or a month. Use a sick day or a vacation period if necessary. Avoid working through lunch hours or coming back to the office in the evening to catch up on work.

4. *Get enough rest and relaxation.* Get sufficient sleep. Use relaxation techniques such as stress management, biofeedback, and imagery exercises. Change pace and wind down after work. Listen to music or meditate. Engage in a vigorous physical activity or become absorbed in a hobby. Leave the strains of the job behind.

5. *Seek satisfactions outside of work.* Open up your life beyond the boundaries of your work environment. Family and friends can offer encouragement when work problems threaten. Outside activities and relationships provide outlets for creativity and challenge.

6. *Seek counseling or other professional help.* There is no reason to feel isolated or alone. Take advantage of any counseling services offered by your work organization or community.

7. *Leave the job or even the occupation itself.* Such decisions are very personal and individual and should be made only after you have tried all other possible strategies and determined that the difficulties on the job have simply become overwhelming. You need to make a searching self-analysis, assessing your goals, values, abilities, temperament, and attitudes. Recycling the career decision-making process and sharpening your job-hunting skills will be necessary.

Work organizations can take steps to counteract job burnout. Strategies to alleviate the conditions that lead to burnout are adapted from Mangano (1982) and summarized as follows.

1. *Divide or rotate the work.* Work can be organized so employees can take turns at various job functions. Then, no one person is overexposed to high-stress situations. Variety in their duties gives workers relief from monotonous tasks.

2. *Plan regular breaks in the work routine.* Coffee breaks during the workday and adequate vacations allow employees to get away from stress. Companies can buy membership in recreational clubs, health spas, and gyms and encourage their employees to use these facilities during lunch hours or after work.

3. *Hire more workers* when the workload becomes too heavy. Despite the additional expense involved, this option should be considered, especially when relatively inexpensive kinds of extra help are available.

4. *Provide adequate job preparation.* Since burnout is linked to unrealistic expectations, a good orientation program can help put the demands and expectations of job performance into proper perspective. Training cannot anticipate all possible situations that may occur on the job, but it is better than nothing at all.

5. *Provide opportunities for staff development.* People need to continue learning throughout their careers, and training should extend beyond the first few days or weeks on the job. It is important to grow professionally and personally at work; staff development programs can contribute positively to this growth. Such programs can take various forms: workshops and seminars on special topics of interest to individuals and departments, regular staff meetings, brainstorming and problem-solving sessions, courses at a university or a local community college, and even social occasions among staff members. Burnout victims are likely to feel isolated and insignificant, and these programs can prevent such feelings from becoming overwhelming. Not every program may be as exciting or productive as intended, but all such events offer workers a chance to listen and be heard.

6. *Give constructive feedback about performance on the job.* Burnout victims often have no idea of how they are doing on the job. It is important that workers receive praise and recognition when they have earned it. Too often, workers gain the attention of management only when they make a mistake or threaten a grievance. If constructive criticism is necessary, it should be carried out in a nonthreatening manner, letting the worker know he or she is a valued member of the team. Praise and constructive criticism should not come only at formal evaluations, when promotions and pay raises are discussed, but should also be offered spontaneously and informally.

7. *Clarify organizational goals and the role each worker plays in achieving those goals.* People want and need to know what is required of them on the job. Job responsibilities that are reasonable, well defined, clear, and consistent help workers identify themselves in a large structure and create a shared purpose between individual and organization. Vague job descriptions can generate as much frustration as rigid, overdemanding requirements.

8. *Provide preventive counseling.* Intervention by skilled counselors can be extremely valuable in preventing job burnout. Counselors should not be viewed as a part of the company; workers need to express their feelings and thoughts freely when they talk with a counselor.

EXERCISE 9-1 *On-the-Job Problems*

Working will bring its share of problems. The problems presented in this exercise may help you anticipate some situations that could develop at some time in your working life. You can do this exercise alone, but if you are in a class or a group, it is often instructive to hear how others would handle the same problem. Teachers may want to divide a class into small groups, assign each group a situation for 10 or 15 minutes, and then have the group report their conclusions to the whole class.

Situation A: Unused Talents

You have just been hired as an administrative assistant at a major state university after graduating with a master's degree in educational administration. For the first month, various "gofer" assignments use most of your time: running errands for senior administrators, getting coffee for the rest of the office, operating the copy machine, picking up mail at the post office, collecting catalogs from other colleges, and other routine tasks. You feel you've been trained for higher responsibilities than these. What would you do?

Situation B: Idealism Versus Materialism

You are a college graduate who majored in humanities and have now worked at a business firm for about two years. While you were in college, you became very idealistic and learned to despise status symbols, conspicuous consumption, worship of money and physical objects, planned obsolescence, useless gadgets, and all the trappings of a materialistic society. The company where you now work, however, is very materialistic. It is absorbed in selling and making a profit on its material products; profit is the bottom line that resolves all questions; it advertises its products with average or sometimes substandard taste; it gives cash bonuses for new ideas; and its executive offices are decorated lavishly, with expensive carpeting and furniture. Your critical, humanistic background leads you to comment freely on the company's obsession with materialism and its lack of human and spiritual values. Some of this criticism gets back to your supervisor, who tells you that you would be better advised to keep your opinions to yourself if you have any hopes of promotions and greater responsibility within the company. What would you do?

Situation C: The Productive Employee

You have been working at a parts assembly plant for only a couple of weeks. Your rate of production has been consistently higher than your work associates'. You enjoy the work and want to impress your employer and supervisor with your skill and hard work. Your co-workers, however, are beginning to harass you because they feel threatened by your high production rate. You want to have a good relationship with your work associates, yet you believe you should do your best and maintain high standards at work. What would you do?

Situation D: No Raise, No Promotion

You have been working for your employer for nearly two years, going all-out and doing high-quality work. You get along well with your supervisor and bosses. Even with your excellent work record and good relationships, you have not received a pay raise or been advanced to a higher position or higher status. Finally, you bring this problem to the attention of your supervisor, who tells you that management is aware of the situation, but the company hasn't made a profit for a year, and the state of the economy is poor. The company hopes things will improve, but there is no guarantee of that. What would you do?

Situation E: The Pink Slip and Reemployment

You and two other employees have been working in a public organization for three years when the three of you suddenly receive a pink slip—a notice that you are being laid off work in three months. You are informed that budget cuts have made this move necessary. The administration regrets the layoffs very much, since they are happening through no fault of the employees involved. Then you discover that several people who have been hired after you will still be employed. You are furious because the seniority principle has not been followed, but the administration claims that these people are working in more crucial positions. About two months later, you and your two co-workers are recalled to your old jobs. Your two colleagues state that they will now work as little as possible after the "shabby treatment" they have received. What would you do?

Situation F: Taking Advantage of an Employer

You have been on the job in an office for about four months when you begin to notice that a co-worker and friend of yours is taking advantage of your employer: taking a few office supplies, making personal long-distance telephone calls on the company phone during office hours, allowing friends who don't work for your employer to use an employee discount privilege, padding expense accounts, and so on. These offenses start small, but they build steadily to a larger scale. What would you do?

Situation G: Blowing the Whistle on Your Employer

You have been working at a chemical company for six months as a toxicologist, researching the effects of various chemical poisons the company produces. Inadvertently, you discover that the company is dumping unacceptable levels of toxic chemical wastes into a nearby river. You discuss this problem with another research scientist, who tells you that the costs of properly storing and disposing of the chemical wastes are prohibitive and might even run the company out of business. What would you do?

Situation H: Perceived Preferential Treatment

You are a new employee and want to make friends with your work associates, but they are suddenly cool toward you because they believe you have been given some kind of preferred treatment in the hiring process (due to your sex, race, relationship to the employer, or social group membership). You feel they are judging you unfairly. What would you do?

Situation I: The Mistake

After graduating from college, you have been working in the advertising department of a local television station for three months. Your job is to prepare copy for a device that projects lettering on the TV screen. Unfortunately, you misspell the name of an advertiser, and the error shows up in the next commercial displayed live for the viewing audience. The advertiser is angry and calls the station manager. At this time, no one is aware of who made the mistake. What would you do?

Situation J: The Difficult Supervisor

You have been working for a good organization in a job that you like very much, but you find it very hard to talk with your immediate supervisor. This supervisor is reserved, distant, constantly finds fault, and has a negative attitude toward others. Your co-workers regard the supervisor as unfair and have as little to do with him (or her) as possible. You want to improve your relationship with this supervisor because you like all the other aspects of the job so well. What would you do?

Situation K: On-the-Job Training That Failed

You have been working for three months in the company's sales and marketing division. The manager had been very eager to hire you—your outstanding college record was very attractive. From almost the first day, you were turned over to the company's star salesperson, a 16-year veteran, for guidance and development. Your mentor took you on sales calls to help you "learn the ropes," but you found the "star" knew the customers so well and had such an easy relationship with them that no product details were discussed and sales techniques were not needed. Now, you believe your on-the-job training has not helped at all. You learned nothing new. Soon, you will be on your own, but you really won't know what to do. What should you do?

Summary

1. Evaluating job offers involves the appraisal of many factors. Some of them are how well the job will fit into your long-range career planning, work values expressed, abilities used, salary offered, advancement potential, reputation and size of the organization, products made or services provided, characteristics of people in the company or department, organizational culture, commuting distance, management style, prospects for company or industry growth, working conditions, location of workplace, and training and development.

2. Working on the job means living up to your responsibilities as an employee and knowing the obligations of the employer. You may link yourself with a *mentor,* a trusted counselor who helps you make your way around the organization. This chapter presents 15 points to keep in mind when fulfilling the often difficult mission of keeping a job. Employers have the responsibilities of letting you know what is expected of you, paying you for your work, and complying with the rules that govern employer/employee relations.

3. Various groups of workers face special problems. Younger workers are concerned particularly with issues involving freedom and autonomy on the job, older workers with feelings of obsolescence, members of minority groups with opportunity and acceptance, women with equal pay and respect, blue-collar workers with low status and automation, and white-collar workers with powerlessness and the need to stay current with the new technology.

4. Job burnout afflicts many workers, notably in the helping professions. Burnout is a feeling of emotional exhaustion on the job. The cycle seems to start with great enthusiasm, followed by stages of stagnation, frustration, and apathy. Individuals and organizations can use several strategies to counteract the effects of burnout. These strategies range from adjusting expectations and applying relaxation techniques to varying job functions and staff development measures.

References

Edelwich, J., with Brodsky, A. (1980). *Burn-out: Stages of disillusionment in the helping professions.* New York: Human Sciences Press.

Freudenberger, H. J. (1980). *Burn-out: The high cost of high achievement.* Garden City, NJ: Doubleday/Anchor.

Grier, W. H., & Cobbs, P. M. (1968). *Black rage.* New York: Basic Books.

Hoyt, K. B. (1989). The career status of women and minority persons: A 20-year retrospective. *Career Development Quarterly, 37*(3), 202–212.

Kennedy, M. M. (1980). *Office politics: Seizing power, wielding clout.* Chicago: Follett.

Mangano, C. A. (1982). *Teacher's guide to burnout on the job.* Pleasantville, NY: Human Relations Media.

Maslach, C. (1982). *Burnout—the cost of caring.* Englewood Cliffs, NJ: Prentice-Hall.

Mellor, E. F. (1987). Weekly earnings in 1986: A look at more than 200 occupations. *Monthly Labor Review, 110*(6), 41–46.

Rones, P. L. (1983). The labor market problems of older workers. *Monthly Labor Review, 106*(5), 3–12.

Slater, P. (1990). *The pursuit of loneliness* (3rd ed.). Boston: Beacon Press.

Twaddle, A. C., & Hessler, R. M. (1987). *A sociology of health* (2nd ed.). New York: Macmillan.

Work in America: Report of a special task force to the Secretary of Health, Education, and Welfare. (1973). Cambridge, MA: MIT Press.

10

The Social and Economic Aspects of Work

Career planning books are written for the individual who faces an occupational choice and the job market. However, we don't live in isolation from other people; the broader social and economic aspects of work must be considered, if only briefly. One of the many definitions of work is "an activity that produces something of value for other people" (*Work in America,* 1973). Because we depend upon other people to produce and purchase goods and services, and because we work with and for other people, we must devote some space here to issues resulting from the human interaction of working.

In this chapter, consideration of such topics as the work ethic, labor relations, job satisfaction, and changing management styles will give you some historical perspective on work in the 20th century. We will also discuss the attempts of pioneering individuals and companies to improve work and working conditions. Finally, what will the future of work be? Twelve forces and trends that influence occupations and organizations are identified and briefly analyzed. To close this book, the last exercise engages your thinking about the social, psychological, economic, and political trends that will influence your life and work in the days and years to come.

What Has Happened to the Work Ethic?

The *work ethic* is the idea that hard work, thrift, and deferment of gratification constitute the most moral, patriotic, productive, and healthy way to live. Martin Luther gave work a religious dimension, declaring that hard work serves the purposes of God. When national wealth became more important than individual welfare under mercantilism, work became a patriotic duty. The pioneering economist Adam Smith saw competition as an "invisible hand" that required people to work productively in order to compete successfully with others in the capitalist era. Productive work would bring high quality and low prices to all. Sigmund Freud emphasized that love and work developed a healthy personality. For several centuries, people have believed that not working was somehow immoral and unpatriotic and made a person into a useless, mentally disturbed member of society (Macarov, 1983).

Surveys show that people profess belief in the virtues of hard work, but their behavior reveals a different message. The work ethic is being questioned by many and abandoned by some. Automation makes some workers feel useless. A majority of people choose early retirement when they are offered attractive pay and benefits. Some choose welfare rather than work. Work days are lost because of strikes. The incidence of industrial sabotage, absenteeism, and turnover is disturbing. Efforts to humanize work often succeed in reducing dissatisfaction but still do not provide basic satisfaction in work.

Symptoms of job dissatisfaction occur despite improvements in pay and working conditions. The sweatshops are gone; extreme dangers at work have been reduced; children are protected; arbitrary wage cuts and dismissals are rare; and workers are better served by laws, company policies, and labor unions. Living standards, real income, health standards, and life expectancy have risen. Workers' personal possessions and bank accounts have increased. Unemployment compensation helps people weather tough times; workers' compensation provides for the injured at work; and Social Security benefits are available at retirement.

However, adequate pay and good working conditions do not necessarily make people feel satisfied with their work. Such external factors help diminish dissatisfaction, but they may not promote actual satisfaction with the job. Intrinsic rewards of working, such as having an opportunity to perform well, to grow in competence, to be recognized for contributing, and to develop self-regard, have more to do with feeling good about work. When these needs and values are not realized on the job, a great deal of alienation toward work can develop. Alienation is a condition reflected in a person's attitude toward self, others, work, and those in authority. A worker feels separated from the organization, does not identify with the work, and becomes increasingly estranged from others and self. In *Working* (1972), Studs Terkel illustrates how frustrated assembly-line workers handle aggressions generated at work with the family, neighbors, and children.

> When I was single, I used to go into hillbilly bars, get in a lot of brawls . . . I just wanted to explode . . . When I come home, know what I do for the first 20 minutes? Fake it. I put on a smile. I don't feel like it. I got a kid three-and-a-half years old. Sometimes, she says, Daddy, where've you been? And I say, work. I could've told her I'd been to Disneyland. What's work to a three-year old? I feel bad. I can't take it out on the kid. Kids are born innocent of everything but birth. You don't want to take it out on the wife either. This is why you go to the tavern. You want to release it there rather than do it at home. What does an actor do when he's got a bad movie? I got a bad movie every day. [Terkel, 1972, p. xxxv]

From Scientific Management to Human Relations and Human Resources

One outcome of the Industrial Revolution was the formation of managerial groups whose basic purpose was to plan and direct the activities of workers in manufacturing goods. Frederick Winslow Taylor, famous for his time-and-motion studies, changed management into a science in the early days of the 20th century. At the Bethlehem Steel Company, Taylor observed workers shoveling coal; the weight of a shovelful varied from 3½ to 38 pounds. Differences like these were inefficient. Which load weight was best? Under scientific management, the answer to this question would not be someone's opinion; it was a matter settled through precise scientific investigation. Taylor and his assistants experimented with the capacity of the shovel until they found 21½ pounds to be the optimal amount of coal per shovel load. Having a specialized tool for each job became a principle of scientific management. Small shovels were designed for heavy material such as ore, and large shovels were made for light material such as ashes. Supervisors were required to study each worker carefully so the workers could be given the work to which they were best suited. In time, only 140 shovelers were needed to do the work previously done by 500—clearly a gain in efficiency and a reduction in labor costs. No one remembers what happened to the other 360 men who became unemployed. Taylor himself lost his job at the Bethlehem Steel Works when a new management group took control and discovered that Taylor expected the workers to be paid more for their increased productivity.

Perhaps some, or even all, of such employment losses were compensated for by the new managerial and clerical tasks that had to be done, although each new job had to be filled by a different kind of worker. Management was no longer simply a matter of giving orders to workers. It had become a science, with its own theories, research, and literature dedicated to the task of organizing and planning work. Workers had to be carefully selected and correctly trained; clerks kept records of each worker's productivity and pay; instructions were given for each day's work. Everything was done according to exact measurement, and nothing was left to chance. Since pure science is neutral, scientific management has no political ideology or economic doctrine. Henry Ford adopted Taylor's methods for automobile manufacturing in the United States, and Joseph Stalin followed suit for the collectivized heavy industries of the Soviet Union. As for Taylor, the justification for scientific management was the bottom line.

> It is a very proper question to ask whether it pays or whether it doesn't pay . . . scientific management has nothing in it that is philanthropic; I am not objecting to philanthropy, but any scheme of management which has philanthropy as one of its elements ought to fail; philanthropy has no part in any scheme of management. No self-respecting workman wants to be given things, and scientific management is no scheme for giving people something they do not earn. So, if the principles of scientific management do not pay, then this is a miserable system. The final test of any system is, does it pay? [Taylor, 1947, p. 171]

As industry adopted Taylor's ideas, work was divided into smaller, simpler tasks and placed under constant supervision. Increased efficiency brought spectacular increases in productivity, and profits soared. Principles of scientific management were extended into the office. Workers benefited from higher wages, but at a price. They had to do their work exactly as they were told. The costs were a greater authoritarianism in the workplace and a standardization of job procedures that counteracted some of the psychological benefits of work. Work became more efficient and productive, but workers also felt more powerless and alienated in their monotonous, dehumanizing jobs. The legacy of scientific management was the assembly line and its robotlike jobs. In their zeal for profits, many employers focused only on the efficiency side of Taylor's message and forgot human and social values. The work force (and the individual worker) was considered only a cog in the gigantic machinery of industry. Machines were often more highly regarded than human beings; after all, they did not tire or break down as often as human laborers would. "Taylorism" is now outmoded, although it is still practiced in many workplaces—perhaps even in a majority of them. Workers are better educated than they were in the early 1900s, and good pay is no longer the sole motive for working. To offset the cold impersonality of scientific management, the *human relations* movement was born.

Industrial human relations dates from 1927 to 1932, when sociologist Elton Mayo and his associates studied the Hawthorne Works of the Western Electric Company in Illinois. Mayo's team of social scientists examined the human factor in work and found that no matter what they did, productivity went up. If the researchers increased the lighting, the work output went up, but the same thing happened if the lighting was decreased. Changes in work schedules and rest periods had the same effect. The results of these experiments were perplexing. Mayo finally concluded that the rises in productivity and morale came from paying attention to the workers in the experiment, not from changes in the lighting or the working hours. His recommendations for management included methods for helping workers feel important and part of a team on the job, improved communication between labor and management so that each could better understand the other, improved employee benefits, and sympathetic supervision that expressed human concern for workers. These ideas fostered warmth and a sense of compassion that had previously been lacking. The human relations movement prepared the way for a shortened workweek, minimum wage laws, the prohibition of child labor, collective bargaining, and a variety of employee benefits that are generally standard in the workplace today (Dickson, 1975).

The human relations movement was a step toward a warmer and more humane work environment, but it was not a complete answer to the problems of working. Some human relations advocates went overboard with their message and forgot to balance their concerns with the technology and workmanship needed to make a profit and stay in business. Also, some workers believed the human relations approach was just another management technique to manipulate them into producing on the job. Human relations supervision was more decent than the old authoritarian supervision, but the job was still the same, dull, low kind of work. Gradually, there was a shift to what has come to be called the *human resources* approach. This approach deals extensively with assumptions about human nature, human motivation, and the nature of the work actually performed. The human resources approach is perhaps best illustrated by the work of three theorists: Douglas McGregor, Chris Argyris, and Frederick Herzberg.

Douglas McGregor argues that there are two basic styles of management, rooted in opposite views of human nature. Behind every managerial decision is a set of assumptions about human behavior. Theory X managers assume that people dislike work and will avoid it whenever possible; management must somehow counteract people's inherent tendency to avoid work. Thus, most people must be forced, directed, controlled, and threatened to direct them toward the achievement of the manager's goals. Furthermore, the average person prefers to be directed, tries to avoid responsibility, lacks ambition, and wants security more than anything else.

Theory Y calls for the integration of individual and organizational goals and operates on a completely different set of assumptions. The physical and mental effort expended in work is as natural to people as play or rest. People freely seek work when it is a source of satisfaction. If work is considered a form of punishment, people will avoid it whenever they can. When people are committed to values and objectives, including those of the organization, they will demonstrate self-direction and self-control in the service of the shared objectives. Given suitable conditions and experiences, people learn not only to accept but also to seek responsibility in work. If they avoid responsibility and lack ambition, it is because they have learned those responses, not because of any inborn human tendency to do so. Workers have a relatively high degree of imagination, resourcefulness, and creativity in solving organizational problems. However, work is organized in modern industrial life in such a way that the abilities of the average person are only partially used. Theory Y assumptions are dynamic, carry the potential for human growth, and emphasize the obligation of managers to achieve the promise of human resources. Theory X gives management an easy way out: if the organization fails, it is because its workers are stupid, lazy, indifferent, uncooperative, and unwilling to take responsibility. Theory Y implies that those undesirable worker traits are caused by management's own methods of organization and control (McGregor, 1960).

For purposes of clarity, both Theory X and Theory Y have been expressed here in sharp, extreme terms. Actually, most bosses fall somewhere between these two extremes, and many are fairly close to the middle. Nevertheless, McGregor suggests, employers and supervisors have a basic tendency to adopt either Theory X or Theory Y, because both theories can be proved rather easily. A Theory X boss can show you stupid, indifferent, lazy, dull workers who do not care about their performance on the job. A Theory Y boss can show you bright, motivated, hardworking people who are willing to take on the responsibilities of work. McGregor concluded that workers are molded according to management's perception of them. A self-fulfilling prophecy takes place; in time, people become the type of workers the boss expects them to become. The assumptions of Theory X result in rigidity and authoritarianism in management. Workers learn to work hard and follow orders in order to protect their jobs and standard of living. The Theory X company wants the worker to know that much has been achieved by its way of running things and that much more could be accomplished if employees would adapt themselves to management's idea of what is required. The worker thus learns that the organization comes ahead of the individual. By contrast, the assumptions of Theory Y encourage flexibility, willingness to experiment, innovation, openness, and the creative resources the worker can contribute to the success of the organization.

Chris Argyris also writes of two basic styles of organizational management. One approach emphasizes the needs of the organization; the other stresses the needs of the individual. People have basic needs such as those for self-esteem, achievement, creativity, and a feeling of participation. When management ignores these needs, workers become frustrated, and problems result. People will use their human energy in beneficial, creative ways when their aims and the goals of the organization are similar. Workers lapse into apathy and destructiveness when their goals and those of the organization are widely dissimilar and when organizational goals receive great attention and high priority at the expense of the personal goals of individuals. Management can go a long way toward improving the workplace when it begins to serve human needs as well as organizational needs; move away from a centralized, hierarchical power structure to a more equalized, democratic power arrangement; develop a greater feeling of trust and openness between people who work in the organization; and carefully redesign jobs and work for individual employees. There are roadblocks in the way of democratizing the workplace, however. For instance, sometimes a real need exists for uniformity in work procedures. Another obstacle is the power needs of some managers and administrators, who may want to keep authority in their own hands rather than share it with the work force.

Thus, in organizations where scientific management has evolved into human relations and human resources approaches, a manager tends to be less of a boss and more of a catalyst, a facilitator, or a developer of the abilities and resources of those workers for whom he or she is responsible. The difference in the two humanistic approaches is shown by the way each conceives of the role of information. The human relations method prescribes that workers be given selected information about the company through newsletters and other communications, whereas the human resources approach allows the work group to determine for itself the information it needs in order to carry out its job and reach its goals (Dickson, 1975). Human relations is considerate and treats its workers decently; human resources emphasizes individual autonomy and responsibility.

Frederick Herzberg has examined the issue of improving jobs from the perspective of the workers themselves. His study revolved around the central question, "What do people want from their jobs?" (Herzberg, Mauser, & Snyderman, 1959). The results of the study extended Abraham Maslow's concept of the hierarchy of needs to include the problems of job motivation. Maslow concluded that a person's basic needs arise in a sequence, beginning with physiological needs, followed by safety needs and then by the higher levels of relationship, esteem, and self-actualization needs. Initially, the physiological needs are the most powerful. Whenever they become basically satisfied, the next need level gradually presses into awareness. As each need level emerges, the individual must find ways to satisfy those needs and continue growth toward self-actualization.

Herzberg found a distinction between factors that make workers satisfied with their jobs and factors that merely keep them from being dissatisfied with their work. Job satisfaction and dissatisfaction are two separate dimensions; they are not opposite ends of a scale. When workers say that they are happy and satisfied with their jobs, they usually describe factors related to their work, to experiences that involve successful performance, and to increased opportunities for further professional growth. On the other hand, when people say they are unhappy and dissatisfied about their jobs, the reasons they give have more to do with the conditions that surround their work than with the job itself.

Factors external to the work itself that can cause dissatisfaction with the job involve salary, benefits, company policy and administration, supervision, interpersonal relations, and working conditions. These factors relate to the context of the job, not to the work itself. When working conditions, supervision, pay, and company policies and administration deteriorate to a point below that which workers find acceptable, the result is job dissatisfaction. A positive trend in these external factors, however, does not lead to positive job attitudes. Herzberg calls such improvements "hygienic measures." They are similar to the principles of medical hygiene. "Hygiene operates to remove health hazards from the environment of man. It is not a curative; it is, rather, a preventive" (Herzberg, Mauser, & Snyderman, 1959). Such measures help us satisfy our physiological and safety needs, but they may not have much to do with our needs for affiliation, esteem, and self-actualization. Hygienic measures with respect to work are not to be discounted. Without them, life would be much more difficult. They do alleviate unhappiness with the job—for a while. Workers, having met their physical and security needs, next press for changes in the intrinsic nature of the work itself. Lack of adequate salary, for example, causes so much dissatisfaction that a period of good feelings follows when the salary is increased. This period, however, is short-lived. With the passage of time from the last pay raise, workers want a raise again; if it is not granted, job dissatisfaction sets in again.

Hygienic measures are needed to make the job acceptable; to make it excellent, qualities Herzberg calls "work motivators" are also required. Work motivators involve the nature of the work itself, a sense of achievement, recognition for accomplishments at work, responsibility on the job, and genuine opportunities for advancement. These factors provide the "psychic income" of working and create the real satisfaction people seek from their jobs. These internal qualities are more closely related to esteem and self-actualization needs than to hygienic measures. The idea of personal growth in one's working life is a far cry from the old notion of work as punishment. It comes much closer to the self-realization motive that many psychologists, including C.G. Jung, Carl Rogers, and Abraham Maslow, have considered to be the ultimate goal of human beings.

Attempts to Improve the Quality of Work

Some work organizations make sincere efforts to upgrade the jobs of their employees. Job-seekers are urged to take notice of companies that care about employee morale, redesign jobs to fit the needs of their workers, share decision-making authority and profits, and experiment with flexible working hours. In addition to those ideas mentioned previously in connection with job burnout, some ideas for improving the quality of work will be briefly covered here.

1. Job enrichment.   The major purpose of job enrichment is to focus on the nature of the job itself and endow it with the characteristics that Herzberg identified as work motivators. Too many jobs are simply too small for the people who take them. Those jobs need to be redesigned to become worthy of the people who fill them. Company objectives must give the goal of good jobs equal status with shareholder and customer satisfaction. Changing routine jobs to give workers more control over their work and trusting them with greater responsibility requires that top leadership and middle management be committed to the idea of enrichment. Some employers say they want workers to accept responsibility on the job but do not delegate real power, preferring instead to keep authority in their own hands.

Some of the characteristics of job enrichment or job redesign are as follows.

- Opportunities for workers to analyze their own jobs and make changes in them
- More variety and less repetition in work functions; more control over the job
- Challenging assignments that give a sense of achievement
- Allowing more interaction with others on the job
- More opportunities for worker self-management and freedom at work
- Rules and procedures that come from the entire group of workers
- Recognition of accomplishments
- Rewards for learning new skills
- Greater emphasis on teamwork
- Reducing differences and status symbols between management and workers
- Setting one's own production goals
- Assembling entire units and completing a whole product

The changes involved in job enrichment cannot be forced upon workers by a well-meaning employer. Workers may be suspicious of the motives for change; it is important to bring employees into the planning of the new ways of working.

2. Organizational democracy.   Living in a society with a political climate that values individual rights does not ensure that democracy will be practiced where you work. Many companies follow authoritarian management courses of action patterned essentially on a military model. The disparity between political ideals in the culture and the power realities within organizations often leads to labor-management conflicts.

The essential idea of democratizing the workplace is to give workers the opportunity to share power with their employers. Beyond power, another concern is communication. In a democratic company, workers have full and free communication, no matter what their rank or status may be. Among the ways organizational democracy can be implemented are electing employees to the board of directors, giving workers real power to regulate their own work processes on the job through autonomous work teams, having workers participate in the selection of supervisors, allowing employees to influence the formation of personnel policies, having workers participate in long-range planning projects, and allowing employee membership on committees to evaluate new job applicants. A rating scale developed in Sweden, designed to measure the extent of worker democracy, lists five levels of worker influence: (1) control over the job itself, (2) control extended to personnel policy such as hiring and the division of work, (3) control over technical matters such as production planning, (4) control over product problems such as quality control and specifications, and (5) sharing managerial control in such areas as long-range planning, budgeting, and the design and planning of new plants. When a work experiment has reached the fifth level, it is in a state of full democracy (Dickson, 1975).

3. Profit sharing and responsibility sharing.
Profit sharing means that an agreed-upon percentage of the company's profits is distributed to employees in addition to their regular salaries and fringe benefits. When jobs have been enriched or redesigned without profit sharing, workers may suspect they are being manipulated, and productivity may slip back to former levels. When increases in productivity are tied to profit sharing, workers feel that they have a stake in the success of the organization. Personal needs (such as esteem and relationships with others) and economic goals (such as increased productivity) can be fulfilled by sharing in both the responsibilities of production and the profits earned from production. Responsibility-sharing implies that workers have decision-making power in their jobs but also that they are accountable for the outcome of those decisions. Most workers are willing to take on responsibility for a greater range of decisions if they are also allowed to share in the results. Profit-sharing arrangements or responsibility-sharing arrangements by themselves are not likely to make significant differences in productivity and profits; these measures work best when they are connected to each other. Profit sharing alone does not increase the size of the profits to be distributed. Responsibility sharing without profit sharing is likely to be regarded by workers as manipulation and to be rejected for this reason (*Work in America,* 1973).

4. Employee ownership plans.
Surveys have indicated that a majority of American would rather work in an employee-owned company than in one owned

by private investors or the government. Worker-controlled organizations occur throughout the world; in the United States, the most common form of worker ownership is the Employee Stock Ownership Plan (ESOP). As of 1989, 10 million workers were enrolled in an ESOP, up from 3 million only a decade ago (Ungeheuer, 1989). Advocates believe ESOPs boost morale and productivity by giving workers a stake in the company's success. Workers have saved their jobs by banding together to purchase the company when it appeared to be going bankrupt or out of business. In many cases, they have made sacrifices by accepting wage concessions in return for stock certificates and by borrowing money to complete the buyout. ESOPs were conceived by Louis Kelso in the 1950s as a way of changing the pattern of capital ownership from a few wealthy individuals to a vast array of employees. However, leveraged buyouts, used extensively in the 1980s by corporate raiders and self-seeking managers, are distortions of Kelso's ideas (Brown, 1987). The ESOP concept is primarily a form of economic democracy that gives workers the experience of ownership and control of their means of livelihood.

5. Self-managing work groups.   Instead of a mile-long assembly line, where each of hundreds of workers performs a simple and monotonous work function, a team of several workers (usually 8 to 12) follows a product from its beginning on the line to its completion at the end. The groups are large enough to perform a number of tasks, yet small enough to allow for face-to-face meetings for decision-making and coordination. Work teams decide among themselves who will do what tasks. Most members learn to do each other's work, both for the sake of variety and to be able to cover for a sick or absent worker.

6. Compressed workweeks.   When most people worked a 6-day week, spending 10 or 12 hours per day on the job, a 5-day, 40-hour week would have seemed like the dawning of the Golden Age. Now you hear of 4-day weeks, with 40, 36, or 32 hours per week, as the standard. Another experiment already tried has been a 3-day, 36-hour week, working 12 hours per day. It is claimed that a workweek of less than five days will lower employees' gasoline consumption rates, cut heat and electricity bills at company buildings, reduce absenteeism, improve efficiency, reduce costs, and give employees a more satisfying work schedule. Some labor unions have opposed compressing the 40-hour workweek into 4 days or less because they want to shorten the workweek to 35 or 32 hours in their own way, and the 4-day week would require people to work over 8 hours a day without receiving overtime pay. Another objection is the possibility of replacing one inflexible work schedule with another.

7. Flextime.   This term, a contraction of "flexible time," reflects the concept of floating work hours. For example, the official workday could extend from 7:00 A.M. to 6:00 P.M. An employee would arrive at work any time between

7:00 and 10:00 A.M. and leave any time after 3:00 P.M. The worker would still need to complete a 40-hour workweek but would have a certain leeway each month. Workers could make up missing hours later, and extra hours could be "banked" as credit for a day off at a later time.

8. Job-sharing and splitting jobs.   The advantage of these work arrangements is to allow time for both family and a career. Five categories of work have been identified under the job-sharing procedure.

    a. *Paired or partnership work:* Two people fill one full-time job, sharing responsibility equally. An elementary teaching job could be shared, for example.

    b. *Shared work:* Two people divide a job, each taking responsibility for half the total work. Unlike paired work, the two do not necessarily have to split the day; rather, they split the total workload of a single job.

    c. *Split-location work:* Work is done both at the office and at home by one person. The work schedule could be worked out in advance so appointments could be met at the office.

    d. *Split-level work:* One full-time job is analyzed into its functional skills and split along different levels of training and ability. (A job where a person is required to compose letters and then type them in final form could be split into two jobs—a part-time writer and a part-time secretary.)

    e. *Specialist:* A person takes a job that requires less than full-time employment, such as a teacher of a specialized subject not in heavy demand.

9. Other time arrangements.   Other options include sabbaticals (a year off from job duties), time off to do social or political work, tailor-made work weeks divided into 2-hour modules, time bonuses (paying workers for 40 hours of work even though they work only 36 hours during certain periods, such as between Thanksgiving and Christmas), varied shifts (two 9-hour shifts and a 6-hour shift, for example), "banking" vacation time, and the 4½-day week.

Where Are We Headed as a Society?

Historians, futurists, and social scientists identify forces and trends in our time that influence the occupations and organizations in which we work. This section of the book analyzes twelve broad social and economic events. A question or two about each of them is posed for you to ponder. Another discussion of economic forces and labor trends can be found Chapter 2 of *Taking Charge of Your Career Direction.*

1. *The United States is, economically, the most important nation in the world, but it no longer dominates the global economy:* What impact will this change have on your life? Increasingly, Americans are becoming aware of and adjusting to the realities of international trade. Asia's Pacific Rim nations—Japan, South Korea, Taiwan, Hong Kong, Singapore, and Malaysia—manufacture attractive, high-quality goods and sell them on the world market, often at lower prices made possible by their lower labor costs. If the great giant of Asia, China, stabilizes politically, its economy could soon become second only to that of the United States (Naisbitt & Aburdene, 1990). Another major player in the world economy is the 12-member European Community organization that seeks to remove the trade barriers once put up to protect themselves from one another. Foreign competition causes anger among many American workers who believe their jobs are threatened by workers in other countries. Some domestic companies call for governmental protection against foreign rivals. Foreign trade works both ways, however. The United States exports many goods and services that create jobs at home. The world economy is credited with giving Americans a wider range of excellent, competitively priced products. How will the global economy personally affect your future work?

2. *An explosion of information is taking place:* Will there be too much? The majority of jobs now involve gathering and using information in one form or another. The main cause of the remarkable increase of information easily available to everyone is the computer. Widespread data collection, analysis, and circulation is uniquely suited to the computer's capabilities. Communications technology shortens the time involved in sending and receiving information; transmitting electronic data takes seconds, and important news is delivered instantly. The advantages of expanded information is obvious, but some people say we will drown in the flood of data, or the result will be "information pollution." Are we accumulating so much information that people will be tempted to simply tune it out?

3. *Increasing opportunities exist for women:* Is this good for society? Over 45 percent of the labor force is female. Women are hired to fill two thirds of all new jobs created. Women may be better adapted than men to establish themselves in leadership positions of the Information Age. New leaders will tend to function as teachers or facilitators, roles traditionally associated with "feminine" traits. Women are in about 40 percent of the 14 million executive, administrative, and managerial jobs, nearly double from 20 years ago (Naisbitt & Aburdene, 1990). As more women move into the workplace, changes occur in peoples' personal lives as well. Fewer women are choosing to marry, and those who marry do so at a later age. More children have working mothers than in the past. Only about 20 percent of all American families now have a father who works outside the home and a mother who is a full-time homemaker. Child care is a major concern, and companies are pressured to provide this service. There is evidence that women are generally healthier and happier than they were 30 years ago,

despite the problems that arise from assuming the dual role of wage-earner and parent. Feminists applaud increasing opportunities and new lifestyles, but are these developments good for children, for women themselves, and for society in general?

4. *The population heads south and west and into the newer suburbs:* Will these trends reverse, and if so, when? The U.S. population is shifting to the south and west, with California, Texas, and Florida leading the way. Smaller states like Arizona, Nevada, and Alaska showed population increases in the 30- to 40-percent range during the 1980s. With this migration of people, economic and political influence has shifted southward and westward as well. Almost as dramatic as this population shift is the movement from cities to the suburbs and even into the nonmetropolitan areas beyond the suburbs. Older suburbs now face many of the same problems as cities do, with their traffic jams, air and water pollution, strained sewage systems, and rising crime rates. Could there be a move back to our cities and to the north and east—and why? Considered elsewhere to be cradles of civilization, can our large cities ever be restored?

5. *Minorities are becoming a larger element in the population:* Will Whites eventually become another minority? Most members of minority groups have been treated as second-class citizens at one time or another; still, they have made their mark on the American culture whether they were native-born or immigrant. Blacks constitute about 13 percent of the U.S. population, and Hispanics will soon become the largest minority group. In terms of percentage, Asian Americans are the fastest growing group. Many Black and Hispanic people lack the skills needed for the new jobs of the present and future. A major challenge confronts American society in trying to help minority groups who are growing at a faster rate than is the American population as a whole. Will the White middle class be reduced to second-class minority status sometime in the future?

6. *Education and the arts occupy center stage:* Will their resurgence be permanent or temporary, and will they be considered essential or a luxury? Our nation has grown increasingly concerned with education. Concerns are expressed about the effects of television on scholastic test results and about the learning achievements of American students when compared with those in other countries. Attention is being directed to the improvement of elementary and secondary education. U.S. higher education, however, is considered to be in better shape. American colleges and universities rank among the best in the world, and foreign students regularly flock to them for educational opportunities that do not exist in their home countries. Large numbers of students are attracted not only to regular degree programs, but also to continuing education courses, workshops, and seminars. Because knowledge becomes obsolete so quickly or is incorporated into computers so readily, many workers will return to the classroom for "booster shots" of training several times during their careers. As for the arts, how do more Americans spend their Sunday afternoons: watching football on television or

visiting a museum? You are correct if you chose the latter. The rebirth of the visual arts, poetry, dance, theater, and music will have tremendous economic implications. New careers and business opportunities in the arts will flourish. However, questions continually arise about the value of education and the arts. In practical terms, how necessary are they? Are they essential to one's life, or are they only luxuries made possible by an affluent leisure society?

7. *A maturing society is still growing older:* What value conflicts will develop with an aging population? Despite modern advertising's emphasis on a youth culture, the United States is experiencing a change in which middle-aged and older people will dominate the society by their sheer numbers. The proportion of older citizens is greater now during than during any previous period in American history. As the year 2000 approaches, the baby-boom generation, those born between 1946 and 1964, is in middle age and is approaching elderly status. The maturing of America profoundly affects the social and economic values and trends of the future. Less attention is likely to be paid to youth as marketers focus more intently on the needs of middle- and older-aged people. Long-term health care will become more important. As people live longer, chronic illnesses will have to be increasingly dealt with. Disagreements between the young and the old are bound to occur, such as the issue of paying for Social Security costs. Workers aged 60 and over who are in good health may want to delay retirement, believing their occupations give their lives meaning, purpose, and an identity they find nowhere else. When age 60-plus people stay in the work force, they take job opportunities from young people. Will the ever-present conflict between the generations grow larger?

8. *Miracles continue to take place in medicine and biology:* Will high health costs also cost jobs in the long run? Illnesses that once killed people are now less of a threat because of advances in medical treatment. The childhood scourges of polio, measles, and mumps have almost disappeared with the advent of new vaccines. Patients survive diseases that at one time were considered incurable. Transplant surgery offers new hearts, kidneys, and lungs to people once condemned to a ceaseless sickbed or death. Where human organs are not available, surgeons use artificial devices. Answers exist for the threat of heart disease through open-heart surgery, pacemakers, exercise and diet, and new drugs. New instruments are developed to help doctors and allied health personnel diagnose and treat health problems— from ultrasound, CAT scanners, radioscopes, and fiber optics to laser technology. Biotechnology changes the genetic composition of plants and animals, and we use their altered life forms to produce more fertile soil, bigger crop yields, leaner meat, and more milk. Gene therapy, by manipulating or replacing defective genetic structures, offers hope and cures to patients with inherited diseases. All these medical and biological advances create new occupational opportunities; however, financial and ethical problems abound in this area. Modern medical miracles and additional health-care

practitioners cause runaway health costs that often go beyond an ordinary person's capacity to pay for them. Will soaring health payments mean that fewer people can afford adequate health care? Could this eventually reduce job opportunities in the medical field?

9. *Technological change and progress continue to drive much of our economy:* Overall, will they create more or fewer jobs? Think of the expansion of jobs taking place in telecommunications, fiber optics, robotics, biotechnology, computer graphics, energy, electronics, and medical technology, just to name a few industries. Throughout history, whenever technological advances have occurred, the nature of work has changed. The microchip downgrades skills in one job and upgrades them in another. Fewer people are needed to do the work in microchip technology, so the total number of jobs declines. Yet the overall effect of new microchip technology is uncertain because it creates other jobs for workers to design, manufacture, transport, sell, and service the new machines (Wegmann, Chapman, & Johnson, 1985). The impact of robotics on manufacturing is also uncertain. Some forecasters see factories devoid of workers, replaced by robots that can measure, cut, drill, assemble, spot-weld, and paint. Robots will become more complex, requiring talented people to construct and market them. Robotics engineers will be needed to design the software that instructs the computer-controlled robots in their tasks. In the short term, new technology appears to cost jobs, but its long-term influences are unclear. Your job may either be eliminated or created by high technology. Beyond your own particular fortune, what will be the general impact of technological development on society: more jobs eliminated or more jobs created?

10. *High unemployment happens in the midst of record job growth:* How can we provide jobs for all? Nearly 50 percent more jobs are being added between 1975 and the year 2000, yet the unemployment rate runs between 5 and 10 percent. With such enormous job growth, why is unemployment so prevalent? The answers involve new technology, increased numbers of job-seekers, deregulation, and foreign competition. Technological changes were discussed in the previous paragraph. Unprecedented numbers of people are seeking jobs in the American labor force. The high birthrates that created the baby boom strained the labor market to such a degree that it could not absorb the demand for jobs. Birthrates have lowered since then, but that decline may be offset by two other large groups of entrants to the job market: women and immigrants. Deregulation policies have increased competitive pressures, and many companies reduce their number of employees in order to survive. The bankruptcy of large companies is front-page news, but many small firms go out of business almost unnoticed. Whether a business decreases the size of its work force or closes its doors, the effect is a loss of jobs. Foreign competitors acquire new technology, have lower labor costs, produce efficiently, and can transport their goods inexpensively; this enables them to offer Americans attractive prices for their

products. As the number of foreign-made products Americans buy exceeds the number of American-made products sold abroad, the foreign trade imbalance costs jobs—although how many jobs is controversial. What can we do to ensure a job to everyone who wants one?

11. *Underemployment, misemployment, and displacement of workers persist stubbornly:* How do we reduce or eliminate these unhappy features of our national work environment? For the college-educated, underemployment is more of a problem than unemployment. Underemployment occurs when a well-trained, highly skilled person works at a job that requires neither the training nor the skills possessed by the worker. A college degree today does not necessarily guarantee a job in the occupation for which the graduate is trained. However, college graduates earn more income than noncollege graduates do over the course of their careers and eventually obtain jobs in their chosen occupations. Nonetheless, it is often a great source of dissatisfaction for a highly educated person to work in a low-paying, low-status job. There is also the tragedy of *misemployment:* 80 percent of American workers are in jobs for which they are not well suited, according to Herbert Greenberg, president of Marketing Survey and Research Corporation (Cornish, 1983). Many people fall into jobs without much thought about their interests, abilities, and values or about finding an organization appropriate for them. When they accumulate seniority and fringe benefits, these people are reluctant to risk these gains, so they stay in the old job instead of changing to one in which they might have more interest and natural aptitude. One of the most perplexing problems of the American economy is the plight of workers displaced by plant closings. Advance notice of a plant closing is required so that job counseling and training in new work skills can be provided. Even when the displaced worker gets a new job, it usually means fewer hours and lower pay than before. Mental depression is likely to occur. Health problems, from headaches to high blood pressure, are common among displaced workers. Economic problems, such as trying to sell a house in a depressed housing market, often make moving to a new location extremely difficult. How can we solve the problems or diminish the anguish caused by underemployment, misemployment, and displacement of workers?

12. *The world's population approaches 6 billion:* Do increases in population mean prosperity or doomsday? The number of people on Planet Earth now exceeds 5 billion and will go beyond 6 billion by the year 2000. At least 10 million people will live in each of 25 cities around the globe. Most populous of all will be Mexico City, slated to number 31 million by 2000. While industries will continue to increase the amount of material goods in most countries, some forecasters say that the world's people will be poorer in many ways in the years ahead. In 1972, the Club of Rome published a report entitled, *The Limits to Growth,* which warned that the earth's resources were not likely to support current rates of economic and population growth much beyond the year 2100, even with advanced technology (Mead-

ows, Meadows, Randers, & Behrens, 1972). This doomsday outlook is countered by assertions that technological advances and proper environmental planning can bring a future of rising affluence, energy, and food for virtually everyone. Which vision will prevail?

EXERCISE 10-1 *The Year 2000*

The last exercise in this book is a series of two statements about the future of work. Each statement in the pair opposes the other. Which statement will be more accurate in the year 2000? The future is difficult to predict, but everyone tries to do it anyway. You might as well join the crowd. Try to explain or illustrate the reason for your response. If you are in a group or class, these are good discussion topics.

By the year 2000, there will be:

_____ More personal satisfaction in working.
_____ Less personal satisfaction in working.

_____ More occupations from which to choose.
_____ Fewer occupations from which to choose.

_____ Increased competition for highly skilled jobs.
_____ Less competition for highly skilled jobs.

_____ Lower unemployment.
_____ Higher unemployment.

_____ More jobs that require greater ability.
_____ More jobs that require less ability.

_____ Greater job security; more protections for keeping your job.
_____ Less job security; fewer protections for keeping your job.

_____ More democratic work environments; workers will make more decisions on the job.
_____ More authoritarian work environments; workers will make fewer decisions.

_____ More work that is interesting and challenging.
_____ Less work that is interesting and challenging.

_____ More jobs where people operate machines and have less to do with people.
_____ More jobs that are involved with people and have less to do with machines.

_____ More men than women in the U.S. labor force.
_____ More women than men in the U.S. labor force.

By the year 2000, there will be:

_____ Greater trust of those who have power in business, labor, and government.

_____ More distrust of those who have power in business, labor, and government.

_____ More flexibility for workers in determining their hours on the job.

_____ Less flexibility for workers in determining their hours on the job.

_____ More leisure time or greater amounts of time spent away from work.

_____ Less leisure time or more time spent at work.

_____ More identification by work role than by other social roles.

_____ Less identification by work role than by other social roles.

_____ Fewer barriers in work opportunities because of sex and race factors.

_____ More barriers in work opportunities because of sex and race factors.

_____ More workers over age 65 in the labor force.

_____ Fewer workers over age 65 in the labor force.

_____ More high-paying manufacturing jobs.

_____ More low-paying service jobs.

_____ More white-collar jobs in the United States than now.

_____ More blue-collar jobs in the United States than now.

_____ More goods-producing jobs in the United States than now.

_____ More service-providing jobs in the United States than now.

_____ More emphasis on the work ethic.

_____ Less emphasis on the work ethic.

_____ Greater choices in personal lifestyles.

_____ More restrictions on choices of lifestyle.

_____ A stronger economy than now.

_____ A weaker economy than now.

_____ Increased need for training and education throughout life.

_____ Reduced need for training and education throughout life.

_____ Increased severity in social problems (pollution, crime, and so on).

_____ Social problems remaining, but they will be less severe than they are today.

_____ More emphasis on individuality and personal expression.

_____ Greater pressure toward conformity to organizational or social goals.

_____ Fewer marriages that end in separation or divorce.

_____ More marriages that end in separation or divorce.

_____ Increased social distance and wider income gaps among people.

_____ Greater equality in social status and personal incomes among people.

By the year 2000, there will be:

_____ Closer family ties and greater social support for the family.
_____ Increased separation between parents and children.

_____ Higher percentages of income spent on necessities of life.
_____ Lower percentages of income spent on necessities of life.

_____ Greater emphasis of self-interest and "looking out for Number One."
_____ Increased emphasis on social welfare and cooperation with others.

_____ Greater respect for religion and increased emphasis on belief in God.
_____ Less respect for religion and decreased emphasis on belief in God.

_____ A more humane way of life.
_____ A less humane way of life.

Summary

1. The work ethic is a belief that the best way to live involves hard work, saving, and delaying present satisfactions for future gains. It is now being questioned as never before because of such factors as automation, early retirement, welfare benefits, alienation, and changing attitudes. The work ethic is certainly not dead, but it has changed; people expect more psychological and economic benefits from their work.

2. Three movements have influenced management styles in the 20th century: scientific management, human relations, and human resources. Scientific management organizes work rationally to create the greatest possible efficiency. This promotes productivity but often has harmful psychological effects on workers. In response to the cold, mechanical efficiency of scientific management, the human relations and human resources approaches were introduced. Human relations brought a more personal touch to management, and the human resources approach emphasized improving the nature of the work itself.

3. Many attempts to improve jobs and working conditions have been and continue to be made: job enrichment and redesign, organizational democracy, profit sharing and responsibility sharing, employee ownership plans, self-managing work teams, compressed workweeks, flextime, job-sharing, and job splitting.

4. The following 12 forces and trends are influencing the way we work and live: the United States no longer dominates the global economy; the Age of Information is upon us; increasing opportunities exist for women; the population is moving south and west and into the suburbs; minorities are becoming a larger proportion of the society; education and the arts are growing more important; the nation has matured, and the elderly are becoming more numerous; advances in medicine and biology are miraculous but create rising concerns about health costs; technological developments con-

tinue to drive our economy; high unemployment is occurring during record job growth; underemployment, misemployment, and displacement of workers persist; and the world's population is booming toward 6 billion people, and from this fact predictions of prosperity or disaster are being made.

References

Brown, A. (1987). Power to the workers: The rise of employee stockholders. *The Futurist, 21*(4), 45.

Cornish, E. (Ed.). (1983). *Careers tomorrow: The outlook for work in a changing world.* Bethesda, MD: World Future Society.

Dickson, P. (1975). *The future of the workplace: The coming revolution in jobs.* New York: Weybright and Talley.

Herzberg, F., Mauser, B., & Snyderman, B. B. (1959). *The motivation to work* (2nd ed.). New York: Wiley.

Macarov, D. (1983). Changes in the world of work: Some implications for the future. In H. F. Didsbury, Jr. (Ed.). *The world of work: Careers and the future* (pp. 3–24). Bethesda, MD: World Future Society.

McGregor, D. (1960). *The human side of enterprise.* New York: McGraw-Hill.

Meadows, D. H., Meadows, D. L., Randers, J., & Behrens, W. W. (1972). *The limits to growth: A report for the Club of Rome's project on the predicament of mankind.* New York: Universe Books.

Naisbitt, J., & Aburdene, P. (1990). *Megatrends 2000: Ten new directions for the 1990s.* New York: Morrow.

Taylor, F. W. (1947). *Scientific management.* In D. S. Pugh (Ed.), Organizational theory: Selected readings. Harmondsworth, Middlesex, England: Penguin Books Ltd.

Terkel, S. (1972). *Working: People talk about what they do all day and how they feel about what they do.* New York: Pantheon.

Ungeheuer, F. (1989). They own the place: Employee stock plans come of age as morale boosters and takeover tools. *Time, 133*(5), 50–51.

Wegmann, R., Chapman, R., & Johnson, M. (1985). *Looking for work in the new economy.* Salt Lake City, UT: Olympus.

Work in America: Report of a special task force to the Secretary of Health, Education, and Welfare. (1973). Cambridge, MA: MIT Press.

Index

To the owner of this book:

I hope that you have been significantly influenced by *Taking Charge of Your Career Direction*, 2nd edition. I'd like to know as much about your experiences with the book as you care to offer. Your comments can help me make it a better book for future readers.

School: _____ Instructor's name: _____

Address of school (city, state, and zip code): _____

1. What I like most about this book is: _____

_____

_____

2. What I like least about this book is: _____

_____

_____

3. Of how much interest and value were the activities and exercises? _____

_____

4. Specific topics in the book I thought were most relevant and important: _____

_____

_____

5. Specific suggestions for improving the book: _____

_____

_____

6. Did you use *Job Search*? _____

7. Did you use the *Student Activities* book with the textbook in class? _____

8. The name of the course in which I used this book: _____

_____

9. In the space below—or in a separate letter, if you care to write one—please let me know what other comments about the book you'd like to make. I welcome your suggestions!

Optional:

Your name: _____ Date: _____

May Brooks/Cole quote you, either in promotion for *Taking Charge of Your Career Direction*, 2nd edition or in future publishing ventures?

Yes: _____ No: _____

Sincerely,
Robert D. Lock